ARCHETYPES OF CONVERSION

ARCHETYPES OF CONVERSION

The Autobiographies
of Augustine, Bunyan, and Merton

Anne Hunsaker Hawkins

WIPF & STOCK · Eugene, Oregon

Wipf and Stock Publishers
199 W 8th Ave, Suite 3
Eugene, OR 97401

Archetypes of Conversion
The Autobiographies of Augustine, Bunyan, and Merton
By Hawkins, Anne Hunsaker
Copyright©1985 by Hawkins, Anne Hunsaker
ISBN 13: 978-1-62564-694-1
Publication date 2/12/2014
Previously published by Bucknell University Press, 1985

For S. H. H.

Contents

Acknowledgments	9
1 Introduction	13
i. Archetypes in spiritual autobiography	14
ii. Generic aspects of spiritual autobiography	22
2 St. Augustine: The Heroic Paradigm	29
i. Narrative and ideational aspects of the quest	29
ii. *Crisis* conversion	44
3 St. Augustine: Archetypes of Family	56
i. The maternal nexus	56
ii. The paternal ethos: *senex* and child	67
4 John Bunyan: The Conflictive Paradigm	73
i. The mode of *logos:* the unacceptable self and the problem of evil	73
ii. Archetype of *psychomachia:* the "static" hero and his crises of temptation	82
iii. *Lysis* conversion: the iterated archetype	92
5. John Bunyan: God and Family	100
i. The problem: wrathful God and guilty soul	100
ii. The pattern: absent mother and negative father	104
iii. Resolution: the preacher	109
6 Thomas Merton: A Modern Paradigm	113
i. *Epektesis* and traditionalism: the spiraling quest	115

	ii. Archetype of *psychomachia:* sanctity and the problem of the self	125
	iii. Father, mother, brother, and the ideal of disinterested love	130
7	Thomas Merton: Sacramental Conversion	139
	i. The private vision	141
	ii. The corporate expression	145
	iii. The communal experience	149

Conclusion	155
Notes	159
Bibliography	181
Index	189

Acknowledgments

I am grateful to the editors of *Philological Quarterly* for permission to use portions of an earlier published essay; to Oxford University Press, for permission to reprint from John Bunyan's *Grace Abounding to the Chief of Sinners;* and to Harcourt Brace Jovanovich, Inc. for permission to reprint excerpts from *The Seven Storey Mountain* by Thomas Merton, copyright 1948, renewed 1976 by The Trustees of the Merton Legacy Trust. Thanks also go to Richard Gollin and Jarold Ramsey, who read the manuscript in its earliest phase, to Philip Hallie for his helpful suggestions, to Ellen Doench, Curator of the Davison Art Center Collection at Wesleyan University, and to my husband, Sherman, to whom this book is dedicated.

ARCHETYPES
OF CONVERSION

1
Introduction

St. Augustine, John Bunyan, and Thomas Merton represent three different phases in the history of Christianity and illustrate the diversity of the Christian experience as it is reflected in autobiography. The fourth-century Augustine stands at the very beginning of the tradition, his religious metaphors rooted in Greek philosophy and poetry; the seventeenth-century Bunyan is a Protestant reformer whose religious experience reflects the theological peculiarities of Calvin and Luther; and the twentieth-century Merton stands at the end of the tradition, consciously identifying his religious beliefs with the early Catholicism of Augustine, and yet expanding into a more universal Catholicism through his interest in Eastern mysticism.

Despite these differences, the spiritual autobiographies of these authors are remarkably similar in regard to certain themes and patterns that can only be called archetypal. For example, the representation of life as a long pilgrimage, or a journey, or a return, or an arduous quest toward some dimly intuited goal is an archetypal image that functions in these narratives as a major structural and thematic element. Another example frequently encountered is the representation of intrapsychic conflict as a battle between two different selves or a warfare between God and Satan for possession of the soul—an archetypal pattern that I refer to as *psychomachia*. Autobiographies of conversion are also remarkably similar in regard to characters. Archetypal figures of the mother, the father, the sibling, and the child appear over and over in these narratives to further or to frustrate the protagonist in his predestined conversion. And the conversion is the crucial element: it figures as the main luminary in this constellation of archetypal images, figures, and patterns. Moreover, the conversion that is central to each book determines its religious meaning, its formal structure, and its archetypal emphases.[1]

i. Archetypes in spiritual autobiography

The word *archetype*, which figures so prominently in my title and in this introduction, requires some explanation. Jung is, of course, the name most commonly associated with archetypes, but the reader who expects to find a Jungian analysis in this study may be disappointed. Indebted though I am to him, my own stance is not that of the orthodox Jungian critic. It is not my purpose here to reify archetypes, or to defend an archetypal interpretation of spiritual autobiography as an end in itself. I regard the concept of an archetypal substructure as an enabling device—a kind of lens through which these autobiographies can be more richly understood.

I find that the concept of archetype proves most helpful in literary criticism when it is used not in the strict Jungian sense, where archetype is differentiated from idea and image, but in the common and broader sense of a convenient "umbrella" term that includes archetypes, archetypal ideas and images, overarching patterns, and universal symbols.[2] The history of the term itself encourages a synthetic understanding. Jung is primarily responsible for reviving the concept and for making it a part of our common vocabulary, but as he himself points out, citing Philo Judaeus, Irenaeus, the *Corpus Hermeticum*, and Dionysius the Areopagite, it is not a term that he has invented.[3] For the most part Jung's concept of archetype is derived from Plato's transcendent Idea. Thus he observes that the term *archetype* is synonymous with the Platonic "conception of the Idea as supraordinate and pre-existent to all phenomena."[4] And in his "Commentary on *The Tibetan Book of the Dead*," he calls archetypes "universal dispositions of the mind. . . . analogous to Plato's forms *(eidola)*, in accordance with which the mind organizes its contents." In the same work Jung points to Augustine as a source for his concept of the archetype: these "categories of the imagination," he writes, have the character of typical images, "which is why, following St. Augustine, I call them 'archetypes'."[5] The derivation of Jung's concept of archetype from Plato and Augustine supports my use of it here as a term that evokes both religious and psychological connotations.

But if it is to Jung that we owe our modern rediscovery of *archetype*, it is also to him that we can attribute some of the problems with archetypal method. The two most obvious of these problems can be discussed simultaneously, since they are closely related. The first is the objection that archetypal criticism is often reductive: it flattens what is unique in life and art into what is stereotypic, and contents itself with a generalized or distorted account of phenomena in terms of whatever archetypal configuration they most nearly fit. The result is a spurious likeness in what is analyzed and a monotonous sameness in analysis. To avoid this it is important that we be concerned not only with continuities in archetypal patterns but also with cultural and individual variations. Indeed, precisely because the critic using an archetypal approach locates what is the same in different works, there is a formal basis for observing differences. In other words, though we may find a similar archetypal motif of quest in Augustine, Bunyan, and Merton, it is formulated differently in each: for one it emerges out of its cultural locus in classical poetry and philosophy, for another in scriptural imagery, and for the third in sacrament and ritual. It is the recurrence of the same archetype within such divergent cultural contexts and such contrasting and idiosyncratic personalities that is finally impressive; to this double impression perhaps only an archetypal criticism can do justice.

The second objection is that archetypal analysis lends itself to the inexact, the intellectually nebulous, and the pseudomystical. This habit of hazy spiritualization is evident in Jung's own definitions of archetypes as "typical modes of apprehension" or "universal dispositions of the mind . . . forms or images of a collective nature . . . entities which cause the praeformation of numinous ideas or dominant representations."[6] Though Jung's facility with evocative language is remarkable, it is a facility that often blurs the actual meaning of what he is saying. Despite his brilliance and his intuitiveness, Jung is often a vague, imprecise thinker, one who abhorred the rigid categories and exact definitions that might have limited his impressive synthesizing abilities.

But despite all its problems, an archetypal approach is especially appropriate for analyzing religious and autobiographical phenomena. A frequent reader-response to spiritual autobiography is the recognition of a certain though elusive thread of meaning that is common to one's own life. This sense of resonance can be explained by the tendency of spiritual autobiography to be saturated with archetypal ideas and images. And this, in turn, is due to the divine context within which an individual writes about his or her spiritual life. What Jung calls the collective unconscious, the repository of archetypes, resembles what the theologian would recognize as the mind of God—the mind of God being at once the ground of our being and the mirror of what we can only infer in ourselves.[7] Merton refers to it as "the infinite depths of an eternal Providence."[8] But for Augustine it is the other side of the mind, the dark side of the mind, the dark side of memory—our state of seeing "through a glass darkly," which will turn after the death of the body into the eternal day of the Heaven of Heavens.[9]

quest and psychomachia

In autobiographies of conversion, the protagonist's development is almost always expressed in the archetypal images of pilgrimage and *psychomachia*. The quest turns the desire for God into a literal journey where the regressive and progressive contours of the psyche are projected onto a symbolic landscape and the inner personae are manifested as real people in the author's personal history; on the other hand, the archetype of *psychomachia* dramatizes the conflict of ambivalent and opposing tendencies in the psyche as the battle between good and evil for the soul.

In Augustine's autobiography the quest archetype tends to predominate. The *Confessions* is organized around the picaresque story of the prodigal youth whose apparently aimless wanderings and futile searches are a part of the providential plan of an attentive, if inscrutable God to lead him to a realization of his true destiny and his true self. In a conversion experience that is dramatic and climactic, confusion gives way to certitude, the sick soul is healed of its ambivalences, and the darkness of doubt yields to the brilliance of faith. Though the representation of this crucial experience involves the mythic and the formulaic, it is at the same time intensely personal and uniquely idiosyncratic.

Grace Abounding to the Chief of Sinners differs from the *Confessions* (and also from *The Pilgrim's Progress*) in that it tends to underrepresent the quest motif, while putting great emphasis on the archetype of *psychomachia*. Thus Bunyan's conversion does not emerge in the narrative as the product of a long search for God, or wisdom, or the true self, but as a lengthy process of repeated cycles of conversion and relapse, or cumulative battles between good and evil principles.

And in *The Seven Storey Mountain*, the ancient image of life as pilgrimage—a linear movement through time—is reinterpreted in the image (also traditional) of the spiritual life as a spiraling ascent. *The Seven Storey Mountain* has reminded a number of its readers of the *Confessions:* "The autobiography of Thomas Merton is a Twentieth Century form of the *Confessions* of St. Augustine," remarks Bishop Fulton Sheen.[10] But this similarity is not an identity; though there are striking resemblances between the two works, there are also striking differences. For example, the Pauline conversion seems to be a significant imaginative model for both (voices speaking, darkness changing to light, imagery of healing). Nonetheless it is far more difficult to pinpoint the exact moment when Merton is converted than it is to do the same with Augustine. The dramatic event of Augustine's conversion is discrete, distinct, and unforgettable, whereas there are a number of incidents in *The Seven Storey Mountain* that could represent "the" climactic conversion episode. Later on in life Merton would come to see this pattern of continuing conversion as itself a valid paradigm of the religious life.

familial archetypes

The characters in autobiographies of conversion almost always have a symbolic function, and can be seen as patterned after the family: the masculine archetype (father, counselor, tutor, God), the feminine archetype (mother, *sapientia*, temptress or spouse, and Church), the fraternal archetype (brother, friend, rival), and the child archetype, symbol of the soul's capacity for resurrection and renewal. It is these personae—figures from both the collective and the personal life—whom the protagonist must confront on his spiritual pilgrimage. Moreover, it is the function of these characters to move the hero away from the natural familial figures toward their sublimatory embodiments in God and Church.

The assertion that an individual's idea of God is shaped by the relationship to the natural parents is now commonplace. Thus for Freud religion derives from "the survival into maturity of the wishes and needs of childhood."[11] In a similar fashion Jung sees religious nostalgia as a regression that "activates the parental imagos" and thus reestablishes the infantile relationship.[12] Developmental psychology draws a similar parallel between infantile experience and religious phenomena: so Erik Erikson, equating religious faith with the primary stage of "basic trust," views religion as a return to an original state of the self embedded in a maternal matrix.[13]

But there are two very different ways to apply the observation that religion and early childhood experience are associated. The first is to see God as an idealized good parent; belief is here a regressive act maintaining a biologically mature individual in a psychologically immature state of dependency, while deflecting any negative feelings that might be felt about this all-powerful parental figure. The God postulated in this relationship is illusory—a reified construct of human need and wishful thinking. This is, of course, the view of religion that Freud suggests, particularly in *The Future of an Illusion* and in his essay "The Question of a Weltanschauung." But a simple reversal suggests more profound ways to interpret the consonance of parental and divine figures—ways for which Freud himself laid the groundwork in his observations on the psychosexual development of the child and in his writings on the significance of the transference. Here the evolving experience of the child may be seen as psychological preparation that is fulfilled and realized in the religious experience of maturity. From this perspective, religious faith and practice can be considered as primarily an expression of the relationship between an individual and God. And the God here postulated is neither an illusory being composed out of displaced parental qualities and projections of self nor an anthropomorphized demiurge. Nor is the relationship between God and person considered a static, fixed polarity of all-powerful creator and dependent creature but, on the contrary, a dynamic, fluid relationship between two "real" beings.

Some contemporary scholars in the psychology of religion use the correlation between religious and early childhood experience in ways that advance our understanding of both phenomena. So the psychoanalyst Paul Pruyser observes: "God's names . . . such as Father, Maker, Sustainer, and Provider, are relevant to the family drama. To me, the statement that a god is a father figure may also imply its complement that biological fathers have numinous qualities."[14] A developmental variant is the theologian Heije Faber's hypothesis "that certain patterns are 'released' in the individual phases of the child's development [these are the Freudian psychosexual stages] . . . and that in, or according to, these developmental patterns corresponding religious structures develop."[15] And then there is the suggestive research of the psychoanalyst D. W. Winnicott on the psychodynamics of early infancy. Winnicott's postulation of an "intermediate area of experiencing"—a "transitional space"—between the infant's awareness of himself only and his developing awareness of others not only provides a locus for religious experience in the development of the psyche, but also defines "illusion" as itself a kind of reality. Thus he writes, "I am therefore studying the substance of *illusion,* that which is allowed to the infant, and which in adult life is inherent in art and religion."[16]

Perhaps conversion could be thought of as a kind of transcendent wish-fulfillment, where the ordinary state of ambivalence gives way to the sense of clarity and inner harmony, and where the usual distance between self and other is replaced by the sensation of oneness. Thus a successful conversion recovers what Winnicott calls "the substance of illusion"; to some degree it is both a rediscovery of the state of early infancy, and its perfection. Unlike pathological regression, the regressive aspect of a conversion experience moves beyond the dualities of self and other, infant and parent, or creature and creator to a position whereby the "illusion" of oneness actually does constitute reality, on the most profound level; the infantile situation thus becomes that toward which we grow in this life, not that from which we grow away.

conversion

The theme of conversion seems to bring together all of these archetypes. Indeed, the way in which the conversion orders the life of the author determines the archetypal content of the narrative. It is in the *Republic* that Plato contemplates the possibility of there being an "art" of conversion: "just as one might have to turn the whole body round in order that the eye should see light instead of darkness, so the entire soul must be turned away from this changing world, until its eye can bear to contemplate reality and that supreme splendour which we have called the Good."[17] The image here is that of the sun as the great source for all life beneath it, and conversion as a tropism of the soul toward its sun. It is an image easily adapted to Christianity, for the Christian idea of conversion is similarly the turning of the soul away from the transitory things of this world toward the eternal things of God. With its imagistic patterns of repeated dyadic units (death and life, sickness and health, darkness and light, blindness and sight), Christian conversion preserves the dualistic habit of thinking so characteristic of Platonism.

William James, in *The Varieties of Religious Experience*, defines conversion in a way that at first sounds very much like Plato's: "the process, gradual or sudden, by which a self hitherto divided, and consciously wrong inferior and unhappy, becomes unified and consciously right superior and happy, in consequence of its firmer hold upon religious realities."[18] The jargon of twentieth-century pychology has replaced the idealistic terminology of the fourth century B.C.; Plato's philosophical dualities of "this changing world" and "that supreme splendour" have been replaced by psychological concepts of that which is "wrong inferior and unhappy" and their opposites, "right superior and happy." But the two philosophers' views on conversion are more alike than they are different. For example, the Platonic dualism of soul and body survives in James's "divided self," which "becomes unified" as a result of conversion; and the Platonic notion of a realm of universals, here called "the Good," is represented by James in the still vaguely Platonic formula "religious realities."

James introduces two important categories into his definition of conversion—the "gradual" and the "sudden"—categories that he has adopted from the work of his predecessor in the psychology of religion, E. D. Starbuck. Following James, scholars in this field regularly favor a division into these two categories: the Pauline model of an abrupt, instantaneous, sometimes mystical event, and the more diffuse model of a gradual, educative process.[19] But James's most suggestive contribution to the psychology of conversion may be his appropriation of the terms *lysis* and *crisis* from medical terminology to refer to the two kinds of conversion: "The older medicine used to speak of two ways, *lysis* and *crisis*, one gradual, the other abrupt, in which one might recover from a bodily disease. In the spiritual realm there are also two ways, one gradual, the other sudden, in which inner unification may occur."[20] The medical matrix from which James draws his terminology of *lysis* and *crisis* is important, for conversion is here implicitly defined as spiritual healing. And if conversion is the healing of the spiritual body, then we might well expect these two models of conversion to function as alternative religious therapies for different spiritual maladies.

James's medical model is a particularly appropriate one, since the metaphors of sickness and healing have been used as descriptions of conversion for centuries. Moreover, these two categories can be extremely useful in understanding how a particular experience of conversion actually structures the autobiographical narrative that describes it. The gradual or *lysis* type James describes as conscious and voluntary: the change "consists in the building up, piece by piece, of a new set of moral and spiritual habits." The abrupt or *crisis* conversion, on the other hand, is unconscious and involuntary, and depends on a yielding up of the will: "The act of yielding . . . is giving one's self over to the new life, making it the centre of a new personality and living, from within, the truth of it which had before been viewed objectively."[21] The conversions of Tolstoy and Bunyan, he observes, are representative of the gradual type, whereas the conversions of St. Augustine and St. Paul are representative of the sudden type.[22] It is this second, sudden type of conversion that James considers the more interesting, and more "authentic." The *crisis* conversion is also more popular, generally, for orthodox Christian scholars, since the yielding up of the personal will, so important to *crisis* conversion, is necessary to any concept of conversion where "grace" assumes a major operative function. In theological terms, "man's extremity is God's opportunity."[23]

In the three autobiographies that I shall be discussing, the conversion that is central to each determines both its religious meaning and its formal structure. The *Confessions* follows the Pauline *crisis* paradigm, although the facts of Augustine's life after his conversion suggest that it may have been a much more gradual process. Undoubtedly, one of the reasons for this discrepancy is that Augustine needed, or wanted, to emphasize the Christian model of conversion, and to de-emphasize the Greek philosophical pattern of a gradual progress through stages toward wisdom. Whatever his reasons, the dramatic potential of autobiography is greatly enhanced by his adoption of the *crisis* paradigm of conversion. In the re-interpretation of his life that is required by the autobiographical process, everything that precedes conversion is seen as either leading up to it or preparing for it in some way, and everything that follows conversion is perceived in accord with the belief that a "new man" has emerged out of that seminal event. Accordingly, the model that emerges is the triadic pattern of spiritual searching, followed by conversion, followed by spiritual certainty.

This triune sequence can be seen as the basic model of the conversion archetype. But there are a number of conversion narratives, among them Bunyan's *Grace Abounding*, that do not demonstrate this structure. If these narratives lack the dramatic arc of a *crisis* conversion—its tension, climax, and resolution—this is because the author's personal experience, or autobiographical recollection of that experience, conforms to a different pattern. In part this is due to the theological and cultural milieu from which both life and autobiography derive. Whereas Augustine's conversion conforms to the Pauline prototype of a sudden, fulminant event, Bunyan's is consistent with Calvinist-Lutheran ideas of regeneration as a lifelong process made up of a series of definite stages. This pattern in *Grace Abounding* might be called the "double conversion," for it consists of a dyadic scheme of *crisis* events within an overarching *lysis* conversion model.

Both the structure of Merton's autobiography and the nature of his conversion are closer to the Augustinian tradition. But Merton's attempt to return to the Christianity of Augustine and the other Church Fathers also involves a conscious repudiation of Protestantism. Both conversion paradigms are thus very much present to his mind—whether as positive or as negative influences—and emerge as influences in the archetypal patterning of his religious experience. In a conversion that is best described as "sacramental," private religious experience is made valid as it is assimilated into the corporate, ecclesiastical rituals of the Roman Catholic Church.

ii. Generic aspects of spiritual autobiography

In conclusion, this study of archetypal patterns in spiritual autobiography must be set against the critical background of current scholarship on autobiography. Autobiographical theory has undergone a good deal of revision within the last thirty years. Recently, interest has veered away from a focus on the self writing the life to a focus on the structure and function of "literary selfhood." One result is the idea that the self is total invention—the only reality being the literary artifact: "the self that was not really in existence in the beginning is in the end merely a matter of text and has nothing whatever to do with an authorizing author. The self, then, is a fiction and so is the life, and behind the text of an autobiography lies the text of an 'autobiography.'"[24]

But the author of a spiritual autobiography almost always regards the self, or the ego, or the finite personality, as a fiction. It is the soul, not the self, that is ultimately "real." And it is from this initial standpoint that the author tells his story. With narratives that *begin* with this assumption, criticism on the ontology of the self is really not very useful. Far more helpful to the study of a literary genre whose subject is the life of the soul is the kind of criticism that emphasizes the recreation or transformation of the self that results from the autobiographical process. Some of the very best criticism of this sort was written in the 1960s and 1970s. In *Design and Truth in Autobiography*, for example, Roy Pascal emphasizes how the imposition of order and pattern in autobiographical recollection serves to change the experiences remembered: he argues that "autobiography is not just reconstruction of the past, but interpretation" and thus, in fact, is "more the revelation of the present situation than the uncovering of the past."[25] In his assertion that the autobiographical process does not simply record the past but organizes and shapes it into a coherent unity, Pascal influenced subsequent critical theory. Thus Dean Ebner writes that autobiography attempts "a shaping of the past, as it were, into a coherent pattern with stages and with self-consistency of character." John Morris similarly observes that "one of the chief purposes of the autobiographer" is "the ordering of his experiences into a shape that answers better than mere continuous sequence to his notion of what his life really means." And in the same vein James Olney observes that the autobiographer writes out of a "vital impulse to order . . . that, in the end, determines both the nature and the form of what he creates."[26]

For all these critics, absolutely essential to the genre of autobiography is the process of ordering, patterning, and shaping the recollected life. To some extent this is also true of religious autobiography. But spiritual autobiography would seem to involve something more than the imposition of pattern and order upon the events of an individual's life, since it is a life that is always seen and understood within the context of a divine meaning. The stance of an individual in the attempt to make sense of his life to himself, or to another, can be seen as quite different from that of the individual who tries to understand his life in relation to a divine presence. Compare the tone, as well as the content, of the remarks of the eighteenth-century Benjamin Franklin and the seventeenth-century Richard Norwood in their explanations of how they came to write. Franklin's autobiography is addressed to his son. Remembering his own pleasure in learning about his ancestors, he remarks, "Imagining it may be equally agreeable to you to know the circumstances of *my* life—many of which you are yet unacquainted with—and expecting a week's uninterrupted leisure in my present country retirement, I sit down to write them for you."[27] Norwood's description of his religious journal is very different: "In the year of our Lord 1639 the 49th year of my age, a day which I had set apart to give unto the Lord by fasting and praying privately, upon some occasion [then] requiring it; amongst other things that day I endeavoured to call to mind the whole course of my life past, and how the Lord had dealt with me."[28]

The key phrase here is *and how the Lord had dealt with me*. Spiritual autobiography is predicated on the relationship between a particular individual, living in a certain place and in a certain time, and a divine reality that is universal and timeless. This relationship between particular and universal tends to present events in an individual's life in a figurative way as signs of underlying archetypal "things." Autobiography is a species of personal history, but spiritual autobiography can be thought of as personal history dilated into sacred history. The subject of an autobiography is an individual who lives (or lived) in a definite time and place, but the real subject of spiritual autobiography is suprahistorical.

Furthermore, the organizing methods of this kind of autobiography, with its theological perspective, will differ in important ways from those of secular autobiography. John S. Dunne, in *A Search for God in Time and Memory*, utilizes Hegel's concept of "dialectical moments" to explain this difference. The method is that of "bringing to mind the time that is out of mind":

> This would be a method first of bringing one's own lifetime to mind, of passing from the "immediate moment" in which one's concerns are confined to the present situation to the "existential moment" in which one's concerns are extended to one's future and one's past . . . and of passing from the existential moment in which one's concerns are confined to one's own lifetime to the "historic moment" in which one's concerns are extended to all time, both the future and the past.[29]

This Hegelian method, set in a religious perspective and given religious terminology, is remarkably similar to the Augustinian figurative model of signs and things. For Augustinian allegory takes real events, real situations, real moments, and uses them, by figural interpretation, to propel author and reader into eternal time and eternal truth, "so that by means of corporeal and temporal things we may comprehend the eternal and spiritual."[30] This is precisely what Augustine is doing in the *Confessions*. Hegel's "existential moment," in which one's concerns are extended to one's past and future, is similar to Augustine's stance in the first nine books (the personal confession) of the *Confessions,* where his theological perspective extends backward to his birth into original sin and forward to his own redemption. Similarly, Hegel's "historical moment," in which one's concerns are extended to all time, both the past and the future, parallels Augustine's stance in the last four books of the *Confessions,* where his concern is with the genesis of the world (the beginning of time) and the final atonement and redemption of all mankind (the end of time).

Although this pattern is most clearly evident in the *Confessions,* it also exists in *Grace Abounding* and *The Seven Storey Mountain.* In the last two sections of *Grace Abounding* (Bunyan's account of his ministry and imprisonment), the scriptural figure of the apostolic preacher is fused with the individual man, John Bunyan. In the section entitled "A Brief Account of the Author's Call to the Work of the Ministry," Bunyan actively fulfills his vocation by acting on others in his preaching; in "A Brief Account of the Author's Imprisonment," he fulfills his vocation by being acted upon, by suffering for the faith. Both sections represent an expansion of personal selfhood into the apostolic pattern of witnessing to the faith by preaching and by willingly suffering persecution. Similarly, the last part of *The Seven Storey Mountain* locates Merton in the monastery, where the personal identity so vividly evoked in earlier sections is absorbed and transformed in his new vocation as monk. When Merton enters the monastery he enters into sacred space and sacred time, and the ordinary routine of day-to-day living becomes supraordinary in contemplation and ritual.

The structural progression in these three spiritual autobiographies from the personal to the sacred, and from one's own time to all time, matches the progress of meaning in Augustine's figural hermeneutics. Indeed, Augustine's concept of signs and realities as set forth in *De Doctrina* provides a basis for the suggestion that there is an archetypal substratum to spiritual autobiography. For example, the biblical event of the exodus of the Israelites out of Egypt to the Promised Land is a "sign" that must be understood as pointing beyond itself. The "realities" that it signifies are those of religious archetype: the exodus itself signifies the archetype of pilgrimage, and Egypt and the Promised Land are signs of the archetype of the two cities—the earthly and the heavenly. Augustine's theory of hermeneutics, Stanley Fish observes, is "not only a way of reading the Bible but a way of reading the World, which, no less than the Bible, is God's book."³¹ And in his *Confessions,* Augustine is "reading" his own life as a text to be interpreted symbolically. Thus his journeyings from Thagaste to Carthage to Rome to Milan and back again to Africa are "signs" pointing to the underlying pattern of the soul's quest for God, in which Augustine's own deliverance from sin to salvation parallels "the education of the human race," which "has advanced, like that of the individual, through certain epochs or, as it were, ages, so that it might gradually rise from earthly to heavenly things, and from the visible to the invisible."³²

Not only is spiritual autobiography different from its secular counterpart in its methodology, but it differs also in regard to its intended reader. Augustine, Bunyan, and Merton all believe that the story of their lives will contribute to the conversion of those who read it. In translating personal events into the language of religious myth and meaning, they hope to lay down an archetypally defined path for future pilgrims. For at some level of consciousness and purpose, the author of a spiritual autobiography offers his experience as a model for the reader. And if the protagonist of spiritual autobiography is indeed not just an individual but a universal, then his experience may well be ours as well: "Everyman" includes us all. One might wish to draw a simple distinction between secular and spiritual autobiography that sees the latter—whether explicitly or implicitly—as hortatory and didactic. But to emphasize the importance of the didactic aim of spiritual autobiography is to distort the work. Also, such a view implies that it is the relationship between author and reader that is the principal one. And this, I am convinced, is simply not so.

It is tempting to observe that the episode during Augustine's conversion when he hears the child chanting *"tolle lege"* and picks up Paul's *Epistles* is itself a miniature of the reader's relationship to the *Confessions.* In other words, we are expected to do the same— to read the *Confessions* in the same way that Augustine read the Scriptures. But if Augustine intended us to "read" the event in this way, he becomes guilty of a certain hubris in attributing to himself the same divine inspiration that belongs only to Scripture. There is another incident in the *Confessions* that parallels the *"tolle lege"* episode and helps us interpret it in a deeper and truer sense. This is when Augustine comes upon Ambrose, deep in study, and goes away for fear of disturbing him (in book 6). Augustine is turned back in upon himself to work out the terms of his quest. These he finds in the study of Scripture, the only "true" literary mediator in that it is the "Word of God," not the words of men.

Thus the reader does not relate to the *Confessions* as Augustine does to Scripture; rather, it is in Alypius, who witnesses Augustine's conversion and who is himself converted, that we are to see ourselves. And Alypius is converted not by witnessing Augustine's conversion, but by mimetically taking to himself a scriptural passage: "[Alypius] requested to see what I had read: I shewed him the place; and he looked further than I had read, nor knew I what followed. This followed: Him that is weak in faith, receive: which he applied to himself, and shewed it to me" (*Conf.* 8.12). Augustine's life is a text to be read and interpreted symbolically, but it is a text to be read by himself. And we, as readers, are encouraged to do the same with our own lives.

The true relationship, then, in spiritual autobiography is not that between author and reader but between the author and his God. This relationship is concretized in very different ways in the three religious autobiographies. In the *Confessions* Augustine actually addresses God, and God speaks to Augustine through the medium of the created word. Thus God communicates to Augustine not only through Scripture, but also in the books of the Platonists and in the voice of the child whose chanting *"tolle lege"* is the catalyst for his conversion. In *Grace Abounding* Scripture is the primary medium through which God and man converse. Thus Bunyan's prayers are either direct biblical quotations or are meditations on scriptural passages. God speaks directly to Bunyan throughout the narrative, but always in the set language of the Bible. In *The Seven Storey Mountain*, Merton's own prayers to God are only referred to indirectly; it is God's address to Merton that appears in the autobiography. What Mazzeo writes about Augustine—"the nature of St. Augustine's thought led him to look more and more to the intelligible, the eternal and the silent"[33]—might also have been written about Thomas Merton. For Merton paradoxically fulfills his Trappist vows of silence by writing about the ineffable, by speaking about the unspeakable.

Thus spiritual autobiography is written not primarily out of a need to convert others, although that is one of its functions, but out of a need to express the inexpressible and to point to the greater realities of the invisible and the eternal. Only in this way is it a "sign." Just as secular autobiography has been explained as the imposition of meaning upon the random events of an individual life, so can spiritual autobiography be described as the expression of what remains fundamentally inexpressible. In other words, the aim in spiritual autobiography is not so much to make meaningful or to comprehend an individual life as it is to believe in its ultimate meaningfulness, whether or not it is a meaning that can be understood. If God reveals himself in and through history, then personal, experiential history is also revelation, and can be comprehended in the language of those archetypes and symbols which reveal its essential meaning in relation to divine reality.

Most critics no longer make a distinction between secular and spiritual autobiography. But I would suggest that such a distinction be retained. For spiritual autobiography, unlike its secular counterpart, is concerned not just with the self but also with the soul in its evolving relationship to God; it is written with a divine audience in view, and its methodology involves a figurative reading of the events of an individual's life. The method of achieving this is one where events in the personal life are imposed upon archetypal patterns of sacred history, and the meaning and purpose of that life is therein seen as coincident with divine purpose. Spiritual autobiography not only serves as a vehicle whereby the facts of a person's life can be shaped into a purposeful (and divinely purposed) unity, but it serves as a vehicle whereby the "meaning" of the self can be perceived through the imagined eyes of God, and thus articulated in the context of the meaning of life itself.

2
St. Augustine
The Heroic Paradigm

i. Narrative and ideational aspects of the quest

In his recent study of religion and autobiography, John S. Dunne observes that Augustine's description of the journey of the soul in his *Confessions* established a paradigm for spiritual experience that has been imitated and passed down through the ages. This recurrent pattern, he writes, is due "to the genuinely archetypal character of the events Augustine narrates, the actual recurrence of such events in human lives."[1] Similarly, Robert O'Connell finds that Augustine, Everyman, and Adam share a "secret identity [that] governs the subtle development of the *Confessions*, harmonizes its themes, blends them into a symphonic unity, discloses their profoundest sense."[2] The hero of the *Confessions*, and of subsequent spiritual autobiographies that model themselves on Augustine's work, is more than just an individual self; the protagonist is, indeed, Everyman, the archetypal soul. Thus it is not surprising that these statements by twentieth-century scholars should have their parallels in the remarks of Augustine's earlier readers. So St. Teresa observes, in her own spiritual autobiography: "When I started to read the *Confessions*, I seemed to see myself in them and I began to commend myself often to that glorious Saint. When I got as far as his conversion and read how he heard that voice in the garden, it seemed exactly as if the Lord were speaking in that way to me, or so my heart felt."[3] And Petrarch, too, remarks that after reading the *Confessions*, "I account myself to be reading the narrative not of another man's pilgrimage but of my own."[4]

The word *pilgrimage* is an appropriate one, for it suggests the archetype of quest—an archetype that combines the inner dynamic of the soul's yearning for God with the outer dynamic of the mythic hero's journey toward some longed-for goal. And this is what spiritual autobiography is all about: the confluence of inner experience—the heart seeking union and the mind seeking wisdom—with an exterior narrative wherein those interior psychological realities are embodied. And insofar as its purpose is to make those interior realities of heart and mind incarnate, the narrative necessarily conforms to archetypal patterns that are common to us all.

Seen as psychological components of the soul in its quest for God, heart and mind are but two aspects of the same process. For our feelings of inchoate longing, vague yearning, and unappeasable desire are the affective and libidinal counterparts to the intellectual search for wisdom and truth. It is important to think of these as psychological phenomena that are "participial": seeking, yearning, wanting, desiring, and searching indicate a psychological process as it is actually experienced—a process that is embodied in the sustained personal narrative of spiritual autobiography.

For Augustine, then, as for subsequent writers who model their works on his, the seeking of the mind and heart for satisfaction finds expression in the archetype of the quest. Indeed, the major metaphor for the conversion of the soul in the *Confessions* is the quest, and the narrative structure of the whole work is evidence of the coordinating effect of that archetype. The literal journeys from Thagaste to Carthage to Rome to Milan embody the intellectual pilgrimage through the various philosophies and religions available to Augustine at the time, and also point toward the affective journey of the *cor irrequietum*—the heart that yearns for an end to its restlessness.

In the *Confessions*, as in the many spiritual autobiographies that will pattern themselves after it, life before conversion is perceived as a kind of labyrinthine maze with numerous false passages and wrong turnings, but one that eventually and inevitably culminates in conversion. Accordingly, the first nine books are the story of Augustine's personal life, of his spiritual wandering in the "distant country" that is the Earthly City. But in the last four books the quest of pagan epic and Old Testament Scripture turns into the metaphor of the Christian pilgrimage, the *peregrinatio*[5] where the "true haven" or "final resting-place" is the City of God—"*regem nostrum et patriam Hierusalem simplicem, castam*" (10.35)—a reality not attainable in this life. It is against this one eternal city that we are to see the many secular cities—Thagaste, Carthage, Rome, even Milan—in the story of Augustine's spiritual quest.

Born in the small African town of Thagaste, Augustine was the son of a Christian mother and a pagan father. Shortly after his father died, when Augustine was seventeen, he was sent to Carthage to further his studies. While he was there he devoted himself whole-heartedly to the pursuit of pleasure, in the course of which he took a concubine, who was to remain with him some fourteen years and bear his son. It was also at Carthage that Augustine underwent his two youthful conversions: the first to wisdom when he read Cicero's *Hortensius*, and the second to Manichaeism. These two proleptic conversions represent the type and antitype of his later, "true" conversion to Christianity.

The arrival in Carthage of Faustus, high priest of the Manichees, was the beginning of Augustine's disillusionment with Manichaeism. From Carthage he traveled, against the wishes of his mother, Monica, to Rome. It was there that he was exposed to the philosophical agnosticism of the Academics, who claimed that true wisdom resided not in the attainment of truth, which was thought to be impossible, but in the pursuit of truth. Peter Brown observes that "this comparatively short period of uncertainty is one of the most crucial and little-known turning-points of his life. For it brought home to Augustine the ideal of 'Wisdom' as a prolonged quest."[6] After only a year in Rome he proceeded to Milan, where he met Ambrose, and not long after became a catechumen in the Catholic Church. From here on, in Milan and with Ambrose, Augustine's *peregrinatio* of aimless wandering turns into one of purposeful search.

Symbolically, the brief time Augustine spent in Rome is a kind of parenthesis between the cities of Carthage and Milan. For if Carthage is, in some sense, the city of Faustus, Milan is certainly the city of Ambrose. The two religious figures function as countertypes of the archetypal figure of "wise old man" or *senex:* Faustus is the *senex in malo;* Ambrose, the *senex in bono*. Thus Carthage and Milan acquire a symbolic importance in the odyssey of Augustine's life: Carthage as a type of the Earthly City and Milan as a type of the Heavenly City. Moreover, there is a direct parallel between geographical place and intellectual quest where Thagaste, Carthage, Rome, and Milan represent literally "real" objective correlatives to Augustine's intellectual and spiritual development from African Christianity to Manichaeism to the doctrines of the Academics, and finally to the Christianity of Ambrose.

Augustine's conversion can be seen as the end of his quest, and, at the same time, as marking its beginning. For if the first eight books describe the religious quest of the author from birth to conversion (the ninth is devoted to Monica's death and biography), the last four books expand the quest archetype into the story of all Mankind—extended into the beginnings of time in the genesis of the world, and anagogically into that "eternal Sabbath" which will commence with the end of time.

That the *Confessions* does not simply record the literal facts of Augustine's life and conversion is demonstrable not only by these last four books, but also by narrative, ideational, and structural elements in the way the first nine books are written. For its author the *Confessions* is a kind of darkened mirror that not only reflects the "signative" facts of a life but suggests also the realities, the "things" beyond those signs. When Petrarch and St. Teresa remark on the identity between Augustine's experience and their own, and when O'Connell and Dunne marvel at Augustine's ability to describe archetypal experience, they are all asserting the universality of the "things," the "realities," that lay behind the literal events described in the autobiography. The intellectual search for truth and the heart's yearning for satisfaction—these are the universals, the "things," of the quest archetype, whose signative nature is a narrative of specifics in geography, events, persons.

To refer to the "signative" aspects of the quest archetype in the *Confessions* is to focus on the literal story of Augustine's life and also on a deeper level of discourse that, as I shall show, derives both from biblical and from classical sources. There is a long tradition of commentary on the *Confessions* that sees Augustine's conversion as exclusively Christian. As Guardini writes, "the God of Christianity to whom Augustine was converted and before whom he recorded his confessions is not the absolute being of philosophy, but the holy, living God of the Old and New Testaments."[7] A more common contemporary approach to the *Confessions* sees it as made up of ideas and images that Augustine inherited from the Greek philosophical tradition, upon which he imposed, sometimes rather superficially, biblical ideas and images. Indeed, some of the very best current Augustine scholarship is dedicated to explicating an underlying Neoplatonic (mostly Plotinian) intellectual framework.⁸ And yet there is more to classical culture than Plato or the Neoplatonists;⁹ too often scholars tend to equate "classical" and "Platonic" (or "Neoplatonic") in their discussions of Augustine's sources. It is important to remember that for Augustine the classical tradition includes Vergil as well as Plato, epic poetry as well as philosophy.

I shall assume here that Augustine stands at the confluence of the two great traditions of classical and Christian thought. The quest archetype of the *Confessions*—the theme of the *peregrinatio animae*—can thus be seen as drawing upon three primary sources: Neoplatonic doctrines of the fall and return of the soul, the biblical story of the Prodigal Son, and epic formulations of the journey of the hero, particularly Vergil's *Aeneid*. And for my analysis the concepts, images, and symbols that Augustine derives from biblical, Platonic, and epic traditions must be considered significant not merely as sources but even more as archetypal analogues: they resonate with the *Confessions* and with one another as well.

For Plotinus, the fall of the soul is a progressive one through declining stages of awareness. Although the inferior stage cannot know what has preceded it, still the soul feels an inherent drive for completion that is characterized by a yearning for its source in its superior stage.¹⁰ Eugene TeSelle nicely paraphrases Plotinus's doctrine: "the soul has gone outside itself *(progressus)* and is poured out *(a seipso fusus)* into the world of multiplicity, from which it needs to return to itself and thereby to God, who is present within the self."¹¹ The Plotinian fall of the soul and its need to return to its divine source have mythic, archetypal overtones: it is the very stuff of which the stories of the quest of the mythic hero are made. What Plotinus says about the fall of the soul could describe Adam and Eve in the Garden of Eden, Aeneas in the arms of Dido, or Augustine in the embrace of his concubine: the soul becomes enslaved to the things of the body, writes Plotinus, "when it becomes fascinated with the brilliant reflections of the divine that it sees in the material world and, losing sight of itself, 'turns' toward them and 'goes forth' from itself and becomes 'present' not to itself but to the body."¹²

The Plotinian theme of the soul's fall and return becomes parable in the story of the Prodigal Son, who also undergoes a fall "outward" and a return "inward"—both allegorized as journeys. Augustine mentions this parable several times; it seems to have functioned as a kind of self-portrait for him in the opening books of the *Confessions* in the same way that the stories of Ponticianus and Victorinus did in the final books. For if the stories of Ponticianus and Victorinus allegorize the joy of the conversion of the soul in its return to God, the parable of the Prodigal Son stresses the sorrow of the soul's fall in its initial, willed departure from God. Augustine quotes the parable at length in 1.18; perhaps it is not accidental that this passage is prefaced with a reference to Juno's speech in the *Aeneid*, which Augustine memorized as a boy, where she laments her inability to prevent Aeneas from going to Rome (1.17). Indeed, it seems likely that Augustine would have recognized the archetypal consonance between the epic and the parable. Later he alludes to the parable in terms that resonate with the *peregrinatio* theme: "Very far verily had I journeyed away from thee *(peregrinabar)* being even barred from the husks of those swine . . ." (3.6). Comparing himself to the Prodigal Son, Augustine writes: "I preserved not mine own abilities entire for thy service, but wandered into a far country, to spend it there upon my harlotries *(meretrices cupiditates)*" (4.16).[13] The allusion here is to the *meretrix* figure of the book of Proverbs, who seduces the soul away from its true love, *sapientia*.

Moreover, Augustine used the parable in the same way that he used the *Aeneid*, to refer to the archetypal city of sin. Thus the distant city toward which the Prodigal Son travels is Augustine's Earthly City, "the streets of Babylon," in which our capacity for love "is of its own inclination changed, being quite altered from its heavenly clearness and depraved" (3.2). Because the soul errs in choosing the wrong object for its love, it is in exile from its true home in God's eternal city. The rhetoric of quest throughout the *Confessions* suggests the scriptural image of the filial soul: prodigal in its willed journey of the affections away from an inherited "good," and penitent in its contrition and yearning to turn back to God.

But of these three sources for the quest archetype in the *Confessions*—the Plotinian, the biblical, and the Vergilian—it is the last that is perhaps the most important. The *Confessions* is permeated with all sorts of resemblances to Vergil's *Aeneid*. Augustine's tacit comparison of the protagonist of the *Confessions* to Vergil's Aeneas is facilitated by the sustained narrative that is the structure both of spiritual autobiography and of epic. In using the *Aeneid* to help shape his own ideas of heroism and quest, Augustine shows how classical fiction is both fulfilled and transformed in what he considers to be Christian fact, and at the same time inevitably moves his literary persona into the realm of myth. This is not to maintain that Augustine's appropriation of Vergilian archetypes in the *Confessions* is necessarily a conscious one. What I do want to suggest though is that the mythicization of self that inevitably occurs in spiritual autobiography—whether it is a conscious or an unconscious process—results here in the creation of a protagonist who in certain ways is very similar to the epic hero.

It is my belief that the archetypal resonance that St. Teresa and Petrarch, Dunne and O'Connell experience in reading the *Confessions*, Augustine found in Vergil's *Aeneid*. In Augustine's time the imaginations of pagan and Christian alike sensed a similarity between the epic adventures of Aeneas and the growth of the soul.[14] Moreover, as a professional rhetorician, Augustine studied and taught Latin poetry, especially Vergil and the commentaries on Vergil. Harald Hagendahl, in his exhaustive two-volume study on Augustine and the Latin classics, provides convincing evidence that the impact of Vergil on Augustine is indeed considerable—though it would appear to be at its lowest ebb in the *Confessions*.[15] The basis of my argument is that Augustine never totally dismisses his early training as a rhetorician, though he may often have wanted to, and that the conscious repudiation of classical thought, especially of Vergil, that is evident in the *Confessions* might well signal an unconscious use of those same classical motifs and themes. As Hagendahl observes, "Since his young days, and by renewed reading, Augustine's mind had been so impregnated with Virgilian poetry that lines and phrases crept in almost of their own accord."[16] Thus it is not inconsistent with Augustine's mature disavowal of classicism that his youthful saturation with Vergil should provide him with a reservoir of images, scenes, and character portrayals that served as formative metaphors in the creation of his autobiography.[17]

Given Augustine's professional immersion in Vergil and the intimate knowledge of the text that his quotations and allusions suggest, we can be nearly certain that he was aware of the parallel between the incidents of the *Aeneid* and certain events of his own life. For example, when Augustine leaves Carthage for Rome, his mother tries frantically to detain him in the same way that Dido tries to keep Aeneas from sailing away from Carthage to Rome. Like Aeneas, who deceives Dido by sailing away from Carthage at night in secrecy, Augustine evades the tearful Monica by also sailing away secretly, at night. And surely Augustine would have observed the archetypal consonance not only between Monica and Dido, but also between the Carthage of his own experience and the

Carthage of Aeneas's experience. Like Vergil, Augustine reifies the "choices" made during the course of a life in the language of geographical place.

If these are similarities too obvious for Augustine to have missed, and if the *Confessions* was written, as Hagendahl suggests, with "a deep-seated hostility to the old cultural tradition,"[18] then we must ask why Augustine would repeatedly allude to events in his life that closely paralleled events in the *Aeneid*. One answer might be that, for Augustine, the Christian "hero" represented the fulfillment of the ideal of the mythic hero—in much the same way that the New Covenant is a fulfillment of the Old Covenant. And this is consistent with the way in which early Christian thinkers used both the Old Testament and pagan literature. Thus the imperial future of Rome in the *Aeneid*, like the Promised Land in the book of Exodus, prefigures the redemptive future of the Church. And likewise, the spiritual quest that is the subject of the *Confessions* becomes the Christian truth, the Platonic "reality," of which the journey of epic and myth is a prefiguration.

Indeed, the *Confessions* might well be called Augustine's spiritual *Aeneid*. Like Aeneas, Augustine is called by divine providence to leave behind the carnal pleasures and worldly ambitions of the Earthly City (in both instances the actual city is Carthage), and to embark on an arduous quest toward the place to which each is destined—the Heavenly City for Augustine, Rome for Aeneas. The symbol of the two cities, and the necessary abandonment or destruction of the one before the other can be attained or created, link the archetype of quest to the experience of conversion. Indeed, Aeneas can be seen as undergoing a type of conversion in turning away from Dido, Carthage, and the pleasures of the senses, just as Augustine's conversion can be characterized in the epic trope of denying personal wishes in favor of providential destiny.

For both Aeneas and Augustine the lures of Carthage, the Earthly City, are focused on a woman: Augustine must abandon his Carthaginian concubine to fulfill his destiny, just as Aeneas must abandon Dido.[19] For Aeneas, Carthage can be seen as itself a "second Troy," in that his experience there represents as it reproduces the sins of lust for which Troy was punished. In this context it is significant that Dido destroys herself by fire—a metaphorical lust that harkens back to the fires, both literal and figurative, that consumed Troy. The response of Augustine's concubine, sent back to Africa and deprived of her son, is a self-imposed chastity: it is a solution that is at the same time self-destructive and self-saving, and illustrates one difference between epic and Christian ideals.

Not only is the journey theme represented in both books as the passage from city to city, but it is also represented as a descent into the underworld for Aeneas or as the journey into the self for Augustine—a journey that can be represented either as ascent or descent. There are several episodes in the *Confessions* that can be seen as archetypically similar to Aeneas's descent into the underworld: his entry into himself in book 7, his ascent with his mother into the visionary apprehension of "the eternal wisdom" in 9, and his contemplative descent through time in the *penetrale* of memory in 10. Aeneas, in his sojourn in the underworld, encounters ghosts from his racial history—the history of Troy; Augustine in the "underground" of his psyche—in his memory—confronts Christian truths that transcend history. Aeneas is accompanied by the Sibyl; Augustine, by his mother with her prophetic dreams. Aeneas finds Anchises in the Elysian fields of pagan Paradise; Augustine glimpses wisdom in "that region of never-wasting plenty"—the Christian Paradise.

Lastly, Augustine's tacit comparison of himself with Aeneas is supported by the particular way in which Aeneas is characterized. Throughout Vergil's poem Aeneas is known as *"pius* Aeneas.*"* It is a significant epithet, for it points to an underlying difference between Aeneas and the other epic heroes, "swift-footed Achilles" and "Odysseus of the many devices." Aeneas is a remarkably passive character in the *Aeneid*. Throughout he is depicted as the pawn of conflicting superhuman forces: his *pietas* is a function of his fidelity to the providential plan of the founding of Rome, despite the obstacles, enticements, and impediments that are devised to prevent or at least delay his fulfilling that destiny. *Pietas* in classical literature often has the dual meaning of filial devotion and patriotism: for example, *pietas* is translated as "duty" in the Loeb edition of Cicero's *De Inventione* and *duty* in turn is defined as what is owed to country and parents.[20] In the figure of Aeneas, *pietas* is expressed in both senses, for Aeneas carries his aged father on his back (literally and also figuratively) in his attempts to be true to the providential vision of Rome. Thus Aeneas's *pietas* toward his fatherland—Rome as the "new Troy"—is in a parallel relation to the Christian soul's *pietas* toward its spiritual "fatherland." In terms of this dual meaning of *pietas,* Augustine's relation to his mother parallels Aeneas's relation to his father, where the maternal city of God, the "motherland," replaces the city of Rome as the country to which the hero is destined. In obedience, however reluctant or delayed, to this *pietas,* both heroes must sacrifice their personal lives.

The archetypal analogy between the *Aeneid* and the *Confessions* is richly suggestive. This confluence does not suggest that Augustine read the *Aeneid* as an allegory or as a source of Christian truth, but quite the contrary: just as the saint's life assimilates and corrects the life of the philosopher sage,[21] so Augustine is creating a true epic of the soul in quest of wisdom and peace, whose Christian meaning supplies the inner truth that Vergil could not know. It is his own life that Augustine interprets as epic and as allegory. Augustine's success, in that he was able to write an account of his experience that could set up profound reverberations for generations of readers, is due to the fact that he was able to grasp the truth of his life in its archetypal dimensions—dimensions that transcend as they reconcile diversities of culture, race, history, religion, and intellectual tradition.

And now we must turn from the narrative to the ideational aspects of the quest archetype: the idea of quest as a return, the symbol of the garden, and the episodes describing the quest in the language of Neoplatonic vision. The Plotinian doctrine of the soul's inevitable fall and need to return, the parable of the Prodigal Son with its departure and return, and the *Aeneid* too, where Rome is "new Troy," all allude to the goal of the quest less as a discovery than as a recovery; a turning backward, a reversion, a remembering.[22] In the *Confessions,* this "recognitive" aspect of quest is linked with Augustine's idea of the power of memory as a repository of potentially dynamic archetypes (10.17). He alludes to it parabolically in mentioning the New Testament story of the woman who, in finding a lost coin, would not have been able to do so had she not remembered it (10.18). The lost coin is symbolic of "the blessed life *(beata vita)."* And the parable leads Augustine to ask: "but this I want to know, whether this blessed life be in the memory? For, never should we love it, did we not know it" (10.20). The *"beata vita,"* which exists in the eternity of memory, is an Edenic archetype.

Thus the Prodigal Son's leaving his father's house for distant lands and the Plotinian soul's emptying itself outward are quasi-allegorical formulations of an archetypal Fall—a primal memory that we share in the dim recesses of our common mind—a *"beata vita"* once known and now lost and forgotten. Indeed, the primal Fall can well be thought of as a kind of forgetting. If this is so, then conversion is a remembering—perceived either as process (the *lysis* conversion) or as an event (*crisis* conversion). But how do we remember that which has been forgotten? Augustine replies that "we have not yet utterly forgotten that which we even remember ourselves to have forgotten" (10.19).

Seeking and remembering are thus two aspects of the same process. The Latin *quaerere*—a common verb in the *Confessions*—means both to search for and to ask or inquire after. Augustine uses *quaerere* in referring both to the woman seeking for her lost groat and to the individual seeking after God. But that which was lost is, in both cases, "only lost to the eyes, but surely preserved in the memory" (10.18). It is the difference between sight, which is outer, and vision, which is inner. The true path of the spiritual quest leads inward; it is a journey into "the fields and spacious palaces" or the "huge court" of memory (10.8).

The quest archetype can thus be seen as a journey of recovery and return where, with the guidance of memory, the energizing forces of heart and mind drive the voyaging soul back and inward toward its destined fulfillment. The yearning of the soul for God, which is so prominent a theme in the *Confessions*, is itself an expression of this nostalgic need to return home, to recover what was lost, to remember what was forgotten. The soul engaged in this quest is traversing a landscape that is indeed interior, and easily allegorized. While its starting point is the personal and the psychological, this level soon opens out (or in) to a level of reality that is transpersonal and archetypal.

An example of this kind of thinking is Augustine's use of the symbol of the garden. There are three key experiences recorded in the *Confessions* that occur in the setting of a garden. The first is the episode in Augustine's childhood of the arbor, where he wantonly robs a pear tree of its fruit—an autobiographical analogue to original sin in the garden of Eden. It is a sin of disobedience where "a company of lewd young fellows" despoil the pear tree and fling the fruit to hogs—an act provoked not by hunger or greed but by a kind of perverse satiety: "Yet had I a desire to commit thievery; and did it, compelled neither by hunger nor poverty; but even through a cloyedness of well-being. . . . For I stole that, of which I had enough of mine own, and much better" (2.4). The spoiling of the pear tree is a despoliation of the self: the fruit flung to the hogs recalls the husks thrown to the swine in that other story of an adolescent—both images representing the prodigality of youth turning to sin "out of a voluptuous and darkened affection." (1.18)

The result of the fornication of the soul in squandering the passions which are its divine inheritance is the desolation of the self. So Augustine ends book 2 and his youth with the passage made famous by that modern pilgrim, T. S. Eliot: "I went astray, O my God, yea, too much astray from thee my Stay in these days of my youth, and I became unto myself a wasteland" (2.10).

The second instance is the garden with its fig tree, which provides the setting for Augustine's famous conversion. It is a scene that looks back to the arbor and pear tree of Augustine's youth, the imagery of sudden illumination during conversion—"instantly... it was as though a light of confidence now darted into my heart"—reversing the "darksome affections" of adolescent sin. Moreover, as the pear tree recalls the tree of good and evil in Genesis, so the fig tree recalls the fig tree in the book of John, under which Nathaniel was seen by Christ before he went to meet the man reported to be the Messiah. About this Leo Ferrari observes: "Augustine's earliest references to this episode do not explain the significance of the fig tree, but do emphasize the conviction that Nathaniel was in a blessed state when under that tree."[23] The symbolism is obvious—it is the theme so common in the *Confessions* of the God who "sees us" before we "see him"—the God from whom we depart, although he has never departed from us.

In the third instance the garden represents the theme of spiritual fruition—the fruit of conversion—in the soul's union with God through vision. This occurs in book 9, when Augustine and his mother stand in a window overlooking a garden and experience together an exaltation of the spirit that culminates in their visionary apprehension of God (9.10). The garden here clearly recalls the transfigured garden of Revelation, with its river of the water of life and its tree of life. Augustine and Monica, in their shared visionary ecstasy, "thirst with the mouth of our heart after those upper streams of thy fountain, the fountain of life" and ascend "as high as that region of never-wasting plenty, whence thou feedest Israel for ever with the food of truth" (9.10). It is an episode that reinvokes the *quaerere* theme, only at the stage of its fruition. For the garden image here marks the maturity of spiritual vision in a language where the oral imagery of the soul as infant suckling at the breast of God is transposed into the erotic imagery of the soul in the ecstasy of union with God. In its synthesis of the passionate and the spiritual, this episode reinvokes both the garden of the pear tree with its sin of prodigality and the garden of the fig tree with its redemption by conversion.

Significantly, the three garden images are placed so as to point to the conversion that is the center and goal of the spiritual quest. Augustine here uses structure itself as an expressive and didactic device in the formation of his autobiography; he does the same thing with the Neoplatonic theme of vision. In both instances the resultant pattern highlights his conversion: the three garden images occur before, during, and after conversion; similarly, the two visionary episodes are placed just before and just after his conversion. Augustine first writes at length about vision in book 7; he does so again in book 9. And the intervening book, 8, is the story of his conversion. It is significant that in looking back over his life, Augustine should perceive these visionary experiences as bracketing his conversion. As structural elements in the autobiography, they indicate progressive stages in the quest for God.

The experience in book 7 is mentioned several times. The first of these references (in 7.10) is preceded by a section where Augustine tells us of his readings in "certain books of the Platonists" (7.9). His description of the effect of those books on his thinking is worth attending to closely, for he writes not only of what he did read there, but also of what he did *not* read (i.e., of "Jesus Christ the Mediator")—thus weaving "then" and "now" in such a way as to form a sort of three-dimensional narrative texture. For the constant alternation of "and therein I read" with "all this I did not read there" presents us with a double image of the autobiographical persona—the observed, to which is added the authorial persona—the observer. In other words, it is a highly complex narrative where Augustine the author, Bishop of Hippo, looks back on the as-yet-unconverted Augustine reading the Neoplatonists, who himself seems to be providentially looked forward to an Augustine who is reading St. Paul. And it is out of this texture of Neoplatonism supplemented by a later exposure to Pauline Christianity—of a synthesis of a past (and double) perceived self and a present authorial perceiver—that Augustine introduces his discussion of vision in 7.10: "And thence [from those books] being admonished to return unto myself. . . ." In the lines that follow, the quest motif links the Neoplatonic doctrine of vision with the Christian dogma of Christ the Mediator: "I entered into my inmost being, thou being my leader, and I was able to do this because thou wast my helper. Into myself I went, and with the eyes of my soul I saw over the same eyes of my soul, over my mind, the unchangeable light" (7.10). The passage also links Vergilian epic with Christian doctrine, for the divine guidance that accompanies Augustine through the depths of his soul is reminiscent of Aeneas's journey into the underworld accompanied by the Sibyl, and also his journey into the future, where he is led by Anchises.

Later on in the same book Augustine expands on his discussion, this time utilizing the Neoplatonic ascent of the soul to discover the "unchangeable light" and even to approach a sense of "that which is"—the Christianized realm of universals and archetypes (7.17). That both accounts are variants on the same visionary experience is underscored by the similarity in his description of the soul's apprehension of the "unchangeable light." In 7.10 it is experienced as the voice of God exclaiming *"ego sum qui sum"*; in 7.17 it is discovered to be *"id, quod est."* The experience is mentioned again in 7.20: "But having read these books of the Platonists, having once gotten the hint from them, and falling upon the search of incorporeal truth; I came to get a sight of these invisible things of thine *(invisibilia tua)*. . . ." In all the accounts of the visionary experience in book 7, Augustine's experience of *"invisibilia tua"* concludes with the soul's falling off, driven back by *"consuetudo carnalis"*—the heavy weight of sin and habit. It is the role of Scripture in his intellectual and spiritual development, he tells us, that will enable him in the future not merely to see God but to hold to what he sees: *"veniat et videat et teneat"* (7.21). Similarly, it is only when he is able to "embrace the Mediator between God and man" that he will acquire sufficient strength to resist the lures of sin and habit and thus find fruition in that divine embrace (7.18, 20).

After his conversion, Augustine describes another visionary experience. It is significant that he achieves this climactic experience not alone, as before, but with his mother. This event occurs at Ostia, just before her death, and is one that Augustine believes to have been providentially arranged (9.10). Furthermore, it is an event that in many ways parallels Augustine's conversion in the preceding book: the fact that Augustine and Monica stand in a window overlooking a garden is surely an authorial reminiscence of the garden where Augustine in the throes of conversion was accompanied by his close friend Alypius. So too, the part that Monica plays in the ecstatic experience of the soul after conversion is reminiscent of Augustine's portrayal of the maternal, yet sexually ambiguous figure of Continence, who appears to him just before his conversion, beckoning to him with outspread arms from that "other side" of his future: "cheerful was she, but not dissolutely pleasant, honestly coaxing me to come to her . . ." (8.11). The language that Augustine uses when he describes the visionary ascent toward wisdom that he shares with Monica is the language of passion—a reminder that his doctrine of illumination is the product both of mind and of heart: "Yet we thirsted with the mouth of our heart *(inhiabamus ore cordis)* after the fountain of life. . . . Yea we soared higher yet, by inward musing, and discoursing upon thee. . . . And while we were thus discussing and thirsting *(loquimur et inhiamus)* after [wisdom], we arrived to a little touch of it with the whole effort of our heart. . ." (9.20). Monica and Augustine attain these peaks of religious ecstasy by the very passion of their seeking; by driving themselves with an *"ardentiore affectus."* Simply to list the first-person-plural verbs in this episode, in the order in which they occur, is to trace the confluence of mind and heart in the impassioned ascent of mother and son toward God: "we talked together. . . we sought after. . . we ranged over. . . we ascended. . . we came unto. . . we passed beyond. . . so that we attained that region of everlasting plenty where you feed Israel forever with the food of truth. . ." (9.10).

Augustine structures his autobiography in such a way that the solitary vision of book 7 and the shared vision of book 9 represent the difference between Augustine the Neoplatonist and Augustine the Christian. He himself summarizes the difference between Neoplatonism and Christianity in the appropriate imagery of quest: the Platonists are like "those that saw whither they were to go but knew nothing of the way," whereas Christianity is "that path which leads into that blessed country, not only to be looked upon, but dwelt in" (7.20). The "blessed country" is the same as the "region of everlasting plenty" that marks the climax of the vision shared with Monica in book 9. Thus the solitary Neoplatonic vision culminates in the abstractions of *"invisibilia tua"* or *"lucem incommutabilem,"* while the Christianized vision with Monica culminates in the concrete (and maternal) imagery of a place of overflowing plenty. It is this metaphorical difference between "beholding" and "holding"—a difference between intellectual and affective knowing—that demonstrates the superiority of Christianity over Neoplatonism for Augustine.

Peter Brown has suggested that during the fifteen years between Augustine's conversion and his writing the *Confessions,* the ideal of the quest of wisdom "as a vertical ascent, as a progress towards a final, highest stage to be reached in this life" gives way to the image of the *iter*, the long highway, and the moments of transcendence become "the consolations of a traveller on a long journey." In support of this, Brown quotes Augustine: "While we do this, until we achieve our aim, we are still travelling"; these moments of transcendence thus become no more than "points of light 'along this darkening highway.' "[24] But these "points of light" can be seen as more than consolations; such visionary experiences reconcile our yearning for God and our inability to possess God fully in this life. In them, vertical ascent and horizontal pilgrimage become different aspects of the same thing. It is the fundamental paradox of the Christian quest archetype, where finding God is at the same time only beginning to truly search for him.

ii. *Crisis* conversion

For generations of readers, Augustine's experience of conversion, as he records it in the *Confessions*, has served as a paradigm for what happens during conversion. Different readers have concentrated upon different aspects of this model. Thus Richard Norwood, writing in his *Journal* (1639) about his own conversion, temporizes in the traditional Augustinian fashion: "Therefore it seemed safest to defer conversion till the heat of youth were a little over. . . . It will be better when the unbridled fury and heat of youth is somewhat assuaged; or if I will needs convert now and forsake all the pleasures of the world in the prime of my youth, yet take thy fill a little and be a little satisfied in worldly pleasures. . . ."[25] Does Norwood find his own experience articulated in Augustine's story of conversion, or does he actually see the *Confessions* as a model in shaping his own experience? Most likely, it is both. On the other hand, St. Teresa uses the Augustinian model of conversion not so much to shape her experience as for contrast. Although she professes herself to be astonished at the identity between Augustine's conversion and her own, in one important passage in her autobiography she remarks that "there was only one thing that troubled me . . . namely that, after the Lord had once called [saints like Augustine], they did not fall again, whereas I had fallen so often that I was distressed by it."[26] What Norwood and St. Teresa, in their different ways, choose to focus upon are two major elements characterizing a *crisis* conversion: the long period of resistance, denial, and procrastination preceding the *crisis* episode, and the total change in life and personality apparently effected by that event.

The paradigmatic *crisis* conversion is abrupt, intense, highly emotional, vivid and distinctly memorable, and often accompanied by physical automatisms such as seeing visions or hearing voices. It is a clear and unequivocal event marking a definite turning point in the convert's transition from one set of beliefs and values to another. William James describes it as an experience "in which, often amid tremendous emotional excitement or perturbation of the senses, a complete division is established in the twinkling of an eye between the old life and the new."[27] B. R. Rees describes it as "a slow wearisome period of gestation followed by a sudden birth of new life, of gathering clouds of self-doubt pierced by an instantaneous flash of illumination."[28] In the narratives where it is described, this kind of conversion suggests the powerful and simple structure of tension—climax—resolution. The first stage is a gradual increase of internal conflict to the point where it seems unendurable. This period of mounting inner tension is usually accompanied by intense conviction of sin and often manifested in states of anxiety and depression. The second stage is the climax and turning point, the sudden establishment of a "new center" in the psyche. A crucial element in this second stage is self-surrender, for it is only by giving up, or letting go, that the powerful forces outside the personal, conscious self can emerge—whether one considers these forces to be profound instinctual urges from the depths of the Unconscious or divine interventions of Grace from above. The third stage is felt as peace, joy, resolution, certitude, freedom. The convert feels as though he has undergone a death and rebirth, or has entered a new world altogether. The sense of renewal is immediate, profound, and supposedly lifelong.

The archetypal model of the *crisis* conversion is Paul's encounter with the numinous on the road to Damascus, an experience where he is violently and suddenly wrenched from one set of beliefs and practices to its opposite. But the sudden conversion paradigm is almost as well-known from Augustine's account. Indeed, Paul and Augustine are often linked as exemplary of this kind of conversion. This is itself of interest, since there would seem to be important differences between their experiences. Augustine's conversion is led up to by a long period of searching for truth, by a sequence of ascending stages in that search, and by the conscious desire for conversion; Paul on the other hand, lacks any such preparatory period.[29] But this discrepancy between the two conversions is resolved if one accepts the existence of nonconscious elements in mental processes. And this is James's own view of *crisis* conversion: "His possession of a developed subliminal self, and of a leaky or pervious margin, is thus a *conditio sine qua non* of the Subject's becoming converted in the instantaneous way." Within this subliminal, or subconscious, area of mental life, James observes, thoughts undergo a kind of "subconscious incubation.... When ripe, the results hatch out, or burst into flower."[30] Arthur Darby Nock uses a different metaphor to describe the same thing: "[In the story of Augustine's conversion] Christianity is throughout presupposed and present in the subject's subconscious ... it is like a chemical process in which the addition of a catalytic agent produces a reaction for which all the elements were already present."[31] According to these explanations, Paul's persecution of the Christians becomes itself proof of an internal conflict; a defense against belief, a reaction-formation. It may be that what Paul does before conversion is analogous to what Augustine does after conversion in his bitter polemics against such heresies as Pelagianism and Donatism.

The hallmark of the *crisis* conversion, then, is a dramatic and sudden turning point. But this experience is not necessarily the only one of its kind in the convert's lifetime. Indeed, it is more common than not for the individual who undergoes a *crisis* conversion to have experienced other such turning points in his life. As Mircea Eliade remarks: "if we look closely, we see that every human life is made up of a series of ordeals, of 'deaths,' and of 'resurrections.'"[32] The *Confessions* nicely illustrates this observation, since Augustine represents his life as patterned in a sequence of conversions: first to a Ciceronian pursuit of wisdom, then to Manichaeism, then to Neoplatonism, and finally to Catholic Christianity.[33]

Just as the stages of his intellectual quest can be represented by the various philosophies or religions to which he gives himself, so too the stages of the affective quest can be represented by the women with whom he is involved. The turning point in the story of Augustine's conversion occurs when he travels to Milan. For it is in Milan, in book 6, that the intellectual search and the affective quest are, for the first time, in harmony with each other. He comes under the influence of Ambrose, listens to his sermons, and begins "to esteem better of the Catholic doctrine" (6.5). As he vaguely realizes at the time, he is "no longer now a Manichee, nor fully yet a Catholic Christian" (6.1). And yet it is a painful time in his life—

a time of stasis, uncertainty, and misery—where he finds himself unable to believe in anything with conviction and certitude.

But if it is in Milan that Augustine comes under the influence of Ambrose, it is also in Milan that Augustine is reunited with his mother, Monica, "whom motherly piety had made adventurous, following me over land and sea" (6.1). As his intellectual life is now to a great extent dominated by Ambrose, so is his affective life dominated by Monica. She again urges him to get married and this time succeeds, persuading him to dismiss the concubine with whom he had been living for fourteen years. The girl to whom he is espoused is too young, and the marriage is delayed for two years. Unable to wait, Augustine takes another concubine. But she cannot replace the first concubine, whom he misses so deeply. He describes his feelings in the language of surgery. She is "cut away from my side, taking my heart with her": though intended to cure the "disease" of lust, it is a wound that refuses to heal (6.15). This pain, and loss, are significant in inducing the *crisis* of his conversion.

Scholars have speculated as to Monica's motives in subjecting her son, for whom chastity had always been so difficult, to such an arrangement. But Augustine himself does not here speculate on her motives, although it is an arrangement that is not dissimilar to the situation he describes in book 2, where his parents do not arrange a marriage for him at the conventional age. In the earlier episode, Monica had hoped that lust could be "cut back to the quick *(resecari ad vivum)*" rather than restrained in the bonds of matrimony; in the latter, his concubine is "cut away from my side *(praecisione factum erat)*" in preparation for his impending marriage (2.3; 6.15). It is significant, in this earlier episode, that he refers to Monica as "the mother of my flesh *(mater carnis meae)*." For in so preventing him from legitimately satisfying sexual desire, she seems to be condemning him to the same life of sin that she has so earnestly warned him against. Monica's stance toward her sixteen-year-old son would appear to be much the same as her stance toward her thirty-two-year-old son: in both incidents she expects of him a chastity that he is unable to maintain.

Although in book 5 Augustine writes that he nearly died from a serious illness, contracted soon after he had arrived in Rome (an illness that may well have had something to do with his guilt over abandoning his mother on the shores of Carthage),[34] it is book 6 that is studded with medical imagery. Not only is lust described as disease and the loss of his concubine represented as a surgical excision, but the intellectual life is similarly presented in the metaphorical language of sickness and healing. Still smarting from his past error in allowing himself to be so childishly misled and deceived by Manichaean promises, Augustine is unable to believe in the teachings of Catholic Christianity, although he does not disbelieve them either: "so it was with the state of my soul which could in no way be healed but by believing; and lest it should believe falsehoods, it refused to be cured . . ." (6.4). When Monica joins Augustine in Milan, she finds him "grievously endangered by despair." Discovering that this despair derives from his being poised between the Manichaeism that he no longer accepts and the Christianity in which he does not yet believe, Monica anticipates the crisis of his conversion in the medical imagery of the times: "she felt sure that through this I was to pass from sickness unto health, some sharper conflict coming between, an additional danger, as it were, such as physicians call the crisis" (6.1). Unable to trust the "good physician" from whose healing hand he would receive the "medicines of faith" (6.4), anxious as to what he could believe as certain truth in Christianity, and reluctant to give up the satisfactions of the body, Augustine postpones from day to day the conversion that he knows is inevitable. Typically, he concludes a section where he seems to be floundering in his quest with a consolation that is partly authorial—Augustine the Bishop of Hippo looking back with pity on Augustine the unbeliever—and partly divine: "behold thou art present to us . . . and dost comfort, and say thus unto us: 'Run on, I will carry you, I will bring you to your journey's end, and there also will I carry you' " (6.16). It is an appropriate introduction to the sections that describe his conversion.

Peter Brown has eloquently described the extent to which the *Confessions* is "the story of Augustine's 'heart,' or of his 'feelings'—his *affectus.*"[35] Given this emphasis, it is not surprising that Augustine's conversion should be primarily a conversion of the heart or the will—the dramatic resolution of the theme of the *cor irrequietum*. But the emotional *crisis* event is preceded by a more gradual, educative conversion of the intellect. Book 8 describes the conversion of the heart; book 7 the intellectual changes that precede it. The intellectual conversion is accomplished when with the aid of Neoplatonism, Augustine turns away from Manichaeism and toward the Christianity of the Pauline Epistles. Augustine himself recognized that there were common elements between Neoplatonism and Christianity. Indeed, in some ways the philosophical doctrines of pagan Neoplatonism would have appeared to him to be closer to the Catholic Christianity of his time than were the religious beliefs of the Manichees, although these were in a sense also Christian. Augustine's readings in Neoplatonism serve two important functions: they help him rid himself of what has remained of his Manichaean ideology, so that he is able to adopt the concept of God as a transcendent being and to reject the idea of evil as a reified substance, and they introduce him to the *"invisibilia"* of the Neoplatonic vision. So prepared, Augustine is ready to "walk in that way, whereby he may at last arrive, and see, and comprehend" (7.22). He then turns eagerly to the writings of St. Paul.

The final stage, the conversion of the heart, is ushered in by an intensification of the inner conflict that has always characterized Augustine's spiritual life: "Thus did my two wills, one old, one new, one carnal and this, spiritual, try masteries within me and between them they tore my soul apart" (8.5). This is the language of *psychomachia*—the battle between two wills, the conflict between the old and the new or the flesh and the spirit. In describing this inner warfare, Augustine shows us Christian theology evolving out of personal experience. It is significant that Augustine's argument against the Manichaean dualism of good and evil occurs when he is actually in the garden, and directly precedes the famous crisis of his conversion. For the ethical and philosophical system of the Manichees set a reified principle of Evil against a reified principle of Good. Salvation depended upon identifying with the Good, and detaching oneself from the Evil of the material world. But Augustine here determines that the sensation he feels so intensely of having two wills at odds with each other does not imply that there *are* two contrary minds or souls, each of a different nature, as the Manichees had maintained; rather, "it is but the one and the same soul," he writes, that contains both the good and evil will (8.10).

This "vast tempest within" sends him fleeing into a garden. His description of his state of mind is framed in the dualisms of paradox: "I was for the time most sanely mad, and dying, to live: sensible enough of the piece of misery I now was, but utterly ignorant of the good which I would soon achieve" (8.8). Tormented in mind and soul he prays out of the "vehement passions of [his] delay" that he delay no longer: "let it be done now; let it be done now" (8.8,11). Voices personifying the pleasures of the body call to him seductively, but he resolutely turns away from them and toward Continence, who stretches forth her arms to embrace him. Confronted with the greatness of his misery, he moves away from Alypius, flings himself beneath a fig tree, and begins to weep disconsolately. While weeping "in the most bitter contrition of [his] heart," he hears the voice of a nearby child chanting "*tolle, lege; tolle, lege* (take up and read, take up and read)." Reminded of the story of the conversion of Antony (who is likewise converted by overhearing a scriptural passage), he construes this to be a divine command, reaches for a book of Paul's Epistles, and opens it at random, where his eyes fall upon the verses that were for him a sign of his regeneration. "For instantly, even as I came to the end of the sentence, it was as though the light of confidence flooded into my heart and all the darkness of doubting vanished." (8.12). It is here that the archetypes of quest and *psychomachia* find a common expression. For the predetermined conclusion of that "tumult in my breast," the surrender of the will that puts an end to the painful inner conflict, is also the goal of the spiritual quest: "That way we go not in ships, or chariots, or upon our own legs . . . but to arrive fully at that place required no more but the will to go to it . . ." (8.8). And thus the classical quest for wisdom, which began when Augustine read Cicero, led him astray with the beliefs of the Manichees, and returned him to the right path in the speculations of the Neoplatonists, culminates in the wisdom of the child.

It is appropriate that Augustine's conversion should occur in a garden; moreover, in a garden beneath a fig tree. The setting is surely a consciously symbolic one, recalling both the Edenic tree of good and evil in the youth of Mankind and the pear tree in Augustine's own youth—both despoiled by a perversion of will.[36] For the *psychomachia* that leads to conversion originates, he writes, not in any Manichaean substantial Evil but as an inherited punishment for the sin of Adam (8.10). Again, ontogeny recapitulates phylogeny: both events present original sin as the sin of disobedience, and as taking wanton pleasure in that disobedience. The fall of the collective human soul occurs when Eve listens to the enticement of the serpent to "take and eat" the forbidden fruit of knowledge that will kill; the resurrection of the human soul occurs when Augustine listens to the child's voice chanting "take and read" and picks up the Epistles of St. Paul, the knowledge that will give life. The child represents Augustine's own capacity for renewal, for behind the image of the child-self is the suggested image of the Christ-child. And indeed, the passage Augustine reads qualifies the solitude of the self with the immanent presence of

Christ: "Not in rioting and drunkenness, not in chambering and wantonness, not in strife and envying: but put ye on the Lord Jesus Christ; and make not provision for the flesh, to fulfill the lusts thereof" (8.12).

Both *lysis* and *crisis* models of conversion were familiar to Augustine—the gradual conversion in the ascent to wisdom of the Platonists, and the sudden conversion in the story of Paul and the conversion-narratives of his contemporaries.[37] Once again we see the confluence of classical and Christian motifs in Augustine's thought, for both models helped shape the autobiographical reworking of the original experience. It is not surprising that the Pauline influence is more obvious: it seems appropriate that the text Augustine is told to "take up and read" comes from Paul's Epistles. The scene of Augustine's semi-miraculous conversion seems in many ways a mimesis of the conversion of Paul on the road to Damascus. Both Paul and Augustine hear voices during their conversion crises: for Paul it is Jesus; for Augustine it is God speaking through Scripture, and the voice of a child—of his own humility—directing him to that divine voice. Both conversions are characterized as a passage from blindness to vision that is facilitated by "a light"; in both, doubt gives way to confidence, skepticism to faith.

These resemblances are more than accidental. The theological reasons why Paul is an appropriate model are obvious, for he is the great theorist of Christian conversion: the experience described in Acts becomes the central dogma of the Epistles. But the archetypal reasons are equally compelling. Indeed, the Pauline conversion is far better suited than the Platonic to a genre that blends the personal and the historic, the actual and the mythic. For Paul's personal experience has typological dimensions that extend forward to the Last Judgment and backward to Old Testament prefigurations of deliverance and judgment. Saul is journeying to Damascus when he is struck blind, and thereafter he spends three days in darkness, taking neither food nor drink. After this symbolic death, he receives baptism—itself a ritual of rebirth—and subsequently takes on another name: in every sense he becomes a new man. In its fidelity to the Pauline model, Augustine's account of his conversion fuses the archetype of quest with that of death and rebirth.

Moreover, the dual form of the Pauline quotation—"Not in rioting and drunkenness. . . . but put ye on the Lord Jesus Christ" is an apt symbol of the dualities of the *crisis* conversion: death and life, old man and new man, sickness and health, darkness and light, doubt and confidence. It also fits William James's notion of *crisis* conversion as a dyadic process. James analyzes the *crisis* conversion as a dramatic change of psychic equilibrium from conscious to unconscious center—"the movement of new psychic energies towards the personal center and the recession of old ones towards the margin." Thus there are, he suggests, two stages in a conversion, although these two stages are experienced as simultaneous. The one he refers to as "self-surrender" and the other as "new determination": "Self-surrender sees the change in terms of the old self; determination sees it in terms of the new."[38] Conversions such as Paul's or Augustine's are thus a simultaneous turning away from sin and turning toward God.

Augustine's conversion in the garden is indeed a moment of high drama—the structural and thematic climax of the book and a paradigmatic example of the Pauline *crisis* conversion—and the reader is led to believe that his life changed radically from this point on. But in fact, the preponderance of Neoplatonism in the subsequent Cassiciacum dialogues indicates that the conversion was much less the dramatic change that Augustine perceives in retrospect than a gradual process of acquiring Christian concepts and ideals.[39] Indeed, the autobiographical book that Augustine wrote immediately after conversion is not the *Confessions* (which was begun eleven years later) but the *Soliloquies*, which "consist[ed] mainly of dialogues between Augustine and his own reason."[40] And the retreat at Cassiciacum, to which he withdrew with a few friends after his conversion, derived far more from the classical model of a "cultured retirement" (*otium liberale*) than from any Christian model.[41] Not only do the events after conversion qualify Augustine's description of the experience in the *Confessions*, but also the incidents of "proto-conversion" recorded in the autobiography—the conversion to Ciceronian wisdom, to Manichaeism, and to Neoplatonism—betray his affinity with the Greek philosophical tradition of change as a gradual advance through various stages toward wisdom. Also, there is psychological evidence that Augustine's conversion was not the radical change from doubt and disbelief to total certitude. Thus the psychoanalyst Charles Kligerman remarks, on the basis of Augustine's vehement polemics against such heresies as Pelagianism and Donatism, that "the instability of his new equilibrium necessitated constant vigilance on the part of Augustine to reaffirm his faith.

This provided the motivation for a lifelong series of powerful polemics, supposedly to convince others, but also to still his own doubts and externalize the conflict."[42]

But what we are concerned with here is not historical truth but autobiographical truth. And this is a kind of truth that inevitably changes the "real" event, though in so doing it may achieve a deeper meaning. As Roy Pascal observes, "the distortion of truth imposed by the act of contemplation is so over-riding a qualification of autobiography that it is indeed a necessary condition of it. . . ."[43] Pascal's notion of distortion in autobiography is similar to the mythic remaking of the self that is so important a part of spiritual autobiography. Thus Augustine's account of his conversion in the *Confessions* is not literal truth; rather, it is paradigmatic truth. We have no way of knowing whether Augustine actually perceived his conversion as having occurred as he describes it in the *Confessions*—either as he experienced it or when he described it more than a decade later—or whether he simply chose to write about it paradigmatically. What is significant here is not the "real" experience, which is irrecoverable anyway, but the model created out of the raw materials of that experience. And this paradigm, for the countless generations who have read the *Confessions* and used Augustine's account of his conversion either to structure their own future experience or to discover a mirror-image of past experience, is that of the classical *crisis* conversion.

Moreover, it is clear that the *crisis* model of an abrupt and climactic illumination occupied a central place in Augustine's own imagination. Significantly, the description of his own conversion is preceded by similar paradigmatic stories of *crisis* conversion: Ponticianus's story of the conversion of his two comrades upon reading a book about the life of St. Anthony, and the story of the conversion of Antony himself, of which Augustine is reminded when he hears the voice of the child. And indeed, Antony's experience is quite similar to Augustine's, for he is likewise instantaneously converted when he overhears the scriptural passage, "Go home and sell all that belongs to you," takes it as a divine command, and proceeds to give away his possessions. Antony's conversion may well have functioned for Augustine as Augustine's own conversion functions to facilitate (or mirror) the conversions of those who read his *Confessions*.

The Pauline model of a *crisis* conversion is useful structurally as well as paradigmatically. For in adopting it, Augustine transposes the tripartite formula of conversion (spiritual unrest, conversion, spiritual peace) into a narrative structure of life-before-conversion, conversion itself, and life-after conversion. It is the dramatic reversal in Augustine's conversion—the passage from old to new man and from personal to transpersonal—that accounts for the striking difference in style and language between the first nine and the last four books of the *Confessions*. It seems as though the autobiography proper ends with book nine; the remaining books are more abstract and more distanced from the life of their author. And indeed, the author's stance toward his reader (and toward his life) seems to have changed between the first nine and the last four books. In the first nine books Augustine is looking back, via memory, on his former life: he is confessing "what I once was *(quis fuerim)*"; the last four books, on the other hand, are meant to be a confession of "what I now am *(quis ego sim)*" (10.3). To some extent, then, the author of the *Confessions* is identifiable with the literary persona of the last four books, and distinct from the "hero" of the first nine autobiographical books. As William Spengemann writes, this is a distinction between "the self-aware narrator" and "the self-deluded protagonist."[44] Moreover, the goal of the spiritual quest undergoes a change in the transition from autobiographical to allegorical narrative: in the first nine books it is conversion; in the last four books it is that total union with God which is to occur after the death of the body or at the end of time.

Book 10 is the transition between Augustine the hero of the quest, his attention focused on the Earthly City that he must leave behind, and Augustine the author of the *Confessions*, his gaze directed toward the Heavenly City that is outside time, in "*aeternitas tua*" (4.16). Augustine's confession here takes him beyond the realm of his own personal memory to that of an archetypal memory, a "reality" that can never be entirely forgotten. Just as he begins his personal confession with the memory of his infancy, so he ends the transpersonal confession with the archetypal memory of the genesis of the world. If books 1 through 9 may be said to progress chronologically from Augustine as infant to Augustine at age thirty-three, books 10 through 13 reverse the process, proceeding backward from memory (bk. 10), moving through time and eternity (bk. 11), and then through an analysis of matter (bk. 12)—itself a further dilation of the personal toward the divine in that "matter" precedes "time"[45]—and finally ending with an allegorical interpretation of Genesis (bk. 13). And it is appropriate that the autobiography should end with a discussion of Genesis.

The purpose of this final book, 13, is to unify the whole work, for the creation in Genesis figures as the archetype of recreation—or conversion. Just as God at the beginning of time "moved upon the face of the waters," so has God, in the conversion of the human soul, "in mercy moved upon our inner darksome and unquiet deep" (13.14).

3

St. Augustine
Archetypes of Family

i. The maternal nexus

The *Confessions* could be said to be a long, sustained fugue on the complementary motifs of restlessness and rest, or hunger and satisfaction, where resolution is achieved in conversion. The theme of rest and refuge is represented in Augustine's Heavenly Jerusalem, "Mother of us all," and the corresponding theme of restlessness is represented as unceasing and often tormented motion—the hunger of body, mind, and heart for satisfaction. We have observed the restlessness of body in the outer narrative of literal journeys, the restlessness of mind in the inner movement from philosophy to philosophy, and the restlessness of heart in the well-known theme of the *cor irrequietum*. But beyond this, hunger is itself a chief metaphor in the *Confessions*—a metaphor that relates the restlessness of body, mind, and heart alike to the archetypal mother, source of nourishment and cause of both satisfaction and frustration.

Augustine's use of hunger as a metaphor for spiritual need often leads him to analogies with the passive state of infancy. Thus he observes that "the Word was made flesh, that by thy wisdom, by which thou createst all things, he might suckle our infancy" (7.18). And again, he writes: "What am I even at the best but an infant sucking thy milk, and feeding upon thee, food which is incorruptible?" (5.1).[1] Augustine's description of his infancy in the early books of the autobiography is meant as a description of the sins of infancy: these are greed, and the infantile emotions derived from greed—anger (when hunger is not satisfied) and envy (at the satisfaction of another's hunger) (1.7). When as a youth he arrives in Carthage, it is the raging of this inner hunger that causes him to be ensnared by his own lustful appetite. Sexual hunger is accompanied by intellectual hunger: his description of his interest in Manichaeism is replete with references to hunger, food, and nourishment. Later in life he observes that he is "still possessed with a greediness of enjoying things present . . ." (6.11). It is Augustine the author, looking back on his youth, who realizes that this is a hunger that is misdirected and thus can never be satisfied. For the restlessness of the soul is a hunger diverted onto lower things—a hunger that achieves satisfaction only when the soul returns its love to its source, to God.

Throughout the *Confessions* the end of the quest is perceived as a haven after a storm; as rest, peace, and, most important, as assuagement of the inchoate yearnings of the heart. The autobiography ends as it begins: "our heart is restless til it rests in thee" (1.1) and "Thou . . . art at rest always, because that rest thou art thyself" (13.38).[2] Jung describes as a major attribute of the mother archetype "the love that means homecoming, shelter, and the long silence from which everything begins and in which everything ends."[3] He might have been describing the Heavenly City, which Augustine rhapsodizes over as an abode of peace—"Jerusalem my country, Jerusalem my mother" (12.16). The theme of rest and refuge introduced in the first paragraph of the *Confessions* is a refrain that is repeated throughout the book: Augustine describes himself as capable "neither of rest nor counsel," directs us to "rest yourselves in him and ye shall rest safely," observes that "there is no rest to be found where you seek it," and elsewhere remarks, "Let us now at last, O Lord, return, that we do not turn aside . . . for in thee only the soul can rest" (4.7; 4.12; 4.16; 6.16). It is true that all these references to "rest" and "refuge" are to God, and not to the Church or the Heavenly Jerusalem. But Augustine's idea of God, in part derived from classical epic and philosophy, in its Christianized form is inevitably bound up in the idea of the Heavenly City, "Jerusalem my Mother." Mother-Church and Father-God are the archetypal divine parents: the Christian community, as "my fellow-citizens in that eternal Jerusalem," is "subject to thee, our Father, in our Catholic Mother" (9.13). Augustine's "fraternal" model of the spiritual family is derivative of the overarching importance for him of the mother archetype. For it is the maternal City of God that is the "home" of the collectivity of Christian souls.

It is the archetypal mother who is the dominant figure in Augustine's religious imagination—an archetype symbolizing both the goal of our redemptive longings and also the hunger that drives us in search of that goal. Jung formulates the archetypal feminine duality as *"mater spiritualis"* and *"mater natura."*[4] Monica functions in both roles of natural and spiritual mother, as Augustine observes over and over during the course of his autobiography. Early in book 1, when a childhood illness brings him near death, he writes that "the mother of my flesh . . . most lovingly travailed in birth of my eternal salvation" (1.11); and at the end of the personal confession, he commemorates his mother for bringing him to birth "both in her flesh, that I might be born again to this temporal light, and in her heart too, that I might be born again to the eternal light" (9.8).

For Jung the mother archetype signifies "the son's relation to the real mother, to her imago, and to the woman who is to become a mother for him": she is thus both "the solace for all the bitterness of life" and "the seductress who draws him into life."[5] In their representation of the archetypal mother as fundamentally ambivalent, Jungian archetypal theory and biblical symbolism come together. For example, there is the duality of Eve and Mary—mother as temptress and mother as consolation. Just as Christ is a perfected type of the Old Testament Adam, so is the Virgin Mary a perfected type of the Old Testament Eve. Another version of the dual nature of the feminine archetype is to be found in the wisdom literature of the Old Testament, where the feminine appears as spouse rather than as mother. The conflict between wisdom and temptation, both personified as women, is an ancient tradition and was certainly familiar to Augustine. In the book of Proverbs, *sapientia* is a female figure admonishing Man away from "the strange woman" or "the evil woman," the *meretrix* who leads Man into the path of sin and death: "Wisdom crieth without; she uttereth her voice in the streets . . . to deliver thee from the strange woman . . ." (Prov. 1:20 and 2:16).[6] Indeed, Augustine refers to his youthful sins with reference to the lures of the Old Testament *meretrix:* "I chanced upon that bold woman, who knoweth nothing, that subtilty in Solomon. . . . She seduced me, because she found my soul out-of-doors, dwelling in the eye of my flesh . . ." (*Conf.* 3.6). If the *meretrix* is an "adulteress" (Prov. 6:26), *sapien-*

tia is "the wife of thy youth" (Prov. 5:18). And furthermore, the designation "wife of thy youth" is amplified in *sapientia*'s archaic origins, for she exists alongside of God before the creation of the world: "The Lord possessed me in the beginning of his way, before his works of old" (Prov. 8:22). Augustine's Heavenly Jerusalem, the maternal and intellectual mind of God whom he presents in book 12.15 (*"mens rationalis et intellectualis castae civitatis tuae, matris nostrae"*), is based on this Old Testament idea of wisdom, a feminine personification prior to and formative in the Creation.[7] So also Augustine's portrayal of Monica, who throughout the *Confessions* rebukes him with tears and lamentations for his wandering ways, can be seen as parallel to the feminine figure of *sapientia*, whose role is to admonish Man against wasting himself among the things of this world.

Thus it might seem that Augustine's own life provides characters that conform to those two great archetypes: Monica to the spiritual mother, or *sapientia*, and the concubine in whose embrace he so long postponed his conversion to the natural mother, or the *meretrix*. Just as the two women are literally antagonists and rivals—for it is Monica who finally forces Augustine to dismiss his concubine—so also in his allegorical reworking of his experience they stand for opposed forces. As allegorical personae, Monica comes to represent the voice of divine love, while the concubine represents carnal love. And yet, as I shall show, Augustine's autobiography "lives" for us precisely because the characters in his life are not so rigidly categorized. Monica is not simply the "spiritual mother." Her characterization is a very complicated one, and includes both variants of the archetypal feminine. Her positive nature as apotheosized mother in the Heavenly Jerusalem we have observed; the negative side emerges in Augustine's description of the role she played in trying to prevent him from going to Rome. His description of the incident is a vivid one: Monica weeps bitterly to see him go and follows him to the water's edge, clinging to him with all her strength in the hope that he will either return home or take her with him. To get away he must tell her a lie. He then persuades her to spend the night in a shrine, and sails away in secret. Her oversolicitous concern he calls carnal affection (*"carnale desiderium"*), for by her weeping and lamenting, he writes, she was "proving herself by those tortures to be guilty of what Eve left behind her; with sorrow seeking, what she had brought forth in sorrow" (5.8). Later on, in his Epistles, he will tell another young man oppressed with such a mother: "Whether it is in a wife or a mother, it is still Eve (the temptress) that we must beware of in any woman."[8]

Augustine's moral allegorizing here works as psychological insight, for it is an analytic axiom that the clinging, possessive, overnurturant mother, which Monica surely was, is a type of the erotic mother. So we see why Augustine's early life seems an inverted pattern of quest where he is trying to escape his mother, whether into fraternal society, or the arms of a mistress, or the intellectual embrace of Manichaeism. He is trying to be born. But in fact Augustine's spiritual journey is one that is from the mother to the mother. What actually happens in the rebirth of conversion is a reentry into the world of the mother, only this time it is the realm of the spiritual mother, the *Catholica*.

Thus in Augustine's quest from the Earthly to the Heavenly City, Monica as spiritual mother beckons him on while Monica as natural and erotic mother holds him back. It is Monica and not the concubine who figures as Dido, left weeping on the shores of Africa as the hero pursues his divinely ordained task.[9] The *Aeneid* deploys these ambivalences in the feminine archetypes with fullness and subtlety. The loving and terrible mothers appear as Venus and Juno, the goddesses who assist and oppose the hero's quest. Even these polar types tend to overlap and blend, for the wrathful and persecuting Juno presides over Aeneas's union with Dido as the "queen of marriages," while Venus, the great patroness of Aeneas's future in Rome, cooperates to delay it in Carthage—in fact, it is she who first inspires love in Dido.

Dido the temptress and Venus the divine mother seem as opposed as their cities, Carthage and Rome. In this perspective Dido suggests Augustine's concubine: both women are seen, first, as a kind of haven from the troubles of the hero's world; second, as obstacles to his achieving his goal; and third, as victims of his abandonment. As Aeneas finds a false refuge in the embraces of Dido, so Augustine finds a false repose in the sensual pleasure his concubine symbolizes. Later Christian allegorizations of classical epic treated the "temptress" (Dido, Circe, Calypso) as a figure of the fleshly appetites. Thus an allegorical reading of the *Aeneid* along these lines would treat Aeneas's abandonment of Dido as a heroic turning away from his own lustful feelings, and his escape from burning Carthage as a resolute departure from the Earthly City of his fleshly nature in pursuit of the Heavenly City. It is certainly possible that Augustine was aware of this way of handling pagan epic. Indeed, his treatment of his concubine in the *Confessions* is carried out along very similar lines: she is presented more as a symbolic figure than as a real person. We are told practically nothing about her, not even her name, although she bore Augustine's child and lived with him for some fourteen years. It is as if her personality and character are absorbed in the process of allegorization so that she becomes simply a type of the lusts of the flesh that divert Augustine from his true quest, rather than a real woman whom he loved and abandoned. Perhaps, too, the exaggerated emphasis in the autobiography on his affection and grief for his mother derives from a certain amount of displaced emotion—displaced from the concubine from whom he so resolutely turns.

As such a displacement suggests, the archetypes of "temptress" and "mother" are interlocking as well as alternative figures: the careful and deliberate shading of one into the other, whereby aspects of the erotic cling to the mother and qualities of the maternal enhance the mistress, is as evident in the *Aeneid* as in the *Confessions*.[10] For Vergil like Augustine links the mother (Venus) and the paramour (Dido) in the image of the cherishing mother. In book 1 Venus carries off Ascanius, Aeneas's son, and replaces him with Cupid, her own divine child. And this suggestive picture of the mother-goddess embracing and caressing Ascanius and lulling him to sleep in her sacred shrine is followed immediately by a similar one of Dido at her feast, fondling Cupid (whom she thinks is Ascanius) upon her lap. The image is rich in erotic ambivalence. Mythically, it is an action whereby the boy-god is enabled to inspire love in Dido; psychologically, it represents a maternal feeling for the child that blends into sexual desire for the father, Aeneas. It is significant that this happens while Aeneas is telling Dido the painful story of the fall of Troy. Dido is here clearly the erotic mother, cradling and comforting Aeneas in the person of Ascanius-Eros, while at the same time falling in love with him. When he has finished his story, and all the guests are gone, Dido returns to the darkened hall and relives the incident:

> . . . she sees, she hears
> the absent one [Aeneas] or draws Ascanius,
> his son and counterfeit, into her arms,
> as if his shape might cheat her untellable love.[11]

Even the flames of sexual desire that rage so fiercely in Dido later on do not burn away all trace of her maternal feeling: when her lover announces his departure, she laments that she has not conceived his son—a "tiny Aeneas" whose face might still remind her of him. And there is some justice to her reproach that his mother cannot have been the goddess of beauty and love: Aeneas partially renounces Venus in renouncing her. Like Augustine, in leaving Carthage, Aeneas leaves one aspect of his mother behind.

Monica and the concubine can be thought of as the opposite sides of the same archetype, an archetype whose poetic ambiguity figures in the characters of Venus and Dido. To compare Dido to Monica and the concubine, to talk of the "erotic mother," to discuss the Heavenly City in terms of an apotheosized mother—all this is to allude to the great dualism of the archetypal feminine, that of carnal versus divine love. In the *Confessions* the relationship between carnal and divine love is expressed in Augustine's sublimation of his sexual love for his concubine and his filial love for his mother into a love of God, imaged as repose in the great maternal city—the Heavenly Jerusalem. The desires of the flesh are here allied with the archetype of the earthly mother, and both together are transmuted into divine love. For Augustine's relation to the apotheosized mother is as child and as transmuted spouse: while he is child to "Jerusalem my Mother," he is mystically espoused by his incorporation within the body of the Church.

The relation of the *"mater natura"* and *"mater spiritualis"* to each other can here be seen as developmental. Perhaps, then, Augustine's journey from the Earthly City to the Heavenly City is not so much a turning away from the one to the other as a transformation out of the order of nature and into the order of grace. In the words of colloquial Catholic theology, "grace builds on nature." And this is the key to Augustine's dualism. The dualism of the Manichaeans, and to some extent of the Platonists too, pits the natural world against the spiritual realm. Augustine, however, refines this concept by perceiving the spiritual as developing out of the natural.

The pattern of his life demonstrates precisely this development. There are two major instances of this in the *Confessions*. The first is when Augustine arrives at Carthage, the city of Dido (and of Venus) and finds himself in the midst of a "hissing cauldron of lust." He describes his progress as one where he begins by seeking out a suitable recipient of his love. *"Quaerebam quid amarem, amans amare":* the impulse to love is there; it is the object that is yet to be determined. Furthermore, he writes that to love and to have his love returned was what he most wanted, and that it would be all the sweeter if he could also carnally enjoy his beloved. Finally, "love was returned and I was with much joy shackled in the bonds of its consummation . . ." (3.1). But before long the powerful energy of sensual love is converted into the love of wisdom when he reads Cicero's *Hortensius*. His description of this mini-conversion closely parallels that of his initial yearnings for love: "with an incredible heat of spirit I desired *(concupiscebam)* the immortality of wisdom. . . . How did I burn then, my God, how did I burn to fly from earthly delights towards thee. . . . That love of wisdom is in Greek called Philosophy, with which that book inflamed me." What he admires most about the book is Cicero's advice "to love, seek, and obtain and hold, and embrace wisdom itself, whatever it was." It is due to Cicero's words that he is "stirred up and enkindled, and inflamed . . . in such a heat of zeal" (3.4).

The second instance where Augustine transforms the sensual into the spiritual occurs during his conversion to Christianity. He writes that when on the verge of conversion, he sees the "chaste dignity of Continence" beckoning to him in an undeniably maternal metaphor, "stretching forth those devout hands of hers . . . both to receive and to embrace me" (8.11). On the other side of his crisis of choice is the voice of his sensuality—the vanities of this world *("nugae nugarum et vanitates vanitatum")*, the chain of sin, which is habit *("consuetudo violenta")*, the "unclean members" of concupiscence (8.11). It is significant that Augustine is here converted not to the beauty of *sapientia*, a venerable object of devotion for the Hellenic and Hebraic mind alike, but to the beauty of *continentia*.

Peter Brown observes that "the relationship between mother and son that weaves in and out of the *Confessions*, forms the thread for which the book is justly famous."[12] It seems impossible to overstate the significance of this relationship.[13] Even Augustine's conversion to Christianity is finally presented as the double conversion of mother and son: "For so thou convertedst me unto thyself. . . . Thus didst thou convert her [Monica's] mourning into rejoicing" (8.12). If conversion represents the death of the natural man with his earthly ties and the rebirth of the spiritual man with heavenly ties, then the relationship between mother and son must undergo the same process. So in the early part of the autobiography, Monica is the mother grieving over her dead son, the *mater dolorosa* from whose tears and lamentations springs the resurrected son: "out of the blood of my mother's heart, through her tears night and day poured out, hadst thou made a sacrifice for me . . ." (5.7). Yet if her tears are those of mourning, they are purposive too: Augustine observes that his mother did not simply bewail him "as one dead, but as if there were good hopes of his reviving." And he continues with a strikingly appropriate biblical allusion: "Laying me forth upon the bier before thee that thou mightest say unto the son of the widow, Young man, I say unto thee, arise; and he should sit up, and begin to speak, and thou shouldest deliver him to his mother" (6.1).

In some sense Augustine has indeed defined himself in his autobiography as "the son of the widow," always perceiving his life in the larger context of his widowed mother's hopes and fears for him. His knowledge of the Christian God is, quite literally, mediated by Monica. For he perceives her as God's messenger: "And whose but thine were those words, which by my mother, thy faithful one, thou sangest in my ears?" (2.3). And furthermore, God speaks to Monica in visions—visions that foretell future events in her son's life. The greatest of these is that of the rule of faith, which Augustine believes to have foretold his conversion to Christianity:

> For she saw, in her sleep, herself standing upon a wooden rule, and a very beautiful young man coming toward her, with a cheerful countenance and smiling upon her, herself being grieved and far gone with sorrowfulness. Which young man when he had demanded of her the causes of her sadness and daily weepings . . . and she had answered that it was my perdition that she bewailed; he bade her rest contented, and wished her to observe diligently and behold, that where she herself was, there was I also. When she looked aside, she saw me standing by her upon the same rule. (3.11)

Looking back on his conversion in the garden, Augustine sees it as the fulfillment of his mother's dream: "For so thou convertedst me unto thyself . . . standing thus upon the same rule of faith, in which thou hadst shewed me unto her in a vision, so many years before" (8.12).

Not only does Augustine refer to Monica's earlier vision in his account of his conversion, but he even supplies a maternal figure out of his own imagination to match the youthful figure of her dream. For the "very beautiful young man coming toward her, with a cheerful countenance and smiling upon her," who appears to Monica in her sleep, is a transposed figure of Augustine himself, transformed by the dream mechanism of wish-fulfillment. And

Augustine's response to this dream-person is Continence, that "fruitful mother of children," whom he imaginatively conjures up just before describing his conversion: "cheerful was she, but not dissolutely pleasant, virtuously alluring me to come to her and hesitate no longer" (8.11). That this is a variant of the mother archetype goes without saying. That Continence is a transposed figure of Monica herself is suggested by Augustine's careful discrimination between a demeanor that is cheerful but not wanton, beckoning but not seductive.

Furthermore, the embrace of Continence is yet another way of imagining entry into the City of God. For, like the Heavenly Jerusalem, Continence is the spouse of God: to embrace Continence is to "cast thyself upon Him" (8.11). Thus does Augustine leave the embrace of his mistresses and enter into the embrace of "thy Church, the mother of us all" (1.11). The foundations of the spiritual mother, the Church, are to be found in Monica: "But thou hadst already begun thy temple in my mother's breast, and laid the foundations of thine own holy habitation" (2.3). Just as grace builds on nature, and the spiritual develops out of the earthly, so does the apotheosis of the maternal principle, "Jerusalem my country, Jerusalem my mother," to which God is "Enlightener, Father, Guardian, Spouse, Delight and Joy" (12.16), have its origins in the "temple" of Monica's heart.

In the figure of Monica, both as individual and as archetype of spiritual love, all polarities meet: Neoplatonic and Pauline, Vergilian and Christian. It is strangely appropriate that the autobiographical section of the *Confessions* should conclude not with Augustine's *crisis* conversion of book 8—his own spiritual death and rebirth—but with his account of the death of Monica, and the accompanying biographical elegy to her. Monica dies in Ostia, midway between Milan and Africa. For Augustine it appears as a triumph of her faith that, whereas she had always hoped that her body would be buried next to her husband's, she should remark, on her deathbed, "Lay this body anywhere . . . this only I request that you should remember me at the altar of the Lord, wherever you are" (9.11). Just as her concern with what happens to her body after death has been replaced by her belief in the resurrection of the soul, so also is the dead husband replaced by the living son in her last wishes.

The *Confessions* is itself meant to be this "altar of the Lord" of Monica's deathbed request—a fulfillment of her dying wish and a sacramental tribute to her memory. Thus Augustine concludes his personal autobiography: "inspire, O Lord my God, inspire thy servants, my brethren . . . that those of them who read this book may at thy Altar remember Monica thy handmaid, together with Patricius her sometime husband . . ." (9.13). The story of Augustine's conversion is the gradual weaning of the soul from the love of that which cannot last, such as friends and mothers, toward the love of that which is incorruptible and eternal. But the kind of love that he is writing about is, in both cases, libidinal in source and sensual in expression: it is rooted in the desire to see, touch, have, and possess—whether the love-object be human or divine.[14]

What Augustine finally achieves, in this narrative response to the death of his mother, is a kind of affirmation of the love of "that which cannot last." His description of his grief is worth attending to in detail, for it parallels his account in book 8 of the celebrated conversion in the garden. Though he feels "a great sorrow flowing into [his] heart," he holds back his tears, checking even the wailing of his son, Adeodatus, "For we did not think it fitting to mark the death with lamentations, tears, and moanings, because this is the accustomed way to lament those that die miserably or who are thought of as utterly perished" (9.12). He continues to maintain a countenance that does not betray the violence of his sorrow, but blames himself nonetheless for the tenderness of his passion: "I grieved for mine own grief with a new grieving *(dolore dolebam dolorem meum)*" (9.12). Restraining his tears throughout the burial, he begs God in prayer to heal him of his sorrow, but the prayer is not granted. He goes to the baths, remembering that the Greek root of the Latin *balneum* meant "that which drives anxiety out of the mind." But the attempt to cure himself is ineffective, as he confesses to God, here addressed as *"pater orphanorum."* Finally he is able to sleep, and wakes up to the memory of some verses written by Ambrose—verses that celebrate God as the healer of physical and mental pain. This event is an inversion of that other "awakening" in the garden to the chanting voice of the child. The *tolle, lege* refrain in book 8 causes him to repress the "violent torrent of tears"; the verses from Ambrose in book 9 cause him to give way to his tears "so that they flowed as much as they desired." He goes on to describe himself as "making of them a pillow for my heart, and it rested upon them *(requievat in eis),*" which recalls that first reference to the *cor irrequietum* at the very beginning of the *Confessions.* Thus Augustine's description of his mourning achieves a paradoxical affirmation of *eros—*of the love of that which cannot last—within a context of *agape.* And so he urges his readers, at the close of book 9, not to deride him for his tears, but rather to express charity in sorrowing with him: "let him not deride me; but if he be a man of any great charity, let him rather weep for my sins unto thee, the Father of all the brethren of thy Christ" (9.12).

For Augustine, the *Confessions* is a sacramental offering of contrition and thanksgiving made within the "large and infinite inner spaciousness" of his own memory (10.8). As a prayer to God it embodies a longing "to touch thee, whence thou mayst be touched; and to cling fast to thee, whence one may cling to thee *(volens te attingere, unde attingi potes, et inhaerere tibi . . .)*" (10.17). Consistently he uses the verb *attingere*, which means both "to touch" and "to attain to," in referring to the yearning to "touch" God. The rhetoric of quest throughout the *Confessions* reflects this poignant yearning, for it is the notion of enjoying God *(ad fruendum Dei)*, a variant on the Plotinian spiritual embrace (the *amplexis*) between God and the soul, which is the true object of that quest.[15] Thus for Augustine the essence of man is identified with the faculties of desiring, and concomitantly he is defined by men and judged by God in terms of the object of his desire. It follows then that the quest of the hero of the *Confessions*, and thence of the archetypal soul, is to fulfill that desire by finding the right object for his love. And the "right object" is defined simply as that which can satisfy this love: in Augustine's words, that to which one can say, "It is enough, and it is good *(sat est et bene est)*" (7.7). The object of this love is, of course, God—but it is not an intellectual idea of deity. It is therefore appropriate that Augustine should end his personal confession with an appeal to charity in his impassioned story of the life and death of Monica. For when he is able to affirm his grief over her death, he is able finally to affirm his great, even too great love for her—that *"carnalis affectus"*—and thus achieve a final unity between *eros* and *agape*.

ii. The paternal ethos: *senex* and child

In the preceding section I tried to show how the transcendent ideas of the City of God, Mother Church, and the Heavenly Jerusalem have their bases in Augustine's transvaluation of his own mother; similarly, Augustine's idea of God is shaped in part by his attitude toward his natural father, Patricius. Moreover, just as the maternal archetype manifests itself in the dualities of "natural" and "spiritual," or temptation and redemption, or hunger and satisfaction, the paternal turns on the dualities of false and true.

Throughout the *Confessions* Patricius is negatively represented. And Monica actively perpetuates this attitude. Thus Augustine writes that his mother "by all means endeavoured, that thou, my God, shouldst be my father, rather than Patricius" (1.11). Augustine's father is mentioned only a few times in the *Confessions;* in each instance the narrative is tinged with criticism. For example, Patricius is represented as immoderately proud of his son. He is praised by his neighbors for sending his son to Carthage to further his education, but Augustine's response is only to blame him for attending to the wrong things: "But yet this father of mine never troubled himself with any thought of how I might improve myself toward thee, or how chaste I were . . ." (2.3). Indeed, Patricius is not at all concerned over his son's chastity, or lack of it. Augustine recollects a scene in the baths where Patricius is delighted to see "how the signs of manhood began to bud in me." Augustine sums up his father as having "but vain conceits of me" (2.3). Patricius dies when Augustine is seventeen: he mentions this fact only in passing and with no show of grief whatsoever, whereas he will soon experience the depths of sorrow in mourning the death of a friend (3.4; 4.4).

The natural fathers of both Augustine and Aeneas are unsatisfactory, though in opposite ways. Patricius typifies the weak or absent father, leaving Augustine to search for the "true" father in one inadequate substitute after another. Anchises, whom Aeneas must carry on his back away from burning Troy, typifies the burden of the strong father who repeatedly misdirects the hero on a quest that cannot reach its goal until the old man dies. Yet if Anchises fails as a *senex* in life, he succeeds in death, where he functions as a kind of spiritual counselor in the episode in the underworld. Furthermore, there are resemblances between the depiction of the divine father in the two narratives. Zeus is a remote and transcendent deity in the *Aeneid;* he never descends to earth, as do Juno and Venus, but always works through his messenger, Mercury. So also is Augustine's God remote and transcendent; communicating to Augustine either through Monica or through the various *senex* figures in Augustine's life. The providential plan of Zeus, whereby it is Aeneas's destiny to found the city of Rome, is not unlike the providential plan of God for Augustine, which is revealed to Monica in her dream of the rule of faith.

Thus for Augustine the paternal archetype is organized around the two extremes of an imperfect but present father and a God who is perfect but transcendent. In his youth Augustine will repeatedly seek out surrogate fathers to bridge this distance between the natural and the "ideal" father—*senes* who either hinder or assist him in his quest for God, the ultimate father.

Jung equates the archetype of the father-figure with the "wise old man," the *senex*, and identifies both as psychic manifestations of the phenomenon called "spirit." This archetypal figure, Jung observes, is one who emerges in situations where insight and purposiveness are needed but lacking in the hero: "The old man always appears when the hero is in a hopeless and desperate situation from which only profound reflection or a lucky idea—in other words, a spiritual function or an endopsychic automatism of some kind—can extricate him."[16] This relationship between *senex* and hero, moreover, is one that is both ancient and common. For example, in poetry and myth the archetype of the father figure emerges as the wise counselor: thus Teiresias functions as an archetypal *senex* to Odysseus and Anchises as a *senex* to Aeneas. Similarly, in philosophy Plato uses the figure of Socrates to validate his own role as philosophic teacher and guide.

Throughout the autobiography Augustine presents himself as an avid seeker after wisdom. He goes about this search in the conventional way, by seeking the right master. And indeed the many *senex* figures in Augustine's life can be seen as representatives of his maturing ideas of wisdom. They include teachers, bishops, a magician, and a doctor, and occur in pairs, as type and antitype of the *senex* archetype. The first pair of surrogate fathers are chosen for him and are childhood manifestations of the *senex*. These are his early schoolmasters, who function as antitypes of the *senex* archetype, or false *senes*. Augustine remembers them bitterly as unjust disciplinarians. As the unjust schoolmaster is an antitype of the true *senex*, the Christian bishop whom Monica tries to coerce into instructing Augustine is a type of the true *senex*. But the bishop refuses, saying that Augustine is "yet unripe for instruction." Monica persists, and the bishop finally exclaims, in one of the most portentous passages in the *Confessions*, "Go thy ways ... and God bless thee, for it is not possible that the son of these tears should be lost" (3.12). It is an aborted *senex* relationship, but it prefigures Augustine's future relationships with the bishops Ambrose and Simplicianus.

Augustine encounters the next pair of *senes* in the course of a poetry contest. Their vocations are those of magician and doctor, and they represent the adolescence of his spiritual quest. The "false counselor" appears in the person of a sorcerer, who offers to ensure with his magic that Augustine win the contest. Augustine rejects his advances—an action that prefigures his later rejection of Faustus. The role of true *senex* is filled by Vindicianus, who awards him the prize for the poetry contest. Vindicianus, an astrologer turned physician, is characterized as *"vir sagax,"* a physician of the soul who "courteously and fatherly" advises Augustine to throw away his books on astrology and waste no further care "upon that vain study" (4.3).

The final and most important pair of *senex* figures in the *Confessions* are both chosen by Augustine and represent the maturity of his spiritual quest. Both are admired exponents of opposing religious doctrines. The false *senex* is Faustus, high priest in the Manichaean hierarchy. The Christian bishops Ambrose and Simplicianus, on the other hand, function as a composite image of the true *senex*. In fact, Faustus might be said to represent the "spirit" or *genius loci* of the entire Carthage experience, and Ambrose the "spirit" of the Milan experience. The two cities and the two men are polar opposites: Faustus and Carthage represent the false and earthly vision, whereas Ambrose and Milan represent the true and spiritual vision. Augustine meets Faustus when he is twenty-nine years old. He has been waiting for him some nine years, fully expecting that Faustus will be the wise tutor who can lead him to total, undoubting belief. But Augustine is disappointed. What happens is a rather surprising reversal of roles whereby Augustine becomes the teacher and Faustus the student. For Faustus, Augustine discovers, appears to be "ignorant of those arts in which I thought he excelled." But if Faustus is unable to resolve Augustine's questions about Manichaean doctrines, Augustine is able to help Faustus in his enthusiasm for literature: "I began upon a course of study with him . . . in that kind of learning, in which at that time being a rhetoric reader in Carthage, I instructed young students; and I began to read with him, either what he himself desired to hear, or such books as I judged fit for his abilities" (5.7). The episode is for Augustine the author an expression of God's providential intervention. Disenchanted with Faustus, Augustine loses interest in the sect, and accepts a position in Rome.

When Augustine finally arrives in Milan and finds Ambrose, he feels that he has at last found the ideal *senex*, the wise counselor who will be worthy of his own great gifts. But Augustine's advances are rejected, for he finds that the great Ambrose is too busy to talk to him. That Augustine was hurt by this rebuff is evidenced in his attempt to excuse Ambrose, suggesting that he had not fully understood the severity of Augustine's condition: "As little . . . knew he of my private heats, nor of the pit of my danger" (6.3). Thus all the conditions of an ideal *senex* relationship are there—Augustine is the Jungian hero-figure "in a hopeless and desperate situation" and Ambrose, he feels, holds the keys to the understanding that will release him. But what he hopes for does not happen: "Ofttimes when we were present . . . we still saw him reading to himself, and never otherwise: so that having long sat in silence (for who dared be so bold as to interrupt him, so intent in his study?) we were fain to depart" (6.3). Augustine must be content to join the multitudes and absorb the wisdom of Ambrose through listening to his sermons. During this entire time he sees himself as tending inevitably toward conversion, yet "hanging in suspense" (6.4).

Rebuffed by Ambrose, Augustine turns to the aged bishop Simplicianus, who is Ambrose's own spiritual father. Simplicianus tells Augustine the story of Victorinus, a parable intended to direct Augustine's attention away from his mentors and back onto himself. Victorinus was a very learned man who accounted himself a Christian (Augustine is by now a catechumen), but who, out of fear and pride, refused to join the Church. When he finally did so, he rejected the possibility of making a private profession of faith and publicly professed himself before multitudes (8.2). The effect of the parable is, as Simplicianus surely intended, that Augustine is "all on fire" to imitate Victorinus (8.5). But Simplicianus has a deeper motive in telling Augustine this story. He sees through Augustine's pride, and "the better to exhort [him] to Christ's humility (hidden from the wise, and revealed to little ones)" tells the story of the eminent rhetorician and translator of Plotinus who "blushed not to become the child of Christ, and an infant at the font, submitting his neck to the yoke of humility . . ." (8.2).[17]

It is the lesson of humility taught to him by Simplicianus, to "become the child of Christ and an infant at the font," that provides the most important link to Augustine's conversion. For the last of Augustine's *senex* figures is not an old man but a child. When he hears the child's words, *"tolle lege, tolle lege,"* interprets them as a divine command, and reads the Pauline passage from Romans, the verses prove to be a revelation—the final self-knowledge toward which the series of *senex* figures and the parables of Simplicianus and Ponticianus have been leading.

The *senex* archetype achieves its persuasive, guiding function in the archetype of the child. Jung is here again relevant, for he observes that the psychic manifestations of the "spiritual helper" can be either the *senex* or the child: "Greybeard and boy belong together."[18] The child archetype is a symbol of the fully and newly realized self, and thus a representation of the potential future; as Jung writes, the appearance of the child archetype "paves the way for a future change of personality."[19] Jung distinguishes between the "retarding ideal," which is "always more primitive, more natural . . . and more 'moral' in that it keeps faith with law and tradition" and the "progressive ideal," which is "always more abstract, more unnatural, and less 'moral' in that it demands disloyalty to tradition."[20] The child archetype, although it might at first appear to be a regressive configuration, is in fact a manifestation of the "progressive ideal." Augustine's painstaking attempts to acquire wisdom and his studies of philosophies and systems are examples of the working of the "retarding ideal"—a kind of "progress enforced by the will," in accord with tradition, and "natural" to a man of his intellectual gifts. As such the retarding ideal is manifested in Augustine's various *senex* figures. It is only when he abandons his will, "becomes as a little child," and turns his back on the traditional approach to attaining wisdom that he can embrace the progressive ideal. And the symbol of this is the child. His final ability, in the garden, to hear and obey the voice of the child marks a reflexive turning to his own inner capacities for renewal. And these capacities are released through the act of relinquishing his own will (Law, the "old man") and accepting the will of God (Grace, the "new man"). In such a way does the *senex* archetype give way to the *puer aeternus*. That Augustine can respond in this way, a response embodied in the child archetype, provides the final link to his conversion, and effects a reconstitution and a redemption of the earthly family within the divine family: Monica and Patricius, Augustine and his sibling friends are transformed into Jerusalem the Mother, God the Father, and the children of the City of God.

4

John Bunyan
The Conflictive Paradigm

i. The mode of *logos:* the unacceptable self and the problem of evil

The "universals" of religious experience that I have been describing as archetypes and discussing in psychological terms were recognized by writers of the seventeenth century in the metaphors and language of religion. The assumption that the life of the spirit will be more or less the same for everyone is characteristic of seventeenth-century spiritual autobiography. G. A. Starr sums up this attitude as maintaining "that there are universal and recurrent elements in human affairs, particularly in vicissitudes of the soul. History repeats itself not only in man's outward, group existence, but in the spiritual life of individuals."[1] This assumption validated both the writing and reading of autobiography for the seventeenth-century seeker after God. It was an era that abounded in spiritual autobiographies, intended as maps to help the would-be-believer chart his journey into the depths and heights of the spiritual pilgrimage. "No man," Bunyan warns in one of his tracts, "can travel here without a guide."[2] And Thomas Halyburton, a contemporary of Bunyan, writes about his own autobiography:

> should the book ever fall into the hands of any other Christian, it may not prove unuseful to him, considering that the work of the Lord, in substance, is uniform and the same in all; and "as face answereth to face in a glass," so does one Christian's experience answer to another's, and both to the word of God.[3]

This mirror quality of "face answering to face" is in a sense the relation between parts 1 and 2 of *The Pilgrim's Progress:* Christiana is both following the trail blazed by Christian, and led by the hero Great-heart, himself the archetype of the regenerate Christian soul.

Henri Talon's perceptive remark, "It is not books that copy books, but souls that copy souls,"[4] epitomizes the curious similarity between one spiritual autobiography and another, explaining why various figures so frequently "see themselves" in another's autobiographical story. We remember St. Teresa's and Petrarch's responses of self-recognition upon reading Augustine's spiritual autobiography. To these we can now add Bunyan's remarks about the importance of Luther's *Commentary on the Galatians* for his spiritual development: "I found my condition in his experience, so largely and profoundly handled, as if his Book had been written out of my heart. . . ."[5]

One of the functions of spiritual autobiography is to serve as a kind of mirror, not only for its readers but for its author as well. For Augustine the model is that of a darkened mirror—the "dark glass" through which we are shown both what he knows about himself and also the 'self' that only God knows.[6] For Bunyan spiritual autobiography is also a kind of mirror: a double mirror, through which he observes both the "acceptable" self and the "nonacceptable" self. In *Grace Abounding,* the unacceptable self is personified in the voice of the Tempter, who articulates all those thoughts and feelings which are repressed and denied, and subsequently projected outward.[7] As I shall show, this too is a mode whereby the soul enters into a relationship with its God. For the ultimate purpose of this pattern of denial and projection is to be able to confront, combat, and defeat forms of intestine evil. Thus Bunyan's "good" and "bad" selves are in a similar dynamic relationship, the one to the other, as are Augustine's "known" and "unknown" selves. Spiritual autobiography functions for Augustine to illumine the obscurity of the self; for Bunyan, to purify its dark recesses.

For both Augustine and Bunyan the end and purpose of the religious life is union with God. But their methods for achieving this are quite different. Augustine does so by transforming carnal into spiritual love: as the Heavenly City, "Mother of us all," sublimates and transvalues the natural mother, so the spiritually seductive figure of Continence is set against the "toys of toys and vanities of vanities" who whisper blandishments and temptations into his ear just before conversion (*Conf.* 8.11). Bunyan, however, achieves union with God by adoptive identification with Christ. This is a process whereby the depraved natural self is gradually converted into the sinless person of Christ in a threefold manner: first by emptying the self of all that is unacceptable (a process that inverts, as it parallels, the kenosis of Christ), second by projecting these negative aspects of the self onto Satan, and third, by combating and defeating them with God's help.

For Augustine the relation between self and God is grounded in the sensation of yearning, and union is achieved by sublimative possession. For Bunyan, though, the relationship between creature and creator is based on a sense of worthiness or unworthiness, and union is arrived at by identification. The differences here point toward two alternative modes whereby the soul comes to God— modes that I will refer to as "*eros*" and "*logos*." The way Jung uses these two terms supports my appropriation of them here for contrasting religious attitudes: "*eros*" is a function of relationship, it is "that which connects"; "*logos*" is a function of the spirit, it is "that which discriminates."[8] The spiritual dynamic of *eros* is the yearning for God and the archetype of pilgrimage that embodies that yearning; that of *logos* is guilt before God and the archetype of *psychomachia*, or conflict, embodying the inner tension between good and evil impulses which produces those feelings of guilt.

Moreover, these two modes characterize other aspects of religious experience as well. For example, a religiosity governed by *eros* will be God-centered, or theocentric; governed by *logos*, it will be self-centered, or autocentric. Though Augustine seeks within his memory for the immanent God, the *eros*-mode requires a deity outside the self who can be desired and sought after. This kind of religious psychology will be constructed out of the sublimation, not the repression or destruction of the "natural" man. The Augustinian conversion embodies the Roman Catholic truism that "grace builds on nature," for it assumes that in our embrace of the divine, the natural man will simply be absorbed, transformed, and assimilated. This is the principle of all archetypally erotic transformation—of love and idealism—that we tend to become what we love; that we "possess" God by loving God with our creaturely faculties. Implicit in all this is an affirmation of the creaturely as basically "good." But in *Grace Abounding* the archetype of the guilty soul replaces that of the longing soul as the inner dynamic of the work: as William Haller observes, the Puritan saint "was a fighting, not an innocent soul. He put on the whole armor of God and went forth to war against the sin that dwells in all flesh."[9] The difference between the Augustinian *eros* and the Bunyanesque *logos* is that of the incomplete self, longing for completion in the divine embrace, and the wrong self, whose sinfulness requires that it be punished and disciplined.

What Géza Róheim has asserted of cultural groups might be said of religious systems: "Human groups are actuated by their group ideals and these are always based on the infantile situation that provides those unseen libidinal ties without which no human group could exist."[10] Mediative religions (those where the experience of God is mediated by rite and sacrament) can be seen as modalities of the spiritual *eros:* they affirm the temporal reality of the world and the body, and utilize the faculties of the senses, as well as the hierarchies and structure of our social systems, to achieve religious ends. Jung would see mediative religions as archetypally maternal in that they affirm, in this way, the things of the senses. But nonmediative religions (such as Bunyan's Protestantism) are analogous to a different phase of psychospiritual development. They urge us to pass beyond the *eros* which affirms to the *logos* which questions. For the primary function of the *logos* principle is discrimination: such religions aim at locating the causes of sin and guilt and bringing them into the light of day. "There is no consciousness without discrimination of opposites," writes Jung. "This is the paternal principle, the *logos*, which eternally struggles to extricate itself from the primal warmth and primal darkness of the maternal womb; in a word, from Unconsciousness."[11] It is appropriate that religions of *eros* emphasize God the Creator; religions of *logos*, God the Savior. Thus the *Confessions* concludes with the work of God in the creation, whereas *Grace Abounding* concludes with an account of the author's ministry in saving souls. At the end of *Grace Abounding* Bunyan writes in his role as preacher, whose introspective forays into the darkness of the self are externalized and reenacted for the benefit of others: "My great desire in fulfilling my Ministry, was, to get into the darkest places in the Countrey . . . because I found my spirit leaned most after awakening and converting Work . . ." (*GA*, 89).

The itinerant evangelist who defeats Satan on the battlefield of the soul is a variant on the warrior archetype. A religious ethos that emphasizes the battle of the soul with the principle of evil, and that casts the hero in the role of warrior, is one that asserts as primary the archetypal relationship between father and son—a relationship often thought to be marked by strong ambivalence.[12]

In *Grace Abounding* the ambivalence of the spiritual child toward the spiritual father is given vivid and concrete representation in the contrasting figures of absolute good and absolute evil—Christ and Satan. Christ, of course, represents the father perceived as good, with whom the son wishes to identify; Satan, the evil father, whose claim on the son is perverted into possession. Thus Bunyan writes of his union with Christ by identification: "The Lord did also lead me into the mystery of Union with this Son of God, that I was joyned to him, that I was flesh of his flesh, and bone of his bone . . . if he and I were one, then his Righteousness was mine, his Merits mine, his Victory also mine" (*GA*, 73). The metaphor of possession, on the contrary, suggests a kind of union that is at the same time consciously forbidden and unconsciously desired. Thus Bunyan writes of Satan: "it was my delight to be taken captive by the Devil *at his will* . . ." (*GA*, 6). In the seventeenth century, giving in to temptation, or falling into sin, is almost always experienced passively—thus the metaphor of being taken captive by the Devil. Because of this experienced passivity, it is psychologically appropriate that possession should blend into apathy, inertia of the spirit, *acedia*, as in the following: "suddenly there fell upon me a great cloud of darkness . . . I was also so overrun in my Soul, with a senceless heartless frame of spirit, that I could not feel my soul to move or stir after grace and life by Christ . . ." (*GA*, 81).

Thus it is the individual's stance toward whatever is perceived as evil, bad, and sinful—both within the self and also within the larger self of our corporate body—that informs the religious dynamic of *logos*. The *Confessions* and *Grace Abounding* are useful as illustrations of these two modes because they are strikingly pure examples—Augustine of *eros;* Bunyan of *logos*. In a religiosity governed by *eros*, the experiential reality will be a deep and unappeasable yearning, with satisfaction as the ultimate goal. Where *logos* is dominant, the experience will center on feelings of guilt about one's own inadequacies and anger over injustice in the world, and perfection will be the ultimate good. Broadly speaking, *eros* is a more primitive attitudinal stance than is *logos:* it occurs more often in individuals with strong regressive tendencies and more often dominates in religious movements that either have a very strong element of sacramentalism or that exist apart from the cultures in which they occur. On the contrary, individuals and religious groups governed more by *logos* will tend to be actively involved in self-improvement or in ameliorating social and economic problems.

As abstractions, *eros* and *logos* are contrasting or complementary aspects of the religious imagination. But only rarely will they be so clearly discernible; more often, religious experience will consist of elements of both these modes. Thomas Merton is a good example of a figure in whom the two are mixed; his strong sense of the sacramental nature of reality tends to align him with a religious *eros*, but his equally strong concern with evil—both in himself and in the world—suggests the mode of *logos*. Ultimately the *eros*-principle seeks to return us to a matrix of peace, tranquillity, cessation of desire; in a sense the *logos* principle seeks the same end—yet it strives to achieve that same end not in spite of, but in the context of a world and self perceived as severely flawed.

At this point any reader who has not already objected to what might seem an optimistic revision of Augustine—that great opponent of Pelagius who is traditionally associated with a dark and pessimistic view of fallen man—will protest this contrast between "guilt" in *Grace Abounding* and relative "innocence" in the *Confessions*. But I do not mean to equate the Augustinian archetype of the soul with an underlying concept of innocence: we are all familiar with the continuity between Augustinian and Puritan theology, especially with the anti-Pelagian emphases that both share on the depravity of human nature, and with the concomitant need for a down-flowing of divine grace to soften the hardness of the unregenerate heart. What I am emphasizing, in these ideas of *eros* and *logos*, is the individual's stance toward God. For Augustine the nature of the soul is to love God. And, given the combination of Platonic idealism and the doctrine of evil as a *privatio boni*, then even Augustine's corruption—his lust—becomes a distortion or a lower form of a deeper and truer love, the love of God. But for Bunyan the nature of the soul is characterized not so much by a capacity for love as by a capacity for hope and fear—a binary set of emotions that ultimately looks back to the initial act of predestination in election and reprobation, and looks forward to the final act of judgment in salvation and damnation. Moreover, for Augustine it is assumed that once the "turning" of conversion is accomplished, God will welcome back the prodigal soul with open arms. The equivalent in parable is the story of the Prodigal Son, whose return occasions the ultimate rejoicing for the father. But for Bunyan the turning of conversion does not imply God's acceptance: on the contrary, it is the occasion for even more terrible trials and tests. The parabolic model for Bunyan (so he fears) is the story of

Esau and Isaac, where the son who gives up his birthright can never find repentance, can never return to the father.

Certainly there are historical determinants to these two religious stances—*eros* and *logos*. Though it would be reductive to account for the striking contrasts between Augustine and Bunyan as simply the differences between early Christianity and Reformation Christianity, nonetheless to ignore the historicity of these writers would be equally misleading. The history of Christianity shows a variety of religious formulations, each developed in response to a felt spiritual need. The metaphor of illness and healing is an established favorite—one that spans differences of religious denomination, culture, and era—for describing the ills of the human condition and the need for some sort of deliverance. The formulations of religious experience—both as experienced in the individual and codified in a religious system—can be seen as diagnosing at the same time that they attempt to cure whatever ills afflict individual and culture. The diagnosis suggested by the principle of *eros* is that of misdirected love; the cure is the conversion of the soul wherein the long journey through life becomes an ascent, and the "signs" of the Earthly Kingdom are transformed into the "things" of the Heavenly Kingdom. On the other hand, the principle of *logos* diagnoses the problem as that of a powerful intestine evil and a concomitant moral paralysis to withstand evil; the cure, again, is conversion—but this time figuring as a form of radical surgery whereby the natural man (the "sick self") is excised and in its place is substituted the spiritual self that is Christ.

It has often been said that the Reformation was a response to the failure of secular and spiritual forms of mediation.[13] But it is also possible to see the failure of the older ecclesiastical structures as due to problems that are primarily spiritual. The theology of Luther and Calvin (of which *Grace Abounding* is a product) can be seen as a response to a pervasive state of spiritual pathology; that is, as an attempt to provide a more adequate spiritual therapy for souls overwhelmed with guilt. The particular configurations of *Grace Abounding* derive from this cultural ethos of new remedies, new therapies, new solutions. Norman O. Brown has written that Luther's Protestantism represents a response to a new experience of evil—new in its scope and intensity, and new in the concomitant feeling of powerlessness in the face of such evil.[14] It is the problem of evil that requires Reformation Christianity to replace the maternal *eros* with the paternal *logos* as its animating psychospiritual force. And this problem of evil can be seen as the result of the inadequate solution arrived at by the early Church Fathers, chiefly Augustine, whereby evil is denied any status in reality and determined to be merely the absence of good. But the doctrine of *privatio boni,* which so neatly solves the theological problems of evil for a Church threatened by the heresy of Manichaeism, does not solve the experiential problem of evil for the individual soul seeking salvation. Indeed, the notion of *privatio boni* can be thought of as a kind of theological repression, because it represents a refusal to deal with evil by simply denying it the status of "really real." Denied a place in the nature of things, evil develops its own negative reality in Hell—the underworld of Man's mythic unconscious—propagates the countless demons and spirits of the Middle Ages, and finally bursts into consciousness in the agonized, guilt-ridden conscience of the Reformation.

The religious consciousness which informs *Grace Abounding* begins with a situation where the individual's sense of sinfulness is so overwhelming as to be unendurable, and where the Church, in its doctrine of evil as *privatio boni,* lacks any effective remedies to deal with it. The therapy suggested by Reformation theology consists of two successive stages: the first, the inculcation of an intense predestinarian anxiety and the second, a functional demonism.[15] It may well raise critical eyebrows to describe anxiety or demonism as a "therapy" of any kind. But we may here call to mind Róheim's observation "that diseases themselves are also attempted cures" and subsequent elaboration: "fundamentally we find that the disease and the cure of the disease are successive phases or identical."[16] Predestinarian anxiety (the first stage) serves to increase guilt to such an extent that it may become manifest, visible, and palpable; the projection of negative impulses onto Satan (the second stage) serves to isolate the source of guilt outside the self. When considered in this way, the predestinarian anxiety of such figures as Luther, Calvin, and Bunyan is at the same time disease and cure; it serves as a propaedeutic phase in an extended therapy which, though it is lifelong, achieves both release and relief in that unacceptable feelings and thoughts are reified, projected onto Satan, and there combated.

Reformation theology opened the way to predestinarian anxiety in the addition of the doctrine of perseverance to the conversion process—a doctrine where the certainty of salvation is paradoxically achieved by cycles of doubt and despair in the march toward perfection. In Haller's words: "So long as sin vexed him [the seventeenth-century sinner-saint], he might know that God was with him. All he had to do was to continue to be vexed, and he was sure to triumph, because all existence is the conflict of Christ against Satan, the foreordained outcome of which is the triumph of the elect."[17] Similarly Bunyan observes that "great sins do draw out great grace; and where guilt is most terrible and fierce, there the mercy of God in Christ, when shewed to the Soul, appears most high and mighty" (*GA*, 78). Anxiety is thus a defining quality of the Bunyanesque archetype of the soul—a soul that is portrayed as vacillating between peace and terror, hope and fear: "my soul did hang as in a pair of Scales again, sometimes up, and sometimes down, now in peace, and anon again in terror" (*GA*, 65). These ambivalent sets of emotions produce an anxiety that is to be finally resolved only eschatologically, in a Heaven of eternal bliss or a Hell of eternal damnation.

Though there can be no total resolution to predestinarian anxiety for the seventeenth-century saint, partial resolution can be achieved by the process whereby the sinful thoughts and feelings so magnified by intense brooding upon them are then projected onto some demonic figure and there dealt with outside the self. This functional approach to Satan is the Reformation's response to the rather passive doctrine of *privatio boni* inherited from the days of early Christianity. It is a technique whereby the ancient principles of negation, death, sin, and despair, having asserted themselves so definitely as to defeat the remedial powers of the Church, are not only recognized but assimilated into the religious scheme of things, and, paradoxically, used as *positive* forces. In *Grace Abounding*, the self not only projects evil onto a reified figure of sin, the Tempter, but uses the negative self and its impulses so projected to tempt the self. Although this would seem to be a process initiated by the negative self (Satan) for destructive ends, it is in fact a process initiated by the true self (or God) for positive ends; in the case of God to refine, perfect, and instruct the soul, and in the case of the self to induce the conflicts and tests by which it may finally come to a realization of the predestined decree that defines its identity.

Paradoxically, the seventeenth-century emphases on temptation and inner conflict as necessary to salvation served to bring the actual components of "this world" (as opposed to the transcendent world of essences and ideas) into sharper focus. One of the most important contributions of Protestantism was to flesh out the narrative austerity of the Augustinian *peregrinatio* by concentrating on what happens to the individual during his pilgrimage—on his hardships and battles, his victories and defeats. In effect, this renewal of focus is a logical extension of the doctrine of the Incarnation. For if the spiritual and the natural are inextricably linked in the person of Christ, then this fallen world is indeed redeemed, and the older medieval distinction between sacred and secular, along with the principle of mediation, must be set aside. The supreme paradox of Protestantism was its wholesale condemnation of all that is "fleshly" while, at the same time, affirming such "fleshly" institutions as marriage, family, business. It is this paradoxical return to a more fully incarnational theology that is the source of the intensity, the energy, the exuberance of the seventeenth-century religious experience that *Grace Abounding* documents; an experience that is not content to deny and ignore evil, the way Augustine did in his attempts to be un-Manichaean, but is courageously committed to fighting the battle with Sin, Death, and Satan. In this transvaluation of spiritual archetypes, the Augustinian image of the *homo viator*, the pilgrim-soul traversing the insubstantial and unreal wastes of this world toward a final destiny in the next, becomes later on the agitated image of the Christian warrior engaged in fierce battle against the mighty forces of Satan. Concomitantly, there is a reassessment of the Christian life that brings into focus the life in "this world"—a new emphasis on the process of living rather than on the end of life.

ii. Archetype of *psychomachia:*
the "static" hero and his crises of temptation

Roy Pascal observes that in a successful spiritual autobiography the author is able to achieve a balanced integration "between outward experience and inward growth or unfolding, between incidents and the spiritual digesting of them."[18] In *Grace Abounding*, however, there is no such balanced relationship between inner and outer realities. Unlike the *Confessions*, where most of the facts of Augustine's life are woven into the texture of the autobiography, *Grace Abounding* is characterized by an exclusive focus on the inner life and the radical elimination of corresponding events of the outer life. Although fascinating in its excited, nervous prose and its pathological obsessiveness, it is a difficult narrative to read. This is partly because it seems so repetitive; the narrative strikes the reader as simply an additive sequence of temptations. But it is also because of the abstract and formulaic way in which Bunyan presents those temptations. That "whether I had Faith or no" and "[whether] the day of grace should now be past and gone" are orthodox Calvinist problems goes without saying; that these doctrinaire problems have their correlates in the nonformulaic truths of the heart is not so evident (*GA*, 18,20). As I hope to show, there is indeed a pattern to *Grace Abounding*, and it is one that is constructed around those temptations.

The title of Bunyan's autobiography tells us much about his idea of the spiritual hero. For in assuming the appellation "chief of sinners," with his great sins and great deliverances, Bunyan is placing himself in a very special category—an attitude that Esther Harding appropriately refers to as "the tendency to inverted self-aggrandizement."[19] In other words, Bunyan sins in the grandiose pridefulness of his self-perceived humility. Much of the content, as well as the tone, of *Grace Abounding* can be accounted for by what one scholar calls Bunyan's need to "blackwash" his autobiographical persona in an attempt to appear more humble, more wicked, more unlearned, more lowly than anyone else. This he accomplishes in the early part of the narrative by observing (and exaggerating) his inferior social rank, his early childhood depravities, and his lack of learning. Of course it was a convention of the times to exaggerate one's sins and Bunyan was doing no more than other Puritan autobiographers, since the greater the original depravity, the more glory to God in the salvation of such a soul: "where guilt is most terrible and fierce," Bunyan writes, "there the mercy of God in Christ, when shewed to the soul, appears most high and mighty" (*GA*, 78). Yet the intensity of Bunyan's language suggests that he really convinced himself that he was utterly depraved, the "chief of sinners," even though his worst transgressions seem to have been swearing and game-playing: ". . . I was more loathsom in mine own eyes than was a toad, and I thought I was so in Gods eyes too: Sin and corruption . . . would as naturally bubble out of my heart, as water would bubble out of a fountain. . . . none but the Devil himself could equalize me for inward wickednes and pollution of minde" (*GA*, 27).

At the tender age of nine Bunyan finds in himself a *psychomachia* of conflicting desires: "even in my childhood [God] did scare and affright me with fearful dreams, and did terrifie me with dreadful visions" (*GA*, 6). His early ambivalence is resolved when the love of pleasure triumphs and the chastising dreams cease as he becomes "the very ringleader" in vice and ungodliness. These froward tendencies are tempered by his marriage later on, which causes him to fall in "very eagerly with the Religion of the times" (*GA*, 8). On one particular morning the Parson's sermon on the evils of breaking the Sabbath awakens deep feelings of guilt in Bunyan. That same afternoon an accusing voice breaks in upon a Sabbath-breaking game of cat: "Wilt thou leave thy sins and go to Heaven? or have thy sins and go to Hell? "(*GA*, 10). Bunyan concludes that it is too late to reform, despairs, and decides he might as well take his fill of sin. A month or so later a woman rebukes him for swearing, whereupon he reforms, begins to read the Old Testament, and tries to keep the commandments—all to the amazement of his neighbors. Not long thereafter he comes upon some poor women speaking of "the New Birth" and begins reading the New Testament. The seeds of Bunyan's conversion have been sown, and thereupon follows a series of temptations: a crisis of uncertainty as to whether he has faith or not, a crisis as to whether he is of the elect, a crisis as to whether or not the day of grace has passed, a crisis as to whether he is effectually called. Each of these crises is instigated by Satan, "the Tempter," and resolved by God, speaking through Scripture. During this time he comes under the tutelage of John Gifford, pastor of the Bedford Church.

Then Bunyan narrates his receiving proof of his election: "Now had I an evidence, as I thought, of my salvation from Heaven, with many golden Seals thereon, all hanging in my sight. . . ." (*GA*, 40). It is symptomatic of the structural defect in Bunyan's autobiography that this important event is narrated in such a way that we can read through the passage scarcely knowing what is happening, unless we reflect upon the significance of such evidence of election for the Calvinist. In other words, if one does not know the Calvinist doctrinal superstructure, the inner sense of the spiritual pilgrimage is lost. This climactic episode does not seem to be anticipated, in either a religious or a literary sense, by the inner events that precede it (the temptations), nor do those events which follow the sign of election seem to be at all affected by it.

Yet after this episode about election, the crises of temptation are represented as longer, more severe, and more luridly persecutory than those which precede it. The very next one, "a more grievous and dreadful temptation then before," is represented as the temptation to sell Christ for the things of this life and comes to Bunyan in the form of an obsessive verbal formula, "Sell him, sell him" (*GA* 41–42). It is interesting that Bunyan tells us in one place that this particular crisis lasted two hours, and a paragraph later that it lasted two years (*GA*, 41). He torments himself with the scriptural story of Esau, fearing that his sin of blasphemy is the "unpardonable sin," the sin against the Holy Ghost, and thus proof of his reprobation. He is delivered several times by comforting scriptural quotations and voices, but falls back again. The conflict in his heart between hope and despair, which he perceives as a conflict between the forces of Satan and the forces of Christ (both represented by scriptural passages), finally reaches a climax in a battle between the two textual passages—the first about the sufficiency of grace ("My Grace is sufficient for thee") and the second about Esau losing his inheritance ("For ye know, how that afterward, when Esau would have inherited the blessing, he was rejected; for he found no place of repentance, though he sought it carefully with tears") (*GA*, 43–66). The battle ends several days later, happily for Bunyan, with the victory of the more favorable of the two texts. The episode is followed by a triumphant exegesis of the Esau story—an in-depth analysis of the causes and advantages of the temptation that somehow reminds one of a victor despoiling his conquered foe. The two remaining sections of the narrative—Bunyan's account of his ministry and imprisonment—are quiet and somewhat more restrained; we sense that he has exhausted himself in the long and turbulent story of his conversion.

Bunyan's election-theology effects a radical reshaping of his account of his inner life. It is like a fairy-tale where he knows, but cannot admit that he knows, that the prince will survive his ordeals and win both kingdom and princess in the end. Behind the personality of John Bunyan, the evangelical tinker of Bedford, is the seventeenth-century version of the archetypal soul—that "elected Everyman" who figures both as Christian pilgrim, journeying from the City of Destruction to the Celestial City, and as Christian warrior, allied with the armies of God in combat with the Devil. The pilgrim and the knight are familiar representations of the spiritual hero: one thinks of Chaucer and of Spenser, of medieval romance and allegory. By the seventeenth century the archetypes of pilgrimage and battle were universal terms that could both evoke and explain the life of the spirit. The image of the pilgrim with his staff aligns the hero with the archetype of *peregrinatio;* that of the knight with his sword suggests the archetype of *psychomachia.* The archetypes themselves are the same as those in the *Confessions,* but the differences in how the two authors portray and emphasize them are significant. In the *Confessions, psychomachia* is a minor theme within the overarching archetype of the Christian life as quest; in *Grace Abounding* this is reversed.

That Bunyan was familiar with both archetypes as metaphorical representations of the spiritual life is evident in his later allegories, where *The Pilgrim's Progress* portrays the archetype of quest in the journey of the wayfaring Christian soul and *The Holy War* depicts the archetype of *psychomachia* in the vicissitudes of the warfaring Christian soul. *Grace Abounding*, however, is dominated by the archetype of *psychomachia:* the journeys of heart and mind are rendered as various bouts with temptation, and the archetypal figures of *The Pilgrim's Progress* are here condensed into the antagonistic voices of Satan and God. And in this the autobiography is structurally more similar to *The Holy War* than to *The Pilgrim's Progress.* In *The Holy War*, the archetype of a *psychomachia* is allegorized as a continual siege upon the soul of Man led by Satan, from which the soul is finally delivered by Emmanuel, the Christ. The pattern in *Grace Abounding* is identical and relentless: assaults on the soul by the Devil and deliverance by Christ.

If *Grace Abounding* is the personal story out of which the later allegories were conceived,[20] its own predecessor can be glimpsed in the Morality Play. For the hero of *Grace Abounding*, divested of his good and bad thoughts, reminds one of Mankind in *The Castle of Perseverance*—a naked figure alone on the *platea* of his small ego, surrounded by the looming personifications of his good and bad impulses. And indeed, Bunyan's religious experience is predicated on a violent disunion between the two parts of the self, the "earthly" and the "spiritual." His conversion entails the radical severance of the one term from the other and their reunion by adoptive identification with the person of Christ: "Now could I see myself in Heaven and Earth at once; in Heaven by my Christ, by my Head, by my Righteousness and Life, though on Earth by my Body or Person" (*GA*, 73). The Augustinian dualisms, both as experienced in the self and perceived in the world, are binary terms in a developmental or sublimative relation to each other, as the archetype of the pilgrimage from the Earthly to the Heavenly City implies. But the dualisms of Bunyan set each term against the other; they are conflictive, as the archetype of *psychomachia* implies: hope against fear, salvation against damnation, God against Satan, the New Law against the Old Law, grace against wrath. For Bunyan the very conditions of the spiritual pilgrimage are those of *psychomachia.* Thus even that great allegory of pilgrimage, *The*

Pilgrim's Progress, begins with the threat of imminent destruction in Christian's fear "that this our City will be burned with fire from heaven."[21]

In *Grace Abounding* Bunyan wryly observes that he is one who is "no stranger to combat with the Devil"—a self-perception that typifies the Bunyanesque spiritual hero. This is not the soul that seeks a loving deity so much as the soul that flees a wrathful God; not the individual who defines himself by a lost innocence that he seeks to remember and thus regain but the individual who defines himself by an invisible and predestined decree—an intolerable spiritual ambiguity that he seeks to clarify by battles lost and won. So early in *Grace Abounding* Bunyan describes himself as willing to be put on trial as to "whether I had Faith or no" (*GA*, 18). Significantly, after this venture of spiritual warfare, the Tempter makes his very first appearance in the narrative: "Wherefore while I was thus considering, and being put to my plunge about it . . . the Tempter came in with this delusion . . ." (*GA*, 18). The next time the Tempter makes an appearance Bunyan parenthetically tells us something of the psychology of this technique of spiritual combat: "indeed, I little thought that Satan had thus assaulted me, but that rather it was my own prudence thus to start the question . . ." (*GA*, 21). Bunyan is here scoffing at his spiritual naiveté; later on he will identify Satan, not "[his] own prudence," as the source of doubt and temptation. What he is describing in this sequence is important because it reveals the process whereby the condition for spiritual warfare, the trial, is created in projecting and externalizing anxiety, doubt, or despair onto the ready figure of Satan.

Bunyan's representation of the conflicted soul in terms of projected and reified constructs of good and evil tends toward a static character portrayal, and thus to a narrative situation representing the conversion of the soul in a sequence of events that is additive, not developmental. Whereas in the *Confessions* and in *The Pilgrim's Progress* geographical movement serves as a metaphor for the development of the soul in its spiritual quest, in *Grace Abounding* there is no such geographical movement. It is tempting to suggest, as did Stanley Fish in his analysis of "anti-progression" in *The Pilgrim's Progress*,[22] that there is no spiritual progression in *Grace Abounding* either. And indeed, a common critical response to *Grace Abounding* as a literary work is that it is so loosely structured that there seems to be no real development at all in the protagonist's inner life. But this impression may be due not to any intrinsic failure of spiritual growth, but to the predominance of the archetype of *psychomachia* in Bunyan's religious imagination and literary formulation. In *Grace Abounding*, what appears to be an absence of spiritual development may be only a failure of form, where the repetition of temptation sequences or the abrupt victory or defeat of the battle images is less successful than the journey image in rendering spiritual life into narrative.

An example of the way that Bunyan depicts the spiritual development of the "static" protagonist of *Grace Abounding* is the episode already mentioned when he is interrupted in the midst of a forbidden Sabbath game of cat: "a voice did suddenly dart from Heaven into my Soul, which said, 'Wilt thou leave thy sins, and go to Heaven? or have thy sins, and go to Hell?'" (*GA*, 10). It is a description of a motionless event: "Thus I stood in the midst of my play, before all that then were present, but yet I told them nothing . . ." (*GA*, 11). From outside appearances—from the spectator's point of view—it would seem as though nothing is happening. But this is not so, for Bunyan is undergoing the initial movings of the conversion process: the event that directly precedes the dramatic interruption of the game is a guilt-inducing sermon, which Bunyan describes as follows: "I fell in my conscience under his Sermon, thinking and believing that he made that Sermon on purpose to shew me my evil-doing; and at that time I felt what guilt was, though never before, that I can remember . . ." (*GA*, 10). In a seventeenth-century conversion, intense guilt-feelings are absolutely necessary, for guilt makes the heart tender, and thus receptive to religious awakening. Not surprisingly, the very next event in Bunyan's narrative is his "great Conversion, from prodigious profaneness, to something like a moral life" when he is reproved for swearing (*GA*, 13). These three events—the guilt-inducing sermon, the voice and vision that interrupt the game, and the conversion from profanity—may seem to lack any relation to each other, but this is because Bunyan presents them not developmentally but sequentially. In fact, they are interlocking spiritual events of great inner significance in the gradual process of his conversion.

Not only is there character development in *Grace Abounding* but also there is indeed spiritual progression, though it is a kind of spiritual progression accomplished by fits and starts—bursts of aggressive, forward movement alternating with periods of passivity and torpor.[23] And in this, Bunyan is very different from Augustine. In the *Confessions*, as we have observed, Augustine's life manifests itself in a series of journeys—literally, from Thagaste to Carthage to Rome to Milan; intellectually, from Manichaeism to Neoplatonism to Catholic Christianity; and affectively from the concubine, to Monica, to the maternal "City of God." In the *Confessions*, then, not only does the quest dominate the archetypal patterning of the narrative, but what is emphasized in the quest is its object—whether this is God or the concubine who deflects Augustine from his true path (though she is able to do so because his love for her is a dim copy of his love for God). But in *Grace Abounding* what is emphasized in the protagonist's spiritual progress is movement itself—or its absence. In this way the quest motif turns into the theme of progress, and the Augustinian ethos of seeking, desiring, and yearning into a more aggressive ethos of moving forward, marching onward, and conquering whatever stands in one's way.

But the imperfect soul cannot sustain so arduous an ideal of spiritual perfection and thus the progressive march of the spirit periodically and cyclically breaks down into periods of stagnant regressive states—the "miry bogs" of *The Pilgrim's Progress*. These states represent a reassertion of a primary ambivalence in the self, where the clear certainty of faith achieved in the battles against evil is once again compromised by doubt and despair. Moreover, these regressive states of temptation and backsliding are not accidental parts of the conversion process; rather, they are internally necessary to achieve that overall progressive transformation of the soul that Bunyan's election-theology requires. For the Christian who has been effectually called is a composite figure uniting in himself an awareness of "the insufficiencie of all inherent righteousness" (*GA*, 103) and the imputed righteousness of Christ. And the right relationship of divine and mortal in the individual is a learned one, a learning effected by means of these intermediate states of spiritual regression. Bunyan is saying as much when he stands back from his narrative and comments on the function of temptation in his march toward spiritual perfection:

> in general [God] was pleased to take this course with me, first, to suffer me to be afflicted with temptation concerning [the things of Christ], and then reveal them to me; as sometimes I should lie under great guilt for sin, even crushed to the ground therewith, and then the Lord would shew me the death of Christ, yea and so sprinkle my Conscience with his Blood, that I should find, and that before I was aware,

that in the Conscience where but just now did reign and rage the Law, even there would rest and abide the peace and Love of God thorow Christ. (*GA*, 39–40)

When Jung writes that "the constant companion of sanctity is temptation, without which no true saint can live,"[24] he could be describing the psychology of a seventeenth-century conversion, where temptation is always the interface of sanctification.

This formulation of the spiritual life, where progressive movements of the soul alternate with their regressive equivalents—hope with despair and joy with fear—is represented in *Grace Abounding* as a structural oscillation between positive and negative religious experiences: the "positive" represented by Bunyan's encounters with various religious figures and the "negative" by his struggles with Satan in the temptation sequences. For example, Bunyan's encounter with the women from the Bedford Church is followed by his temptation as to whether or not he has faith, which in turn is followed by his vision of the Bedford women and his regeneration, then the linked temptations as to the question of his election and whether "the day of grace should now be past and gone," then his initial encounter with Gifford the pastor, then the crisis of the "negative call," where he is pursued by the scriptural passage "Simon, Simon, behold, Satan hath desired to have you," then his spiritual apprenticeship under Gifford, and so forth.

Moreover an outline of the text reveals that this structural oscillation between progress and regress itself constitutes a definite pattern—one that consists of two series of temptations and two conversion episodes:

introduction	childhood and youth (pp. 5–6)
temptations:	a series of some six temptations (pp. 15–40)
FIRST CONVERSION:	receiving evidence of election (p. 40)
temptations:	"Sell him, sell him" (plus related temptations) (pp. 41–66)
SECOND CONVERSION:	the battle of the two texts (p. 67)
conclusion:	analysis of the last temptation (pp. 74–82)

The progress of the soul in *Grace Abounding* is demonstrable in the difference between the two kinds of temptation series and the two conversions. The first series of temptations occurs before the experience of receiving evidence of election; their purpose is to bring Bunyan to a realization of his utter helplessness and the necessity of taking on the imputed righteousness of Christ in order to be saved. The second series of temptations occurs after the evidence of election; they represent both the period of testing and trial that is lifelong for the Calvinist elect, and also the "right way" to withstand temptation. Bunyan himself tells us this when he steps out of his narrative at the end of the second temptation sequence and comments on his text: "I will now (God willing) before I proceed any further, give you in a word or two, what, as I conceive, was the cause of this Temptation; and also after that, what advantage at the last it became unto my soul" (*GA*, 74).

The progress of the soul in *Grace Abounding* is recorded in the fact that the temptation sequences increase in severity and length after the first conversion until a climax is reached in the temptation that leads into the second conversion; then they taper off. For example, the temptation where Bunyan is haunted by the phrase "Simon, Simon, behold, Satan hath desired to have you" (occurring fairly early in the narrative) is described with some intensity: "a very great storm came down upon me, which handled me twenty times worse then all I had met with before . . ." (*GA*, 30–31). The subsequent temptation, to "Sell Christ," is described as even *more* intense—"a more grievous and dreadful temptation than before" (*GA*, 41). Bunyan resists assent for one year, but finally in a weak moment permits the blasphemous thought and its verbal formula, "sell him, sell him," to enter his consciousness—a "passive" sin that causes him to suffer agonies of guilt and despair for two-and-a-half years (*GA*, 44). This sin of assent to a blasphemous thought is embroidered with the guilt of a multitude of scriptural saints and sinners, and tesellated with such fearful distinctions as being the "Unpardonable Sin"—the sin against the Holy Ghost—and as being evidence that he is indeed an Esau doomed to reprobation. Finally, as the Tempter continues to afflict him, the two opposing armies of good and evil meet together, head on, in the battlefield of the heart. The forces of despair and damnation are represented by the Old Testament story of Esau; the forces of hope and salvation by the New Testament idea of grace. The battlefield is first set up in Bunyan's imagination: "Lord, thought I, if both these Scriptures would meet in my heart at once, I wonder which of them would get the better of me" (*GA*, 66). The psychological state represented by *"I wonder"* is followed by "I had a *longing* mind that they might come both together upon me" and then succeeded by "I *desired* of God they might" (*GA*, 67; emphasis added). Several days later the battle begins: "they boulted both upon me at a time, and did work and struggle strangly in me for a while; at last, that about Esaus birthright began to wax weak, and withdraw, and vanish; and this about the sufficiency of Grace prevailed, with peace and joy." The victory is that of hope over fear, exultation over despair, the New Law over the Old Law, "the Word of Life and Grace" over "the Word of Law and Wrath" (*GA*, 67). It is a process of spiritual exorcism, for along with the departure of the ghost of Esau, "Moses and Elias must both vanish, and leave Christ and his Saints alone" (*GA*, 67).

iii. *Lysis* conversion: the iterated archetype

Augustine's spiritual autobiography is structured around his conversion in the garden: everything that precedes this turning point either leads up to it or prepares for it, and everything subsequent to the conversion is based on the "new man" born out of that climactic event. But Bunyan's autobiography does not have this structure. In *Grace Abounding*, the single arc of Augustine's conversion is replaced by a series of arcs, as the Augustinian *crisis* is repeated over and over again. And this is one's initial response to *Grace Abounding:* that it is a series of temptations, falls, and deliverances, where the two conversion-episodes appear as manifestations—with exclamation marks—of the iterated archetype.

Structure in *Grace Abounding* seems poorly realized, and this is one reason why it is less successful as a narrative than the *Confessions*. Augustine's *crisis* conversion, with its single, transforming event, is admirably suited to the dramatic potentials of spiritual autobiography. But Bunyan's *lysis* conversion is by definition diffuse, cumulative, and repetitive—a conversion model that does not readily lend itself to the narrative dimensions and dramatic potential of spiritual autobiography.

But if *Grace Abounding* lacks the clear arc of spiritual turmoil-conversion-spiritual peace, it is because Bunyan's personal experience of conversion, and the theology behind that experience, conforms to a different model.[25] In the seventeenth century there was a significant minority of religious thinkers who recognized the discrepancy between the way conversion was represented in the exemplary lives of the saints and prophets, and the manner in which it was actually experienced by ordinary people. In other words, personal experience often failed to live up to the paradigmatic expectations created by *crisis* conversion. In a fine book called *The Heart Prepared,* Norman Pettit shows how the English preparationists sought to give to their congregations a model whereby conversion could occur without violent transformation or dramatic supernatural intervention. The conversion of Lydia served for some as a scriptural example of a more gradual conversion. The account in Acts 16:14 is as follows: "And a certain woman named Lydia, a seller of purple, of the city of Thyatira, which worshipped God, heard us: whose heart the Lord opened, that she attended unto the things which were spoken of Paul." For the Puritan preachers Richard Rogers and Richard Sibbes, the conversion of Lydia both explained and justified conversions that did not conform to the Pauline model, since it exemplified an individual for whom conversion came gradually, and after the Lord "opened" her heart.[26]

Those who were sympathetic to this model of conversion could claim a similar emphasis on the gradual aspects of conversion in Calvin's theology. For though the doctrinal Calvinist equivalent to Augustine's *crisis* conversion in the garden is the sure knowledge of salvation—the knowledge that one has been effectually called—the important difference between the two is that the acquiring of this knowledge, for a Calvinist, is not an event but a process, and a lifelong one at that. In Calvin's own words, ". . . God assigns [believers] the race of repentance to run during their whole life. . . . that they may employ their whole life in the exercise of repentance, and know that this warfare will be terminated only by death."[27]

This emphasis on conversion as a gradual process, or a lifelong struggle, is analogous to James's definition of *lysis* conversion, of which Bunyan's is cited as an example: the "gradual" or "conscious and voluntary way," which "consists in the building up, piece by piece, of a new set of moral and spiritual habits."[28] And yet Bunyan's religious experience, as he presents it to us in *Grace Abounding*, cannot be summed up as simply a gradual and voluntary process of unification. As he himself writes in his preface, it is a record of "my castings down and raisings up"—and few were so repeatedly cast down and then raised up again as was Bunyan during the course of his conversion.

The fact that the conversion in *Grace Abounding* is problematic is demonstrated in the various attempts of Bunyan scholars, though they acknowledge that the Calvinist conversion is not an event but a process, to try to find in *Grace Abounding* the turning point, or definitive episode to which they can affix a sense of structure. Thus Margaret Bottrall, although she observes that *Grace Abounding* "is a recapitulation of the long quest for salvation that culminated in Bunyan's conviction that he was one of the elect," nonetheless asserts that "by his own reckoning" his spiritual rebirth began on that day when he encountered the Bedford women. Roger Sharrock, too, though he recognizes that in *Grace Abounding* "there is no single sudden dawning of grace to wipe out entirely the darkness of unregeneracy; conversion is a long process of struggle"—still maintains that "there is a clear turning point. . . . This was when he listened to the poor women of Bedford sitting in the sun and 'talking about the things of God.'" Ola Winslow, though observing that "his conversion story is the great story of his life, and it was life-long," nevertheless perceives that lifelong process as beginning with the divine interruption of the game of cat. Richard Greaves observes that "a turning-point of a sort came when the rebuke of 'a very loose and ungodly Wretch' caused him to turn once again to a fervent religious life." For Dean Ebner, it is the battle between the two scriptural passages that is the actual conversion: "this point in his narrative [is] both the zenith of his spiritual experience and the structural climax of the autobiography."[29]

This great need for there to be a single, dramatic episode in a conversion is indeed striking, especially when accompanied by the stated recognition that there is no such definitive turning point. Equally striking is the confusion as to precisely when this turning point occurs. Certainly, the *crisis* model exerts a formidable suggestive power over our expectations of conversion. The Augustinian and Pauline examples have been imitated both in life and in literature to such an extent that they have unconsciously shaped our very definition of conversion. Thus in *Young Man Luther*, Erikson points out that though tradition has led us to expect a single, dramatic event, Luther's conversion occurred over the course of three quite distinct experiences: "The fact that Luther experienced these clearly separate stages of religious revelation might make it possible to establish a psychological rationale for the conversion of other outstanding religionists, where tradition has come to insist on popular faith."[30]

James's definition of *lysis* conversion as a "gradual process" might seem precisely the "psychological rationale" called for by Erikson. But James's terms, *gradual* and *voluntary*, do not adequately describe conversions like Bunyan's; they are too vague and too general. Indeed, it would seem here that James's psychological view is, paradoxically, too unpsychological: it does not suggest what is going on in the mind of the convert. Perhaps a more precise way of discussing *lysis* conversion might be to consider it in terms of structure and function. For *lysis* and *crisis* can be thought of not only as descriptive terms but also as morphological categories, each having its own specific form and function. Let us then redefine *lysis* conversion, at least for the purposes of this study, as a gradual form of regeneration that often includes two or more *crisis* events. Moreover the number of *crisis* episodes in this more diffuse kind of conversion is not random but is shaped by particular theological arguments and dominant cultural patterns of thought.

The *lysis* paradigm of seventeenth-century conversion can be thought of as both a gradual awakening and an experience of two conversion-episodes. The orthodox Puritan conversion is most often considered either as a sequence of progressive, graduated stages (predestination, justification, adoption, sanctification, glorification, etc.) or in dyadic terms, the most common being justification and perseverance, or justification and sanctification. Both these alternatives are dogmatic equivalents of *lysis* conversion, whether it is defined as a gradual (and graduated) process of spiritual maturation or as a double conversion. Similarly, in *Grace Abounding* Bunyan's conversion is represented as a process that unfolds gradually over a long period of time and also as a process in which there are two specific transitional nodes—in other words, where there are two conversions. The first of these is the episode when he receives evidence of his election—the envisioned scroll "with many golden Seals thereon, all hanging in my sight" (*GA*, 40); the second is the later episode when the New Testament passage about the sufficiency of grace defeats the Old Testament passage about Esau's losing his inheritance.

At this point, one might want to question the assertion that there is a dyadic structure to *lysis* conversion. Why two events? Why not three, or four? And why the selection of these two particular episodes in *Grace Abounding* as the two conversions? A dyadic paradigm of conversion is variously described in the religious literature of the seventeenth century.[31] Thus, although Calvin writes of conversion as a lifelong process—"an incessant conflict with the vices of our corrupt nature"[32]—he also treats it as a process consisting of the two stages of mortification and vivification, the death of the fleshly nature and rebirth in the spirit—a pattern that derives from the two parts of the atonement, the crucifixion and resurrection. In Calvin's own words, conversion consists "in the mortification of our flesh and of the old man and in the vivification of the Spirit." He goes on to align these two aspects of repentance with "our participation in Christ": "For if we truly partake of his death, our old man is crucified by its power, and the body of sin expires, so that the corruption of our former nature loses all its vigour. If we are partakers of his resurrection, we are raised by it to a newness of life. . . . .".[33]

A two-stage conversion is also to be found in the Puritan theologian William Ames, whose work precedes Bunyan's by some forty years, and whose transposition of the original "Calvinese" may be said to be typical of the English theology of the times. Ames observes that conversion "is twofold, relative and absolute (or real)." The relative change he identifies as justification and adoption—it marks a "judicial or moral change," and concerns the remission of sins both past and future by which "a believer is properly freed from the guilt of sin"; the "real" change is both the manifestation and the consequence of the "relative" change of state—it frees the believer from the "sordidness and stain of sin" and restores "the purity of God's image." The distinction is a fine one: the relative change concerns guilt; the real change, purity. What Ames seems to mean by this distinction between "relative" and "real" is the same as that between potential and actual, or a promise made and a promise carried out. Thus sanctification (and also glorification) is "the carrying out of the sentence of justification."[34]

These two stages in conversion, the "relative" and the "absolute," correspond to Bunyan's own idea of repentance as having two aspects, which he compares to the stairs leading to the chambers of Solomon's temple:

> That by which we turn from nature to grace, and that by which we turn from the imperfections which attend a state of grace, to glory. Hence true repentance, or the right going up these turning Stairs, is called repentance to salvation; for true repentance stopeth [sic] not at the reception of grace, for that is but a going up these Stairs to the middle Chambers.[35]

The iterative theology of repentance—nature to grace/grace to glory—is structurally represented in *Grace Abounding* as the two conversions. Thus the first conversion, when Bunyan receives evidence of his election, is the equivalent to the turning from nature to grace; a "relative change" whereby the elected Christian undergoes a kind of death to self as he takes on the imputed righteousness of Christ. And appropriately, Bunyan follows this sign of his salvation with a reference to the crucified Christ: ". . . [I] should often long and desire that the last day were come, that I might for ever be inflamed with the sight, and joy, and communion of him, whose Head was crowned with Thorns, whose Face was spit on, and Body broken, and Soul made an offering for my sins . . ." (*GA* 40). The second conversion, the battle of the two texts about Esau and grace, represents the turning from grace to glory; an "absolute change" wherein the soul effects a real victory over its sinful elements. Implicit here is the soul's identity with the triumph of Christ over sin and death, and thus this episode is followed by a vision (several pages later) of the risen Christ: "But one day, as I was passing in the field. . . I saw with the eyes of my Soul Jesus Christ at Gods right hand, there, I say, as my Righteousness . . ." (*GA*, 72).

In the language of Calvinist dogma, the progress between the two conversion episodes is represented dogmatically as that between election and sanctification (or glorification), and it is imaged forth in the transition between the early allusion to the crucified Christ and the later vision of Christ risen. The life of Christ here figures as a formative model in determining the shape of individual conversion. And this is in accord with the archetypal model of *lysis* conversion, where "education" or modeling oneself after a divine ideal replaces birth as the central redemptive metaphor, and the *logos* is split into those two antinomies of "the Word of Law and Wrath" and "the Word of Life and Grace" (*GA*, 67).[36] The two postures of Christ exemplify the two contrasting attitudes of the autobiographical persona. The crucified Christ represents the youthful hero at the beginning of his soteriological journey, burdened by guilt both acknowledged and unacknowledged; the exalted Christ represents the mature Bunyan's deliverance from guilt—a certitude that affirms the self only by looking beyond it. The conversion of the soul in *Grace Abounding* is always a paradoxical one because from God's vantage point of predestined election the soul has already arrived, but from the individual's vantage point of faith and humility he is always still traveling, his gaze fixed on "yonder shining light."

I have been discussing the seventeenth-century *lysis* model as one that consists of two conversion experiences. But William James suggests that all conversion is inherently dyadic: "In the mind of the candidate for conversion," he writes, there are two motions: "first, the present incompleteness or wrongness, the 'sin' which he is eager to escape from; and, second, the positive ideal which he longs to compass." In a footnote several pages later, he observes that these two phases only seem to be different experiences; they are in reality the same thing: "Self-surrender sees the change in terms of the old self; determination sees it in terms of the new."[37] Although James does not take this step, it seems to me that whether an individual conversion takes the shape of the *lysis* or the *crisis* model is related to the positioning of these two phases. In other words, in a *crisis* conversion, negative reality and positive ideal coalesce and occur at the same time. But in a *lysis* conversion, these two motions (the turning away from sin and the turning toward God) are not only separated, but the space between them is extended and prolonged. The allegorical equivalent to this "space" is the three days Christ spends in the harrowing of Hell (the time between crucifixion and resurrection). The psychological equivalent is the sense of anxiety and uncertainty where the individual is neither in one world nor in the other, but is suspended between the two realms of despair and elation, damnation and salvation. For Christ, the symbolic passage from "old man" to "new man" took three days, but for the ordinary human being it takes a lifetime. It is this created psychological space that is the unique contribution of the Reformation to the Christian theology of redemption.

The kind of spirituality characteristic of Bunyan and his contemporaries, one that is obsessed with guilt and sin, requires a model of conversion that is not only excessively punitive but also where there is a good measure of suspense and anxiety about redemption—in other words, a model where one can never be "too sure." *Lysis* conversion is especially appropriate for the sinner-and-saint of the seventeenth century because its iterative and dyadic structure serves to deny him the too-pleasurable release of a climactic conversion experience. The notorious Calvinist anxiety, where one can never know whether conversion has taken place at all, thus stems from the very nature of *lysis* conversion. This is because there is no single turning point, no certain event upon which to focus a certainty about salvation. The structural diffuseness of *lysis* conversion is evident in the attempts of Bunyan scholars to explain the autobiography by identifying some particular event as the focal point in Bunyan's conversion, and in the anxiety about salvation that permeates *Grace Abounding*. It is important that we recognize that this structural diffuseness is not a product of faulty craftsmanship but a literary counterpart to the theological anxiety underlying *lysis* conversion—where salvation is perceived not in birth imagery, as the simultaneous death of the "old man" and rebirth of the new, but in the language and metaphor of education, as a gradual process of error and relearning, or fall and recovery, or wrongdoing and punishment whereby the soul matures into a regenerate state.

Perhaps a final reason why *crisis* conversion exerts so compelling an influence on the religious imagination, despite the apparent fact that the gradual model is often more true experientially, is that a dramatic, fulminant conversion is more resonant to the archetype of death and rebirth. Like birth, and death too, the conventional triadic arc of *crisis* conversion has an innate and compelling dramatic shape—the tension-climax-resolution that underlies Western drama from Aristotle on. *Lysis* conversion lacks this strong and unifying pattern. Though it reflects real and poignant religious experience, doctrinal truth, and the same archetype of death and rebirth (though it is an extended death and rebirth), *lysis* conversion lacks the dramatic focus and structural stability of a single, climactic turning point—a deficiency that is manifested in Bunyan's experience of a near-tolerable degree of anxiety, ambiguity, and uncertainty, and in the corresponding structural diffuseness of the autobiography. Death and rebirth are opposed phases of a single, archetypal event. The *crisis* pattern preserves this unity; the bipolar *lysis* pattern splits it in two.

It would seem as though a conversion is more compelling when it is experienced or perceived as a single, dramatic event. The attractiveness of *crisis* conversion is very much a part of our twentieth-century religious ethos, but so too is the belief that life consists in a sequence of changes or transformations as one passes through the enabling portals of various life-crises from one stage to the next. The existence of both *crisis* and *lysis* models will become evident in Merton's autobiography, a narrative that bears the imprint of the Augustinian *crisis* conversion, but where the converted soul is experienced as dynamic and ever-changing, always impelled onward to reach a new stage of spiritual integration.

5

John Bunyan
God and Family

i. The problem: wrathful God and guilty soul

Unlike Augustine's God, whose remote ineffability must be approached through a progression of *senex* figures and a maternal ethos, Bunyan's God is almost too near—a closeness manifested most often in wrath and judgment. So Bunyan writes in his autobiography: "Now I should find my minde to flee from God, as from the face of a dreadful judge; yet this was my torment, I could not escape his hand" (*GA*, 52). Augustine flees from God too, but the metaphor of flight refers to evasion of destiny—in the same way that Aeneas evades his destiny by staying too long with Dido in Carthage. Bunyan, however, flees from the "face" of God, a face of anger and wrath that is mirrored, as we shall see, in the faces of the Elders of the City of Refuge who wait to judge him. Bunyan is fleeing not only from a reflection of his guilt, but also from a self-imposed ideal of himself, projected onto God, which he cannot live up to: "This, I say, would come in upon my mind, when I was fleeing from the face of God; for I did flee from his face, that is, my mind and spirit fled before him; by reason of his highness . . ." (*GA*, 52).[1]

The severe countenance that characterizes Bunyan's image of God reflects a stance of extreme severity toward the self. For Bunyan sees God as harshly punitive, afflicting his elect with remedial guilt and abasing humility. Calvin's somewhat masochistic formula is that "it is impossible but that a soul, impressed with a dread of the Divine Judgment, must inflict some punishment on itself."[2] Bunyan's guilt-feelings achieve just that: a fear of divine retribution which is alleviated by self-imposed punishment. If self-punishment seems a necessary part of this model of conversion, so too is failure. Built into the Calvinist scheme of repentance is the abysmal failure of any autonomous effort to improve oneself. Before true repentence can take place, the elect must be convinced of their total powerlessness to achieve anything good and of their total dependence on God. It is significant that Bunyan, allegorized as Christian, traverses the Valley of Humiliation with great difficulty.

The dyad of wrathful God and guilty soul is closely related to the seventeenth-century emphasis on God the redeemer. Whereas Augustine in his *Confessions* tends to emphasize the creative side of God, Bunyan focuses more on the redemptive aspects.[3] The archetype of the child, which plays so important a role in the story of Augustine's conversion, is congruent with this emphasis on the themes of birth and nurturance, and their expression in the archetypally maternal. The child archetype is also present in *Grace Abounding*, but in a radically different sense: Bunyan is the disobedient child who must be punished, over and over, by an angrily paternal God. Calvin's favorite figure for the relationship between the elected Christian and God is adoption. The theology of adoption is contingent upon Christ's imputed righteousness. Just as we are saved not through our own merits but through the response of faith to God's atoning sacrifice of his Son, so also we become the adopted sons of God by assuming Christ's imputed righteousness, by mystical identification with Christ and patterning our lives after his. In other words, Christ functions as an ego-ideal posited by a kind of divine superego: "as God the Father has reconciled us to himself in Christ, so he has exhibited to us in him a pattern, to which it is his will that we should be conformed."[4] But no human being is able to do this. Again, punishment is built into the very scheme of things because the conditions upon which God posits his love are ones that the ordinary human being is incapable of fulfilling. And furthermore, not only is the life of Christ intended as a pattern for us to follow, but God's treatment of his Son serves as a model for his treatment of us, his adopted children:

> Having begun with Christ his first begotten Son, he pursues this method towards all his children. For though Christ was above all others the beloved Son, in whom the Father was always well pleased,

yet we see how little indulgence and tenderness he experienced; so that it may be truly said, not only that he was perpetually burdened with a cross during his residence on earth, but that his whole life was nothing but a kind of perpetual cross. . . . Why, then, should we exempt ourselves from that condition, to which it behoved Christ our head to be subject; especially since his submission was on our account, that he might exhibit to us an example of patience in his own person?[5]

Not only are we to pattern our lives after the life of Christ, but also our conversions after his death: repentance is thus modeled on the atonement.

Augustine's religious sensibility, by attributing to God archetypally maternal qualities such as nurturance, by setting the deity in the feminine context of the maternal Heavenly Jerusalem, and by preserving the feminine *sapientia* of the Old Testament, achieves a balance between the archetypally paternal and the archetypally maternal. But Bunyan's divine pantheon is overwhelmingly masculine: for him the "divine family" consists of a God who projects his infanticidal impulses onto his Chosen People and then punishes them for crucifying his Son. In systematically deleting from Christianity the cult of the Virgin, and in erasing the softer and more nurturant qualities of God, Protestantism effects a major distortion of what had been the Christian idea of God for a millennium. In eradicating the archetypally maternal, Reformation Christianity emphasizes the *logos* mode of relating to God over the *eros* mode. Education, not ecstatic union, is now the substance of the religious life; knowledge, not peace, becomes the touchstone of God's saving grace. It is appropriate that Bunyan should exclaim, at the very end of his conversion narrative: "O now I know, I know!" (*GA*, 82).

A religious sensibility that is governed by the mode of *eros* usually focuses on the sins of the flesh; one characterized by the mode of *logos*, on the other hand, tends to focus on the sins of the spirit. For Augustine the sin of lust is the chief deterrent to his spiritual quest. But Bunyan scarcely mentions lust. In the entire conversion narrative of *Grace Abounding* there is only one passage referring to sexual temptation, and this occurs in reference to his brief interest in the antinomian sect of the Ranters (*GA*, 16). For Bunyan it is not lust (a sin of the flesh) but despair, and the guilt that occasions despair (both sins of the spirit), that are the most formidable problems. "O the unthought of imaginations, frights, fears, and terrors" writes Bunyan, "that are affected by a thorow application of guilt, yielding to desparation!" (*GA*, 58). It is appropriate that Bunyan's equivalent to Augustine's and Aeneas's Carthage is Doubting Castle, where, as Christian, he is imprisoned by the Giant Despair.

In the *Confessions* Augustine feels contrition for things he has *done* (or left undone); Bunyan, however, feels guilt for something he has *thought*. Again, the first focuses more on sins of the flesh and the second on sins of the spirit. Bunyan's obsession with blasphemy is understandable in this context of intense guilt, for it is symptomatic of fiercely ambivalent attitudes about God. We remember that Bunyan's very worst temptation was to assent to the blasphemous thought, "Sell Christ for this, or sell him for that; sell him, sell him" (*GA*, 42). Calvin points out that while Augustine calls temptation a sin only when it is consented to or acted upon, "we, on the contrary, deem it to be sin, whenever a man feels any evil desires contrary to the Divine law; and we also assert the depravity itself to be sin, which produces these desires in our minds."[6] By moving the boundaries of responsibility (or moral reality) back into the self so that sin accrues not just to a wrong action but also to a wrong thought, repression of the sinful thought becomes likely, as well as feelings of guilt when the repression weakens. And the constructs of psychoanalysis and of Reformation demonology are here congruent, since the wrong thought can be banished from consciousness either by repression or by projection onto the figure of Satan.

It is a convention of twentieth-century thought, informed by the psychoanalytic therapies, to consider the guilt-feelings of the ordinary person as negative emotions, ones that contribute to neurosis, cause suffering, and are generally destructive of interpersonal relationships. But in the seventeenth century guilt was appreciated as a symptom that could alert the experiencer to some underlying spiritual sickness. Feelings of guilt were like fingerprints left by a burgler, or the early signs of an illness. The objective, then, was not simply to erase the guilt, but to use it as a clue or diagnostic sign of internal disorder. It is within this context that Bunyan excoriates those theological panaceas of his time that aimed at nothing more than removing guilt, as treating the symptom and not the disease: ". . . I had seen some who . . . seeking rather present Ease from their trouble, then Pardon for their Sin, cared not how they lost their guilt, so they got it out of their minds . . ." (*GA*, 28). The only effective cure, Bunyan asserts, is to use the "Wounds of Conscience" (i.e., guilt) to discover and root out the sin itself. He offers his own experience as a model for an effective religious therapy: "[God] did quite not only deliver me from the guilt that by these things was laid upon my Conscience, but also from the very filth thereof, for the temptation was removed, and I was put into my right mind again . . ." (*GA*, 36).

The true healer of the soul is aware that "unless guilt of conscience was taken off the right way, that is by the Blood of Christ, a man grew rather worse for the loss of his trouble of minde, than better" (*GA*, 28). Moreover, "guilt of conscience" is a token of election. Bunyan writes, appreciatively, that "the guilt of sin did help me much, for still as that would come upon me, the blood of Christ did take it off again . . ." (*GA*, 39). The right way to "take off guilt" is not simply to remove it, but to exaggerate both the diseased state of soul that produced the guilt as well as the helplessness of the individual so afflicted, so that the sinner will turn in desperation to Christ, the physician of the soul, and thereby remove both sin and guilt in assuming Christ's imputed righteousness. Given a theology where guilt is valued in this way, God exercises his love in accord with the ethic of judgement and the principle of *logos*, "not in a way of comfort," as would a divine expression of love under the *eros* principle, "but in a way of exceeding dread and terrour" (*GA*, 76).

Augustine's Christianity of *eros* could be said to refer to a spiritual infancy in the life of mankind where the mother is the primary object in the catechumen's world, and Bunyan's Christianity of *logos* to a spiritual childhood where standards and rules are imposed as well as punishment for failure. Augustine's God may be in some sense as unapproachable as Bunyan's, but his is a God surrounded by the penumbra of the archetypally maternal, the Heavenly Jerusalem, a kind of love that simply forgives and welcomes back the errant soul. But the God of *Grace Abounding* is a deity with impossible standards, whose love must be gained by a faith constantly tried and proved. The response of Bunyan's God to that basic question of the religious life, which Christian poses at the very beginning of *The Pilgrim's Progress*—"What shall I do to be saved?"—is the response of silence. Such a silence has two meanings: the first is that there is nothing the individual can do to be saved because he is overwhelmingly guilty; the second is that there is nothing the individual can do to be saved because Christ has already done all.

ii. The pattern: absent mother and negative father

We have been observing the coincidence between Bunyan's and Calvin's idea of God: for both, the divine image is overwhelmingly masculine—an imbalance manifested in the soul by an exaggerated sense of guilt. But the God of *Grace Abounding* is as much a product of Bunyan's personal psychology as it is derivative of seventeenth-century theology. And the pattern of familial archetypes in *Grace Abounding*, like the portrait of God, is that of the negative father and the absent mother. Bunyan's conversion can be seen as a resolution of this problematic parental configuration.

Margaret Bottrall writes that "Bunyan would have echoed St. Augustine's dictum that life does not begin with father and mother but with God and sin."[7] Bunyan tells us very little about his natural parents: the determining forces in his life are truly "God and sin"—the divine and the demonic. He mentions his father in only three instances. The first is his low social rank, "my fathers house being of that rank that is meanest, and most despised of all the families in the Land" (*GA*, 5). The second is when Bunyan asks his father "whether we were of the Israelites or no" and his father answers in the negative (*GA*, 9). The question has both a literal and a symbolic meaning; Bunyan's father fails in perceiving only the literal sense of the question. The symbolic meaning is related to the problem of election. For the question as to whether Bunyan is himself an Israelite comes up when he reads the Old Testament: "finding in the Scriptures that [the Israelites] were once the peculiar People of God, thought I, if I were one of this race, my Soul must needs be happy" (*GA*, 9). The passage has overtones of the much-repeated scriptural passage about Esau and his lost inheritance, for Rebekah is told by God in Genesis 25:23 that "two nations are in thy womb, and two manner of people shall be separated from thy bowels." In Calvinist exegesis, this would refer to the two "nations" of the elect and the reprobate. The third instance is when Bunyan is reproved for swearing; "wherefore" he writes, "I wished with all my heart that I might be a little childe again, that my Father might learn me to speak without this wicked way of swearing . . ." (*GA*, 12). In all three instances, Bunyan's father is portrayed as failing him: in regard to social status, in religious understanding, and in moral standards.

Bunyan portrays his father in mildly negative terms; Augustine's portrayal of his father is unambiguously negative. The real difference is to be found in the corresponding portrayal of the mother. For whereas Augustine balances the negative father with the positive mother, Bunyan does not seem to recognize the maternal archetype at all—either positive or negative—as a significant force in his spiritual life. Thus it is not surprising that Bunyan never mentions his mother, although her death when he was fifteen years old must in some part have determined the subsequent development of so intense a religious sensibility. Though feminine characters in the autobiography are few, they do appear at critical moments to act as catalysts for spiritual change. It is striking that the dyadic pattern of the conversion process is repeated or mirrored in the dyadic ordering of two particular, and apparently random incidents. Thus there are two and only two encounters with women, both of which bear upon his conversion. The first is negative: Bunyan is rebuked for swearing and at least partially renounces it. The second is positive: he is led by the Bedford women into a "very great softness and tenderness of heart" whereby he begins his long process of reformation (*GA*, 15). These parallel incidents exemplify the way experience is ideologically ordered in conversion narratives.

In the initial episode, a woman whom Bunyan describes as "a very loose and ungodly Wretch" reproves him for swearing—a deeply felt reproof that puts him "to secret shame" (*GA*, 11–12). The episode is important, for it tells us much about Bunyan's psychology. The fact that the role of rebuke and correction is played by a woman is significant, for it adds a negative dimension to the nearly absent feminine archetype. Moreover Bunyan's shame and guilt are so great that he is able to give up a lifelong habit: "thought I, I am so accustomed to [swearing], that it is but in vain for me to think of a reformation. . . . But how it came to pass I know not, I did from this time forward so leave my swearing, that it was a great wonder to my self to observe it . . .(*GA*, 12). This can be interpreted as signifying a total repression of an impulse that then incubates in the recesses of the unconscious mind and surfaces much later in dimensions that border on the psychotic. Thus the "wicked way of swearing" of his youth, which he so easily renounced, may have seeded the blasphemous seizures of his maturity, as when "a very great storm came down upon me . . . first all my comfort was taken from me, then darkness seized upon me; after which whole flouds of Blasphemies, both against God, Christ, and the Scriptures, was poured upon my spirit, to my great confusion and astonishment" (*GA*, 31).

But to give up bad habits is not enough, as Bunyan realizes when he encounters several poor women from the Bedford congregation who introduce him to what he now sees as the real meaning of reformation—rebirth. It is a seminal event in Bunyan's life, and its significance for his conversion is made apparent in a vision:

> About this time, the state and happiness of these poor people at Bedford was thus, in a kind of Vision, presented to me: I saw as if they

were set on the Sunny side of some high Mountain, there refreshing themselves with the pleasant beams of the Sun, while I was shivering and shrinking in the cold, afflicted with frost, snow, and dark clouds; methought also betwixt me and them I saw a wall that did encompass about this Mountain; now, thorow this wall my Soul did greatly desire to pass, concluding that if I could, I would goe even into the very midst of them, and there also comfort myself with the heat of their Sun. (*GA*, 19)

It is a vision rich in symbolism, both religious and psychological. The "Sunny side of the Mountain" (recalling the manifest incident when Bunyan meets the Bedford women "sitting at a door in the sun") is the "new world" of regeneration to which they introduce him. Searching for a way to join them in his vision, Bunyan finally comes across "a narrow gap, like a little door-way in the wall, thorow which I attempted to pass" (again recalling the "door in the sun" where he encounters the women). Bunyan describes how he gets through the doorway in the language and imagery of birth:

the passage being very straight, and narrow, I made many offers to get in, but all in vain, even until I was well nigh quite beat out by striving to get in: at last, with great striving, me thought I at first did get in my head, and after that, by a sideling striving, my shoulders, and my whole body. (*GA*, 19–20)

But what strikes us here is not so much the analogy between conversion and birth as the extreme awkwardness of this rebirth. Perhaps this emphasis reflects limitations of the Bedford Church, within whose credal structure Bunyan experienced his conversion. This is the view of Esther Harding, a Jungian critic of *The Pilgrim's Progress*, who observes that "his depression, even despair, witness to the violence he was doing to his own nature by trying to force it into so narrow a creed."[8] Augustine's moment of conversion is facilitated by Continence, who beckons to him in a spirit of chaste joyousness. But the Bedford women are simply "there," on the other side of the Mountain; and as such, they represent more the goal of his spiritual endeavors than his helpers along the way.

The mountain in the vision, a symbol of the Bedford Church, looks forward to Bunyan's allusion at the very end of the conversion section to "Mt. Zion . . . the City of the living God . . . the heavenly Jerusalem" (*GA*, 82). The symbols of city and church both represent the archetypal feminine: they come together in the Heavenly City, which is both city and church. The relation between the mountain in Bunyan's vision and the Mt. Zion of his later allusion is the same as the relation between the church militant and the church triumphant. Thus Bunyan's rebirth, like Augustine's, is into the maternal body of the Church. The archetype of the two cities would at first seem to function in more or less the same way for Augustine as for Bunyan: Augustine's Earthly City is Bunyan's City of Destruction, and Augustine's Heavenly City is Bunyan's "City of Refuge" in *Grace Abounding* and "Celestial City" in *The Pilgrim's Progress*. But there is a significant psychological difference between Augustine's and Bunyan's rendition of the two cities. For Bunyan's religious vision is more Christological; he replaces a vision of the apotheosized mother with a vision of the exalted Christ, as befits a religiosity dominated by the archetypally paternal. Thus for Bunyan, the church triumphant is the "whole Body of God's Elect," identified through mystical union with Christ: "Now I saw Christ Jesus was looked on of God, and should also be looked on by us as that common or publick person in whom all the whole Body of his Elect are always to be considered and reckoned . . ." (*GA*, 73). Another difference is that Bunyan always tends to substitute the father for the mother. Very near the end of *Grace Abounding,* Bunyan envisions a fearful comfort where the Apostles "did look with scorn upon me, and hold me in derision," reminding him of the truth of redemption as set down unequivocally in Scripture: "These, as the Elders of the City of Refuge, I saw were to be the Judges both of my Case and me, while I stood with the avenger of blood at my heels, trembling at their Gate for deliverance; also with a thousand fears and mistrusts, that they would shut me out for ever" (*GA*, 66). It is a fearful image: the language of love and transport in Augustine's description of the heavenly Jerusalem is transmuted in *Grace Abounding* into the language of fear and terror.

Thus for Bunyan the Celestial City is personified as the apotheosized *animus*—the positive aspect of which is Christ, and the negative, the Apostolic Elders of the City of Refuge. But in Bunyan's imagination, positive and negative exist side by side. In *Grace Abounding* it is sometimes hard to discriminate between the divine and the diabolical—the Elders of the City of Refuge glowering down at Bunyan are hardly recognizable as citizens of the City of God. Similarly, in *The Pilgrim's Progress* the mouth of Hell is placed right next to Heaven's gate. Two pilgrims arrive together, and one is welcomed into paradise while the other is cast into perdition. But there is a consolation to even so dark a vision as Bunyan's. For religions of *logos* offer a tough-minded kind of

John Bunyan: God and Family

truth—not the sublime truth of Platonism, but truth in the sense of fidelity to life as it is experienced. While we (and Bunyan, too) might wish for a greater psychological distance between positive and negative, or good and evil, or salvation and damnation, nonetheless a religious vision that preserves, however precariously, the experiential ambiguity between these pairs of opposites is one that is true to the normal uncertainties and psychological ambivalences that characterize everyday life.

iii. Resolution: the preacher

We have observed that in the *logos* mode, union with God is achieved by identification with Christ. It is in Bunyan's final identification with John Gifford, when he himself becomes a preacher, and by his self-characterization as both mother and father to his congregation, that he is able to transcend personal limitations fixed by problematic familial patterns and reinforced by the severely "masculine" religious ethos of seventeenth-century Protestantism. But before he can arrive at this resolution, Bunyan makes a pilgrimage through the various religious options of his time (as did Augustine before him). It is not surprising that each of these stages in the spiritual journey should be represented by a male figure. The feminine archetype, representing situations of internal change, tends to dominate during events of crucial moral or spiritual transition; the masculine, representing external religious options, takes precedence during episodes when Bunyan confronts religious belief-systems with some organization and structure.

The first of these stages is the Anglicanism of his childhood. He tells us he adored the ecclesiastical ritual of the Church and was in particular enamored of the priest:

> had I but seen a Priest, (though never so sordid and debauched in his life) I should find my spirit fall under him, reverence him, and knit unto him; yea, I thought for the love I did bear unto them . . . I could have layn down at their feet, and have been trampled upon by them; their Name, their Garb and Work, did so intoxicate and bewitch me. (GA, 9)

The second stage is marked by Bunyan's acquaintance "with one poor man that made profession of Religion" (GA, 12). Through the influence of this man he begins to read the Bible, particularly the New Testament. But when this religious intimate "turned a most devilish Ranter," Bunyan terminates the relationship (*GA*, 16). At about the same time, Bunyan breaks off a friendship with a young man "to whom my heart was knit more than to any other," because he cursed and swore (*GA*, 16). It is a symbolic act, signifying his putting off the "old man"; it is surely not accidental that a propensity to foul language should characterize both this young friend and also the particular vice that Bunyan is able to renounce.

Bunyan is now ready for the third stage in his spiritual quest—the "true path" that will lead him to his spiritual home. This stage is initiated when he comes under the spiritual tutelage of Gifford, the pastor of the Bedford Church. His encounter with Gifford ushers in the Calvinist stage of true humiliation: "from that time," Bunyan writes, "[I] began to see something of the vanity and inward wretchedness of my wicked heart . . ." (*GA*, 25). The relationship between Bunyan and Gifford becomes that of master and disciple, as Bunyan is "led from truth to truth . . . even from the birth and cradle of the Son of God, to his ascension and second coming from Heaven to judge the World" (*GA*, 37). The parallel in *The Pilgrim's Progress* to Bunyan's encounter with Gifford is Christian's confrontation with Evangelist, who points out the right direction and thus literally initiates his spiritual pilgrimage. Symbolically, both Gifford and Evangelist represent the "inner guide," the archetypal *senex* who appears when the hero is caught in a dilemma of indecision and indirection as an endopsychic personification of the right choice.[9] Of this archetypal function, Joseph Campbell remarks that "the higher mythologies develop the role [of supernatural helper] in the great figure of the guide, the teacher, the ferryman, the conductor of souls to the afterworld."[10] In guiding Bunyan through the dangers and intricacies of the Baptist-Calvinist pilgrimage, Gifford is to Bunyan as Evangelist or Great-heart to Christiana: the inner guide made incarnate in the role of preacher, the ordained psychopomp who guides the initiate into understanding of Scripture "from the Cradle to the Cross." These teachings are the magical amulets, the enchanted keys, which in *The Pilgrim's Progress* enable Christian to escape from the dungeon of Despair, and which in *Grace Abounding* enable Bunyan to decipher the cause and purpose of his many temptations, and his failure to resist them.

Bunyan receives from Gifford what Augustine is denied by Ambrose and Simplicianus. It is Gifford who mediates between Bunyan and the angry, threatening God-image of the beginning of the autobiography. If the figure of Great-heart represents the mature Bunyan—Bunyan the preacher—it is also a representation of John Gifford. For Bunyan grows up under the spiritual tutelage of Gifford to take his place as pastor of the Bedford Church: in the allegory, Bunyan and Gifford coalesce into the figure of Great-heart. Thus the real equivalent to Gifford in the *Confessions* is not Ambrose or Simplicianus but Monica. The paternal aspects of the preacher role, which Bunyan learns from Gifford and later inherits, are made obvious in Bunyan's account of his ministry: "If any of those who were awakened by my Ministry did after that fall back (as sometimes too many did) I can truly say their loss hath been more to me, then if one of my own Children, begotten of my body, had been going to its grave; . . I have counted as if I had goodly buildings and lordships in those places where my Children were born . . ." (*GA*, 88). And indeed, Bunyan perceives his congregation as his children, beginning his autobiography by so addressing them: "Children, Grace be with you . . . that you may see my Soul hath fatherly care . . ." (*GA*, 1). Moreover, the preacher figure not only conforms to the paternal archetype but extends itself to subsume the maternal archetype as well. So Bunyan writes, "In my preaching I have really been in pain, and have as it were traveled to bring forth Children to God . . ." (*GA*, 89). The analogy is explicit: those whom Bunyan has "awakened" by his ministry are like children to whom he has given birth, having been inseminated with "the Gift" of apostleship by God (*GA*, 82–83). Thus the highly masculine spiritual world of Bunyan's psychological gestalt is modified in such a way as to move the preacher figure toward androgyny. Furthermore the androgynous preacher is here an image of the deity, for the divine parent must contain within its oneness both maternal and paternal archetypes.

In *The Pilgrim's Progress,* the seventeenth-century preacher/saint is represented in the emblematic portrait which Christian first sees in the House of the Interpreter: "It had eyes lift up to Heaven, the best of Books in its hand, the Law of Truth was written upon its lips, the World was behind its back; it stood as if it pleaded with Men, and a Crown of Gold did hang over its head."[11] The picture is curiously reminiscent of the emblematic description of Christian at the very beginning of *The Pilgrim's Progress:* both carry a book, Christian has "his face from his own House" and the portrait-person has "the World . . . behind its back," and the "great burden" weighing Christian down has been replaced with "a Crown of Gold" in the Interpreter's portrait. Furthermore, the Interpreter glosses the portrait in terms that unambiguously link preacher with both maternal and paternal archetypes: "The Man whose Picture this is, is one of a thousand, he can beget Children, Travel in Birth with Children, and Nurse them himself when they are born."[12] The androgynous evangelist in the portrait is the archetype of the "inner guide"—he is "the Preacher" as Evangelist, Great-heart, John Gifford, or John Bunyan himself, pastor of the Bedford Church. The analogous figure to the androgynous preacher in Augustine's *Confessions* is, of course, the child, "*quasi pueri an puellae*," who appears at the critical point in his conversion and directs him toward the Pauline Scriptures. Androgynous portrait, parental evangelist, and child—all these symbolic figures represent the unification of the self that is experienced in a conversion.

Gifford is a pivotal figure for Bunyan. He tempers the wrathful, punitive God of Bunyan's religious experience in that he functions both as father-figure and as an accessible ego-ideal that Bunyan can and does model himself after. As the "Law" of God is tempered by the "Mercy" of Christ, and the Old Testament covenant of works replaced by the New Testament covenant of grace, so does that awful panoply of hostile Apostolic Elders finally give way to "an innumerable company of Angels" (*GA*, 82). Similarly, when the haunting spirits of Esau and Moses and Elias depart, "and leave Christ and his Saints" to remain, the face of the wrathful Calvinist God recedes behind the figure of Jesus.

6

Thomas Merton
A Modern Paradigm

Merton wrote *The Seven Storey Mountain* when he was thirty-three years old—seven years after he entered a monastery and ten years after his baptism in the Roman Catholic faith. The autobiography is most commonly seen now as an early work of an author with talent, charisma, and great potential, but with very real religious and personal limitations. In recent years Merton's stature as a religious writer and social critic has risen sharply—a revaluation based on what critics often see as the "late Merton." The difference between "early" and "late Merton," for most of these scholars, is the change in social consciousness. As John Teahan observes, "no aspect of Merton's thought has been more discussed in the secondary accounts than his attitudes towards the world."[1] This change comes in the late 1950s, about a decade after the publication of *The Seven Storey Mountain,* when Merton's publications took on a concern with sociopolitical matters. Some see Merton's change of interest from the spiritual to the sociopolitical as a radical break with the past, others as a "gradual unfolding" of concerns already implicit in earlier works.[2]

As recognition of the "late Merton" increases, appreciation of Merton's early autobiography—at least among some critics—diminishes. And Merton himself repeatedly expressed dissatisfaction with his autobiography—both in its contemptuous anti-worldliness and romantic notions of monastic life and in the authorial persona that he would subsequently have to live with. Later on in his life Merton would look back on the author of *The*

Seven Storey Mountain as "a sort of stereotype of the world-denying contemplative."[3] In the light of his own dissatisfaction with the book, as well as the criticisms that the book seemed to invite among those in religious orders,[4] one might wonder why Merton never chose to revise the book in its later editions. Perhaps he is here far wiser and more charitable toward himself than are his critics, for he shows humility and tolerance in allowing the work to stand as it is. Merton, I think, would have seen that there was a real continuity between the autobiography of his youth and the works of his mature years, a continuity of both positive and negative aspects in his personality and life. In this way *The Seven Storey Mountain* becomes for him a kind of *confessio* in the Augustinian sense—both "accusation of oneself" and "praise of God."[5]

Perhaps the distinction between an "early" and a "late" Merton is itself too simplistic. My own stance toward Merton stresses the unity of his life and thought. For although it is true that Merton's writings in the 1940s and early 1950s are concerned principally with the interior life or the monastic setting and his writings in the late 1950s and early 1960s with racism, poverty, and war, nonetheless it is also true that Merton's writings in the 1960s, just before his death, reverted to a concern with the contemplative. Furthermore, a sophisticated reader of Merton can find all these concerns present throughout his writings, in one form or another. Our willingness to divide Merton's body of writings into an early phase of unworldly introversion and a later phase of social concern (the two are generally related as negative and positive) may indicate more about the values of our own age than it does about Merton. Not only is it characteristic of our time to value work or writing or thinking that shows an immediate relevance and active involvement in social and political problems, but we often tend to interpret an individual's life in terms of a narrow and naive developmentalism. Merton is such a fascinating modern religious figure because, though both his life and his writings do lend themselves to this kind of thinking, yet they also resist being contained by it: in a sense, his "life-pattern" always seems to exist beyond those interpretations which seek to organize, explain, and ultimately limit it.[6]

The Seven Storey Mountain is severely flawed in many ways. The book appeals to us not only because it is the youthful work of an individual who was to become a major presence in twentieth-century religious thought, but also because it testifies to the difficulty shared by so many in sustaining a religious vision in the modern world. A number of explanations have been offered for the popularity of this book: my own view is that its popularity is in some way bound up with its flaws. The life of the "super-Catholic-Romantic-Monk" (it is Merton's own self-characterization) appeals to us not because it represents a "model" for us to follow, but because it functions as a kind of mirror, showing us our deep religious hunger as well as our inability to satisfy that hunger within organized religion and in a manner consistent with the moral imperatives of our culture.

i. *Epektesis* and traditionalism: the spiraling quest

As a twentieth-century spiritual autobiography, *The Seven Storey Mountain* is at the same time contemporary and anachronistic, of our own time and not of it. Augustine's pilgrimage took place in an age where the search for a transcendent truth was communally sanctioned; where Neoplatonism, Manichaeism, and Christianity could be seen as variant forms of a pervasive philosophic or religious idealism. Bunyan was born into a world that was obsessively religious; the form his conversion takes is one that was fully sanctioned by the Calvinism he espouses. Merton, however, is born into a world that he considers radically irreligious, where he can only intuit what is missing by the forcefulness of his hunger. Merton's sacramentalism is the solution to this problem, and at the same time symptomatic of a deeper malaise. For his emphasis on a life of sacramental mysticism only exacerbates the problem of rendering the modern secular world spiritually significant. The "heroic" task of the modern pilgrim is not only to recover what is sensed as a lost personal relationship with the divine, but also to restore to a world that has lost all faith the sense of joy and purpose and meaning that are the products of belief. For Merton, the modern world is characterized by violence, selfishness, and an overriding, stifling secularism. It is a world where the vision of the divine and the numinous can be glimpsed only in the debased reflections of artistic or aesthetic vision—a world where Merton, characterizing himself as a sort of "modern Everyman," lives in perpetual desire for what has been lost: "That world was the picture of Hell, full of men like myself, loving God and yet hating Him; born to love Him, living instead in fear and hopeless self-contradictory hungers" (*SSM*, 3).[7] Merton cannot redeem the time: it seems he can only withdraw from it into another and holier age.

Merton's withdrawal from twentieth-century society into the monastery is one instance of the attempt to be "in the world and not of it"; his autobiography is another, written just seven years after he entered Gethsemani. In part 1, the story of his childhood and youth, Merton documents a pattern of restless movement, literal and psychological, in the nomadic life with his father after his mother dies and in his desperate attempts to find something to believe in after his father dies. Part 2 is the story of his college years at Columbia, and his conversion to Roman Catholicism at the age of twenty-three. Part 3 begins anticlimactically, when Merton's plan to be a Franciscan monk ends with his rejection from the Order. His future now turns on a choice between the vocations of Catholic social worker and Trappist monk. He decides finally on the monastic calling and enters Gethsemani when he is twenty-six years old.

But the resulting impression of a life that has attained its final pattern and form is misleading. For as a monk Merton was divided among his writing—a vocation his superiors variously assigned and encouraged or discouraged and censored—his intense desire to lead a more eremitic life, and his active involvement in pacifist and racial causes. About the same time that he was ordained priest he renewed his interest in Eastern mysticism, an interest that was to increase steadily in the years to come. There is much debate as to how satisfied Merton felt with conditions in the monastery. The fact that in 1955 he formally requested a transfer to the Carthusians (the petition was denied) is certainly indication of some degree of spiritual restlessness.[8] It was only in 1963, after a long delay, that Merton was permitted his own hermitage at Gethsemani. Three years later he undertook a pilgrimage to Buddhist centers in India and Tibet. While in Bangkok he was accidentally electrocuted by an electric fan in his hotel room. Merton died on December 10, 1968; it was the same day he had entered the monastery twenty-seven years before.

The curious synchroneity of Merton's spiritual and physical deaths is an appropriate testament to his sacramentalism. We sense that he would have approved. For the pattern of Merton's life is shaped both by the intuited goals of a spiritual quest and by a series of events, particularly journeys, that tend to repeat themselves. What Merton tries to do is to transform the cycle of repeated patterns in which we all participate into a movement that is both upward and onward: in going back he must believe that he goes forward. The paradigm for this paradoxical motion he finds in the second part of the *Divine Comedy*, in the seven-story mountain that gives his autobiography not only its title but its allegorical form. The motion is a spiral, the winding stair that becomes the model of spiritual progression for the regenerate hero of Merton's autobiography. And indeed, the Dantean spiral of the *Divine Comedy* is the enabling myth of Merton's autobiographical life.

At a first glance *The Seven Storey Mountain* can be seen as resonating nicely with the tripartite structure of the *Divine Comedy:* part 1, the preconversion history of the "natural man," is the equivalent to Dante's "Inferno"; part 2, the conversion, to Dante's "Purgatorio"; and part 3, the postconversion material, to Dante's "Paradiso."[9] The *Divine Comedy* seems a structural metaphor for the autobiographical life; its eschatological dimensions are contained in the autobiography as larger perspectives that define as they judge the individual life. However, to outline so neat a structural parallelism between the two works is simply untrue to the life-pattern that makes up Merton's story—a pattern of movement where randomness is always the interface of purposiveness, where the high, transcendent deity tends to disappear into clouds of inscrutability, and where the vision in the dark glass of the religious imagination always threatens to resolve itself into merely an ordinary picture of the ordinary self.

The Seven Storey Mountain more readily lends itself to a comparison with the *Confessions* than to the *Divine Comedy*. And indeed, Merton has been hailed as a modern St. Augustine.[10] The similarities between the two are striking: both organize their autobiographical narratives around the picaresque story of the prodigal youth whose life is dramatically changed by conversion; both represent the *peregrinatio* of the soul by means of literal journeys and the various stages of their quest by specific geographical places; both authors portray themselves as characterologically disposed toward conversion, in that the final conversion to Catholic Christianity is preceded by a series of minor conversions to philosophical or religious or political belief; both infer a parallel between their own lives and that of a specific mythic or historical figure—Aeneas for Augustine, and Dante for Merton.

But the very different conclusions of the two narratives indicate an important difference between them. Augustine concludes with a joyous affirmation of the soul at rest in God's eternal peace: "Let it be asked of thee, sought in thee, knocked at in thee; so it will be received, so discovered, and so it will be opened." (13.38) The very last words of *The Seven Storey Mountain* tell us much about Merton's spiritual quest: *"Sit finis libri, non finis quaerendi"* (let this be the end of the book, not of the searching). Augustine ends his *Confessions* emphasizing the repose and quiet in which the spiritual search culminates; Merton, on the other hand, emphasizes the search itself. The *Confessions* achieves a real sense of closure—the closure of assurance and consolation. But *The Seven Storey Mountain* is open-ended: its conclusion betrays the author's awareness that his quest is just beginning.

The attitude that the spiritual life is one of continual conversion and ongoing change is characteristic of Merton at all stages of his writing. It achieves formal expression in the notion of *epektesis*, which Merton appropriated from Gregory of Nyssa. John Bamberger summarizes the idea beautifully:

> The idea of *epektesis* is that the perfect spiritual man is not the one who has "arrived" at a high degree of moral perfection and contemplative knowledge of God. Rather, he is the man who, having attained a high measure presses on in pursuit of still purer, more vital experience of God's light and truth. The perfect man is the man who is ever moving forward, deeper into the mystery of God. Heaven itself, in this view, consists in an eternal progress into the love and light and life of God, where each fulfillment contains in itself the impulse to further exploration.[11]

As I shall show, Merton's modern paradigm of conversion is constructed in accord with this principle of *epektesis*.

Merton's conscious allusion to the journey motif throughout his writings has been skillfully commented on by Elena Malits in her recent book *The Solitary Explorer*. The idea of the "journey into the unknown," she observes, was Merton's "favorite metaphor" for the Christian life, and especially the monastic vocation.[12] Just as the archetype of quest served as an expression of the Augustinian *peregrinatio*, and the theme of *psychomachia* embodied Bunyan's polarized religious vision of good and evil, so here the symbol of the spiral can be used to represent Merton's idea of *epektesis*. It is an ancient image—one thinks of St. Bonaventure, and, of course, Dante.[13] In addition to the conscious allusion to the spiraling journey of the *Divine Comedy*, the symbol of the spiral modifies the linear motif of the Augustinian quest in two important ways: first, in its suggestion of a dialectical movement from one idea to its opposite to a higher unity, and second, in an implicit epigenesis, where the spiritual traveler progresses through encountering the same situation over and over, though at a higher level each time. Both these latter ideas should be familiar to the reader from the last two chapters: the tension between opposites and the principle of repetition are central motifs in Bunyan's archetype of *psychomachia*. Thus the symbol of the spiral can be seen as itself a variant on the quest archetype—modified so as to include the principles of antagonism (resolved by a dialectical structure) and of repetition. Used as it is in *The Seven Storey Mountain*, the ancient image of the spiral becomes a strikingly modern metaphor of the Christian life.

Merton's autobiography succeeds so well because it is at the same time faithful to ancient themes and images of the Christian life and distinctively modern. The idea of *epektesis* is itself an instance. For though it may be rooted in the writings of an early Church Father, it also resonates nicely with the assumptions of developmental psychologists in the tradition of Erik Erikson. Moreover, *The Seven Storey Mountain* makes several important contributions to the genre of spiritual autobiography. In a genre that traditionally concerns itself with the soul, Merton introduces the theme of the self: "More than any other contemporary religious personality and writer" observes Elena Malits, "Merton has taught us to appreciate the theological significance of the quest for self-identity. He reintroduced and legitimized the use of 'I' in religious inquiry. . . ."[14] Second, Merton delighted in paradox—a frame of mind or perspective that he may well have added to the pantheon of Christian virtues. Paradox was to become Merton's way of reconciling his ambivalences about the monastic life and about himself. It is in the autobiography that we see the beginnings of this—in his egocentric obsession with the "non-self," in his anagogical vision of religious rebirth, in his curious equation of freedom and love. And third, there is Merton's wry sense of humor. Not only is this a distinctively modern element in spiritual autobiography—nowhere in Augustine or in Bunyan does one find the distanced and balanced sense of self, mission, and belief that occurs increasingly throughout Merton's writings—but it is a distinctively modern trait that seems to be unambiguously positive.

What strikes the reader most about *The Seven Storey Mountain* on coming to it from the autobiographies of Augustine and Bunyan is the sheer amount of detailed information that Merton presents about his life. In part the reason for this may be the influence of the novel in twentieth-century literature—a genre where attention to detail has been elevated to an art form and that often takes the form of a retrospective first-person narrative of the hero's life. Often, indeed, the modern novel is lightly concealed autobiography, as in Joyce's *Portrait of the Artist as a Young Man*. If the mythicizing tendency of spiritual autobiography makes it approximate the methods of fiction, fiction in our time frequently approximates autobiography. Merton wanted to become a writer; moreover, he made several attempts to produce a novel. In a sense *The Seven Storey Mountain* can be seen as the religious counterpart to the novel that Merton was never able to write. Furthermore, there is the tendency of spiritual autobiography to move into fictive dimensions. Perhaps, then, the modern spiritual autobiography manifests these latent fictive tendencies by merging autobiography and novel.

But there is another explanation for the mass of factual detail with which the reader is confronted in *The Seven Storey Mountain*. Augustine and Bunyan are able to select out of their lives facts that are significant and relevant for the protagonist's spiritual development. But Merton is unable to do this because, even in retrospect, the facts of his secular life (like the secular world itself) seem to have no central meaning. Augustine's imagination is close to the mythicizing imagination; thus the archetypal configurations of both Scripture and epic easily coalesce with the facts of his own life story. But for Merton sacred and secular exist side by side in separate realities; sacred events are defined as sacred because they occur in an overtly religious, even ecclesiastical context, and as a result there is no hallowing of the ordinary.

Merton is not the only modern author who senses the radical division between sacred and secular, who consequently sees the ordinary self and the secular world inhabited by that self as empty and devoid of meaning and attempts to fill that void with the mythos of long-dead cultures. *The Seven Storey Mountain* can be seen as closer to Eliot's *Wasteland* or *Ash Wednesday* than to Dante's *Divine Comedy* in its rendering of the "modern myth" as a broken image—one that does not reflect but refracts the medieval synthesis in its use of the fragments of the Dantean vision. Characteristic of both modern autobiography and modern poem is the habit not only of nostalgically alluding to an older cultural-literary model but also of dramatizing disintegration and disorder. And anti-meaning is itself a form of meaning. Thus there are two myths operative here: the first is that of "modernism," the myth that reality is absurd, or meaningless, or incoherent; and the second is the mythology that is opposed to this as a more attractive alternative. The latter we perceive as myth—Teiresias, Tristan and Isolde, Ulysses, Aeneas and Dido—but the former we do not. In his famous comments on "the mythical method" in Joyce's *Ulysses*, T. S. Eliot observes: "in manipulating a continuous parallel between contemporaneity and antiquity," Joyce has discovered "a way of controlling, of ordering, of giving a shape and a significance to the immense panorama of futility and anarchy which is contemporary history. . . ."[15] In a sense this is what Merton in his autobiography is doing with Dante—indeed, with all things medieval.

Is Merton, then, using Dante in *The Seven Storey Mountain* in the way that Augustine uses Aeneas in the *Confessions*? I think not. For Augustine's method, though it is certainly mythical, does not aim at setting up a parallel between his own life and that of Aeneas; nor does he see the unregenerate self and the larger society of which it is a part as "in opposition to" the mythic dimension. Instead, the autobiographical life of Augustine and the epic life of Aeneas participate in the same myth; implicitly, Augustine treats his own life as the Christian fulfillment of pagan epic. Like Eliot, Merton often appears to be trying to inject transfusions of myth into an etiolated experiential reality. In this he is very different from Augustine. For Augustine the natural world, like the unredeemed self, is sanctioned because it is God's creation. Augustine's problem with the earthly kingdom, like his difficulties with his mother, is not that it seems empty and meaningless but that it is all too able to draw his love—and exclusively so. But for Merton the secular world is defined in the very first paragraph as "the picture of Hell," and the secular man or unconverted self as the denizen of this Hell. If Augustine's problem is with an all-too-present mother, Merton's world is defined by the absence of a mother, and of all that the archetypally maternal stands for—passion, tenderness, attachment, relatedness.

Another difference is in the nature of the texts that they appropriate: the *Aeneid* is clearly a mythic text for Augustine, but the *Divine Comedy* is already defined, both for Merton and for Eliot, as sacred and not mythical. In other words, because the *Aeneid* is mythic, it is capable of conversion into a religious frame of reference; the *Divine Comedy* is not, because it itself constitutes a religious vision. The word for what Merton is doing—and Eliot too—is *allusion*. Merton alludes to the *Divine Comedy* throughout his autobiographical narrative—in title, structure, and content—but he does not and cannot recreate Dante's great vision or modify it to accord with his own needs as Augustine did with Vergil's. The two worlds of *The Seven Storey Mountain* and the *Divine Comedy* exist side by side in parallel formation; they are separate realms for Merton the writer even as the secular and the spiritual existed as separate realities for Merton the autobiographical persona.

When Augustine moves from the pagan city of Carthage to the Christian city of Milan, the geographical symbols of travel become literally valid representations of the inner journey of the soul; there is an intrinsic consonance between inner and outer realities. But the theme of outer travels and inner pilgrimage, though present in *The Seven Storey Mountain*, does not have the same progressive symmetry as it does in the *Confessions*. Though there is a good deal of movement from place to place in Merton's autobiography, the spiritual journey is represented not so much in his travels as in his repeated tendency to seek out old abandoned chapels and ruined monasteries. And furthermore, in Merton's imagination the Heavenly City does not even really exist alongside the Earthly City—the two seem to belong to radically different times, the one modern and the other ancient, the one thoroughly secular and the other exclusively spiritual. Thus what is represented spatially in Augustine's autobiography is represented temporally in Merton's. For Merton the Heavenly City—the spiritual vision—is something that has been lost; it survives as a pale copy in artistic sensibility and in the architectural vestiges of its own ruins. Merton's pilgrimage to the Heavenly City can thus be seen as a pilgrimage backward through time. And his early wanderings through old abbeys and churches is proleptic of his ritual death to the secular world and rebirth to the world of thirteenth-century monasticism.

Merton's conversion does not effect a reconciliation of the principles of spirit and nature, the mythic and the real, but the creation of another world—an alternative where one can be "in the world but not of it." Myth and fact exist in an interrelationship for Dante, as for Augustine; but for Merton the factual world consists of a multiplicity of accidents without essences—a world that has been emptied of mythic reality. Hence the theatricality of the form that conversion takes for Merton: he requires a new name, new clothing—a thirteenth-century religious life in the twentieth century. And such radical nostalgia is always problematic.

Despite Merton's enthusiasm for the Middle Ages, writes Aelred Graham, "he is no medievalist in love with the past. He is a modern man—with a difference: a modern man in reverse." From one possible viewpoint, Merton's medievalism can be seen as a necessary though doomed evasion of his place in intellectual history; necessary because he is driven to seek outside his own era for values, and doomed because he cannot really put himself in another historical period. But Merton's spiritual quest can be seen as more than simply religious nostalgia. From another point of view Merton's medievalism can be perceived not in terms of moving from one relative (the twentieth century) to another (the thirteenth century), but through relatives to an absolute—past the "accidents" of time and place to the essence of the eternal and the permanent. But, it will be argued, in the modern world of multiplicities there is no fixed essence, no "Absolute." And therefore is this idea of a transcendent essence (or even an archetypal substratum) not really a form of intellectual betrayal, an illusory consolation? This is certainly a major problem in the modern spiritual situation: what the converted soul formulates as "ultimate reality" or even as its particular goal at any given moment often turns out to be illusion when it is reached, though it is an illusion that propels the searcher onward toward an even higher level of truth. The notion of *epektesis* embraces linear, developmental movement, but it locates this kind of change, which is by nature unending, within the context of an Absolute that does not change.

As his title indicates, Merton conceived of the journey of the soul through life as a spiraling movement. Although the only consistent pattern in the autobiography seems to be that of repetition, it is repetition on a higher level and with a deeper meaning. It is thus appropriate that there should be a striking parallelism between parts 1 and 3 of the autobiography, both in structure (each part has four subsections) and in the theme of travel.

Part 1 of the autobiography shows Merton as a child accompanying his father from France to America, from Provincetown to Bermuda, and back to England. As he and his father leave the French town of Montauban to search out a more ideal locale, Merton observes: "The afternoon we took the peculiar, antiquated train out of Montauban into the country, we felt something like the three Magi after leaving Herod and Jerusalem when they caught sight once again of their star" (*SSM*, 34). Merton's memory of these journeys is studded with churches, castles, monasteries, old chapels. One function of these architectural memories is to give a sense of fixedness to a childhood where traveling from one place to another seemed to be the rule, not the exception. So Merton writes about the medieval town of St. Antonin: "The church had been fitted into the landscape in such a way as to become the keystone of its intelligibility" (*SSM*, 37). The pattern of Merton's life, as he matures, shows the extent to which he has introjected the paternal model of artistic quest. Even after his conversion, when he substitutes a religious ideal for an artistic one, Merton journeys on through the vocations of Franciscan monk, Catholic of the Third Order, and finally, Trappist monk.

The journeys in part 3 are as diverse and as manifold as in part 1. Merton travels to Olean for a vacation with his friends, to Cuba as a sort of pilgrimage, to St. Bonaventure's to teach, to Gethsemani for a visit, to Harlem to serve the poor, and back to Gethsemani in the end. The difference between the two sections of the autobiography is in the nature of the journeys: part 1 shows us *peregrinatio* as aimless wandering; part 3 shows us *peregrinatio* as purposeful seeking. In addition, the fact that Merton, in part 3, no longer needs to search out ancient chapels in the midst of the secular world underscores the difference. If he has found real, functional chapels, he also feels that he has discovered the spiritual city, the spiritual locus, within himself.

Part of the problem of the form of spiritual autobiography is its ending. Biography terminates with the death of the subject. Where, though, does an autobiography end? Especially a spiritual autobiography? How does the religious protagonist announce that "I am there" without arrogance? Augustine's goal is the Heavenly City—he evades the problem by opening his individual life out into the great pattern of creation. When Augustine undergoes his *crisis* conversion in the garden, the autobiography ends. There is nothing more to say about Augustine, the man: his secular identity is incorporated in the universals of eternal time and eternal space. Thus the last four books of the *Confessions* concern not the life of Augustine after his conversion, but the metaphysical history of the world. Merton's goal, too, is the City of God—which he locates in a liturgical past that is curiously present.[16] But there is no sense of conclusion, or finality, with Merton's conversion. The three parts of *The Seven Storey Mountain* demonstrate that spiritual autobiography, like the religious life, does not stop. There is no sense of arrival; only a sense of repetition. The restless movement of Merton's father as an artist is the secular version of what turns out to be the ultimate truth for Merton, that the religious quest is also unending. It is fitting that soon after he enters the monastery he begins to move out of it in the figure of an outward spiral: first in taking walks (with special permission) in the woods outside the enclosure, then building a hermitage away from the cloister, and eventually traveling into the mountains of Tibet. So in his conversion Merton returns to a thirteenth-century Catholic past, keeps moving, and comes out somewhere in a twenty-first-century ecumenism.

ii. Archetype of *psychomachia:* sanctity and the problem of the self

The portrait of the postconversion Merton is one of a consciously paradoxical figure, and as such is a powerful redefinition of the ordinary picture of the regenerate Christian who is at peace and in harmony with himself and the world. And this is Merton's own self-characterization.[17] The "model" that is Merton's legacy to the twentieth century would seem to be that of creative paradox. As one of Merton's brothers at Gethsemani observes, "He was a kind of dividing spirit, a sign spoken against, a sort of question demanding an answer. . . . he was unsettling, disturbing, not comfortable to live with. Put into other words, there was a kind of truth about him that got under your skin, into your heart."[18] It is this ethos of paradox, of contradiction, of open-ended questioning that turns the archetype of the quest into a spiral.

In his later writings Merton tends more and more to portray himself as a living paradox. It is not an image that diminishes the self, this paradox; in fact it recalls the recognizably childish fantasies of "unlimited possibilities of human heroism," with himself as the hero, which he describes at the very beginning of the autobiography. There are hints of this incipient spiritual aggrandizement of the self at the end of *The Seven Storey Mountain*, such as his rapturous description of the contemplative life as "this highest of all vocations" and as "the vocation to transforming union, to the height of the mystical life and of mystical experience, to the very transformation into Christ . . ." (*SSM*, 418). Merton feels himself to be called to this "highest of all vocations," though somewhat in defiance of his religious superiors. It is in response to Merton's rather grandiose conception of his humble vocation that Dom Aelred Graham observes, with an irony perhaps appropriate only to a fellow religious: "Of Merton would not the words be verified that he himself had applied to another?—'The waters had closed over his head, and he was submerged in the community. He was lost. The world would hear of him no more."[19]

Although *The Seven Storey Mountain* is conventional in its story of the transformation of a soul undergoing conversion, it is remarkable in that the self is the dominant and compelling theme for Merton. Whereas Augustine's conversion turned on the transformation of *cupiditas* into *caritas*, Merton's conversion effects a sublimation of his youthful ambitions for heroism into the mature ambition to be a saint. Thus in part 1 he shows us Merton the egotistic "hero" before conversion; in part 2, Merton aspiring to sainthood and in the transition of conversion; and in part 3, Merton the monk, supposedly having conquered or renounced his egotism and yet clearly still struggling with it. Though the conversion of part 2 should transform the hero of part 1 into the monk who has renounced all thought of self, the result is the hero in sacramental form. It is those passages in the autobiography about the need for high ideals which epitomize the peculiar self-aggrandizing nature of the spiritual quest for Merton: "I needed a high ideal, a difficult aim . . . that hopeless desire for what I could not have, for what was out of reach" (*SSM*, 228, 328). This goal, this high ideal, even in its religious form, becomes itself a ladder of ascending ideals: first, it is the priesthood; second, it is sainthood; and finally, it is "the peak of the mystical life," which "is a marriage of the soul with God" (*SSM*, 415). As Aelred Graham implies of Merton, "there can be selfishness in the pursuit of virtue, egoism in the highest form of religion."[20] Although critics have been harsh in exposing these tendencies toward spiritual aggrandizement in the autobiography, few have thought to commend Merton for so resolutely confronting and articulating the problem of the self. Perhaps this is one more reason for the popularity of the book: Merton appeals to the ordinary reader not only because he shares their problems but because he dramatizes the attempt to confront them.

There is a kind of egotism in the way Merton perceives himself from the very beginning of the autobiography. On the second page he writes that from both parents he received "capacities for work and vision and enjoyment and expression that ought to have made me some kind of a King. . . . If happiness were merely a matter of natural gifts, I would never have entered a Trappist monastery when I came to the age of a man" (*SSM*, 4). Clearly, Merton still sees himself as an individual of exceptional natural gifts.[21] In the early chapters of the autobiography Merton depicts himself as much taken with the ideal of the mythic hero. Of his two favorite childhood books, one is a collection of stories called *Greek Heroes:* "it was from these things," he writes, "that I unconsciously built up the vague fragments of a religion and of a philosophy, which remained hidden and implicit in my acts . . ." (*SSM,* 11.)[22] His other favorite was a geography book. He sees both as linked in the common theme of "travel, adventure, the wide sea, and unlimited possibilities of human heroism, with myself as the hero" (*SSM,* 13).

If the ideal in Merton's childhood was the mythic hero, the reality in his adolescence became the secular hero. Part 1 records Merton's "growing up" as a spiraling descent into a concept of self defined only by the debased (and debasing) ideals of the secular world: that he characterizes this world as "the picture of Hell" suggests Dante's journey in the *Inferno.* Monica Furlong sees "the tragic early death of his mother" as a definitive turning point in Merton's life: "In a literal sense it was the beginning of his travels. . . . But in a deeper sense, it symbolized the loss of a center. . . ."[23] The journey takes another turn downward when his father gives up the chapel-home that he had been building for his sons on the slopes of the mountain at St. Antonin. Merton traces his decline thereafter through experiences of isolation in the homes of most of the families with which he is placed and experiences of brutality and loneliness in the various schools he attends. He then describes his arrival at a plateau of toughness and insensitivity, his ensuing rebelliousness and prodigality, and finally his descent into the depths of a solipsistic inferno where he sees himself as "the complete twentieth-century man . . . a glib and hard-boiled specimen" who "now belonged to the world in which [he] lived" (*SSM,* 88, 85). Part 1 ends with its hero defeated by the "futile search for satisfaction where it could not be found" (*SSM,* 164). Merton concludes this chapter of his life and autobiography with: "Such was the death of the hero, the great man I had wanted to be" (*SSM,* 164). It is a recognition of some formality, a reminder that the descent into Hell (which is recognition of sin) must be completed before the ascent of Purgatory can begin.

In part 2, as the spiritual and symbolic quest replaces the geographical and literal journeyings, the biblical story of Moses and the Exodus out of Egypt becomes Merton's archetypal model.[24] And similarly, the idea of heroism is sublimated into the ideal of sanctity. Merton discovers that what he really wants is to become a saint. It is an ideal that has vocational implications and is concretized in the desire to become a priest. And in part 3, when Merton enters into his "final" identity as a monk, the ideal and the real selves seem to come together. But the obsession with the ideal self, though sublimated in the spiritual life, ultimately points to a religiosity of as-yet-unresolved narcissism. The life of a Trappist monk does not resolve the problems of selfhood for Merton; rather, it exacerbates them.

Merton's quest for God keeps on invoking phantoms of the self. Thus in the monastery the shadow of the mythic and secular hero reasserts itself in the "special identity" of the writer. Merton observes in his epilogue that "my vows should have divested me of the last shreds of any special identity. But then there was this shadow, this double, this writer who had followed me into the cloister" (*SSM*, 410). This dark premonition would seem to have been resolved in *The Sign of Jonas*, written about three years after *The Seven Storey Mountain*, where he optimistically deals with the writer-self not as an obstacle to spiritual perfection but as one of the conditions upon which spiritual perfection depends: "If I am to be a saint—and there is nothing else that I can think of desiring to be—it seems that I must get there by writing books in a Trappist monastery."[25] Some ten years later, in his preface to an anthology of his writings, this disquieting duality between Merton-the-writer and Merton-the-contemplative has become an irreconcilable ambivalence. He sees it as his cross, his own special penance, and observes: "It is possible to doubt whether I have become a monk (a doubt I have to live with), but it is not possible to doubt that I am a writer, that I was born one and will most probably die as one."[26] The problem of the self persists, whether as a sense of dual identity, the writer and the monk, or in a Buddhist affirmation of the essential nothingness of the self.

Merton's religious quest turns on a complex of values that is ultimately and paradoxically self-referential—a spiritual ethos where the highest value is placed on the self in the attempt to transcend the self. For Bunyan the problem of the self was portrayed as a *psychomachia* where the "good" self joined with the army of Christ against the "bad" self, whose unacceptable desires and doubts had been projected onto the figure of Satan. For the modern imagination the archetype of *psychomachia* has undergone several important changes. First, the evil once located in the self and projected onto Satan and his demonic legions is now projected onto capitalism, or poverty, or sociopolitical institutions, or war itself. Thus the archetype of the warfaring Christian becomes that of the crusader for social, racial, political, economic, or pacifist causes. This way of thinking is very much present in *The Seven Storey Mountain,* although it is represented as something that Merton must transcend.[27] It occurs negatively in his youthful conviction that "it was not so much I myself that was to blame for my unhappiness, but the society in which I lived"—an attitude that he recognizes as wrong-headed (*SSM,* 133). It occurs postively in his adolescent "conversion" to communism and his later attraction to the life of a Catholic social worker in Harlem.

A second difference between the older and the modern notions of *psychomachia* is that the position once taken by the "evil self" is now that of the "egocentric self."[28] So seen, the conflict is not between good and evil selves, but between self-centeredness and the ideal of selflessness. The principle that mediates between these two ideas of self is often a sort of "outmoded Aristotelianism,"[29] or a simplistic version of Jungian individuation, whereby the good life is thought to result from discovery of and fidelity to the "true" self. But this way of dealing with selfhood only effects a restitution of the same egocentric state, though at a higher level, in that the self remains the object of its own love. And the self taken as its own love-object almost always tends to produce the feeling of ontological unreality—the sense of an absence of self. Merton's solution later on in life to the problem of spiritual egocentrism is to resolve all identities—whether of hero, writer, saint, monk, or priest—into that larger apotheosized self that is both God and "nonself."

It is significant to Merton's theology of the self that the pattern of his life is one of a series of failed relationships—relationships that are either inadequate or incomplete in some way. The surprising number of deaths mentioned in *The Seven Storey Mountain* (father, mother, grandmother, friends, brother) both constitutes and symbolizes this pattern. Appropriately, "the world" is for Merton a condition where he knows there is something missing, although he is never quite sure what that "something" is. And if the life so confronted is at the same time an outer and an inner reality—a sociohistorical era and a state of mind—then the secular (and meaningless) world that Merton so despises is only a larger figure of the secular (and absent) self.

If Merton's egocentrism is an attempt to fill the vacuum created by all those early failed relationships, his ideal of "God's disinterested love" is an attempt both to replace the fragile image of the self with the image of God and to redeem those failed relationships with a God in whose countenance can be found the lineaments of mother, father, and brother. But the tendency of Merton's religious life is always to return him to that inner vacuum. Thus the sense of emptiness within is reinvoked in the metaphor of the religious life as a "furnace of contemplation"—a paradoxical image of a divine "disinterested" love perceived as consuming and annihilating—and later apotheosized in his Buddhist-inspired theology of the "non-self."

iii. Father, mother, brother, and the ideal of disinterested love

The disparity between Merton's descriptions of his father and of his mother is significant. He introduces his father with a short biography, telling us his name, his history, and describing his vocation. His mother, however, is introduced in the briefest of terms; the biography is reduced to the simple statement, "my mother was an American" (SSM, 5). We are told nothing of her background, nothing of her vocation (she was also an artist), not even her name. What he does say is mostly critical. The filial portrait of both parents emerges as that of the idealization of a weak father and the negation of a strong mother.[30]

Merton's mother died when he was six; his father when he was fifteen. Surely the need to deny the values of the mother while identifying with those of the father is related to the pattern of their deaths. Unable to experience fully the security of the dependent child, Merton's response is to place the highest value on its opposite—freedom, or independence, or autonomy. But his loyalty to this ethic betrays an unconscious yearning for a maternal matrix of security and dependence, and thus his quest is characterized by a restlessness that always seeks a conclusion and yet always is impelled onward. The inner dynamic of Merton's autobiography is neither that of the yearning soul seeking union with God, as it is for Augustine, nor is it that of the guilty soul fleeing the face of an angry God, as it is for Bunyan. Instead, it is one of a curiously defined freedom—freedom conceived of as "God's disinterested love."

In the opening sentences of the book, Merton introduces the human condition in terms of freedom and imprisonment: "Free by nature, in the image of God, I was nevertheless the prisoner of my own violence and my own selfishness, in the image of the world into which I was born" (*SSM*, 3). Freedom is restored by resolving this ambivalence into an allegiance to God alone. For Merton, at this time in his life, this is what conversion is all about. Entering the monastery both "realizes" that conversion and is symbolic of what surrender to God means—a condition attained by turning away from "The World" in both its internal and its external aspects. It is fitting that in the very last chapter Merton should describe the conditions of entering the monastery as a death to the world, which he calls "my new freedom." And the essence of this freedom, he writes, "is nothing else but the exercise of disinterested love—the love of God for his own sake . . ." (*SSM*, 372).

The notions of "freedom" and "God's disinterested love" can be seen as both reflecting and resolving a childhood ambivalence about emotional attachments. So Merton observes: "As a child, and since then too, I have always tended to resist any kind of possessive affection on the part of any other human being—there has always been this profound instinct to keep clear, to keep free. And only with truly supernatural people have I ever felt really at my ease, really at peace" (*SSM*, 57). In this passage the covert psychological meaning of *freedom* as escape from intimacy emerges out of its more overt philosophical context. For Merton "the freedom of disinterested love" is not the perfection of human love but its negation. In writing of the French Catholic family, the Privats, with whom he lived for a short time as a child, Merton defines love as what it is not: "That is why I was glad of the love the Privats showed me, and was ready to love them in return. It did not burn you, it did not hold you, it did not try to imprison you in demonstrations, or trap your feet in the snares of its interest" (*SSM*, 56). Ordinary human love is rejected as acquisitive and destructive, for the Privats are placed in a special category—"sanctified by leading ordinary lives in a completely supernatural manner" (*SSM*, 56).[31] Merton's concept of God's disinterested love would appear to be linked to this negative evaluation of "ordinary" human love.

If Augustine and Dante begin with *eros* and in their approach to God sublimate *eros* into *agape*, Merton begins with the ideas of freedom and love and comes up with the ideal of disinterested love. Merton, then, is the man who finds it difficult to love or to be loved; Augustine is the man who is unable *not* to love. And if it can be said that grace builds on nature, then these are the variants of the "natural man" upon which grace must build. Merton returns to Augustine to go beyond him. For his conversion sends him in the opposite direction—toward the consummation with God that purifies but also consumes all that is earthy and natural in the self. Augustine's theology of vision, or illumination, becomes in Merton a mysticism infused with dramatic anagogical overtones.

Merton's early experience of the loss of his parents, and his inability to resolve fully those experiences, might well be the basis of the theological ambivalence inherent in this concept of disinterested love. In the early pages of the autobiography he carefully describes his feelings about their deaths—in both instances presenting himself as left to cope as best as he could with the fact of death by himself, without the help of another human being or of ecclesiastical ritual. Characterizing his response as a child to the fact that his mother was about to die, he writes: "I did not miss Mother very much, and did not weep when I was not allowed to go and see her" (*SSM*, 14). His inability to cope with his father's death some years later only recapitulates the earlier response to the death of his mother. The uncustomarily short, terse sentences convey an absence of feeling: "The sorry business was over. And my mind made nothing of it. There was nothing I seemed to be able to grasp" (*SSM*, 84). The mature Merton accounts for this lack of feeling by justifying it—seeing his inability to grieve as an inevitable consequence of a faulty (i.e., non-Catholic) religious upbringing: "What would have been the good of my being plunged into a lot of naked suffering and emotional crisis without any prayer, any Sacrament to stabilize and order it, and make some kind of meaning out of it?" (*SSM*, 15). When his mother has died and the family returns home from the hospital, Merton focuses upon the memory of his father grieving, alone. Although he never actually criticizes his father for not being more supportive, the language of pathos in which he characterizes himself as a six-year-old child, abandoned to "the heavy perplexity and gloom of adult grief," betrays a desire, however well-concealed, to blame his father (*SSM*, 14). Perhaps, in seeing his difficulties at this time as caused by an inadequate religious education, Merton is displacing blame from the father whom he so needs and admires.

Merton consistently idealizes his father throughout the autobiography. But the actual paternal image, whose contours are only dimly suggested underneath and around Merton's strong need for a positive father-figure, is one of a weak, often unsupportive, often absent father. For example, the "offhand" tone in which Merton writes of the instability of his early life with his father may imply a good deal of unacknowledged negative feeling: "It is almost impossible to make much sense out of the continual rearrangement of our lives and our plans from month to month in my childhood. Yet every new development came to me as a reasonable and worthy change. Sometimes I had to go to school, sometimes I did not. Sometimes Father and I were living together, sometimes I was with strangers and only saw him from time to time" (*SSM*, 18). It is not surprising that Merton, as a child, should overlook the faults of the surviving parent. What *is* surprising is that as an adult he should still maintain this ideal father-image.

Merton represents his quest as the religious counterpart to his father's life as an artist. Though he sees the spiritual quest as an interior journey—the call to "the Promised land," which is "the interior life, the mystical life" (*SSM*, 226), like his father he always seeks an appropriate geographical setting that can serve both as a goal for his spiritual journey and as a symbol, or objective correlative, of that "Promised land." Merton's youthful preoccupation with churches and monasteries is a manifestation of this—of his search for the spiritual city within the earthly city—and also of his need to find, quite literally, an ideal place, the "Heavenly City" on earth.[32]

The story of their home together in the French town of St. Antonin epitomizes the relationship of father and son. It is a house built with materials from an ancient chapel and located on the slopes of a hill surmounted with another old chapel, around which were the ruins of a series of shrines marking the fourteen Stations of the Cross. Given this evocative setting, it is not surprising that "home," for Merton, should always connote not so much a place but a time, "the deep, naive, rich simplicity of the twelfth and thirteenth centuries" (*SSM*, 171). Perhaps it is the father's peculiar aesthetic-religious vision of the "ideal home" that provides the model for his son's eventual choice of a Trappist monastery, with its roots in thirteenth-century French monasticism, as his own home. But it is the outcome of the story of the St. Antonin house that is important here. When it is almost finished and ready for occupancy, the project is suddenly abandoned. The reasons he gives for this are twofold: first, his father's nomadic life made the house impractical, and second, his father's lady-friend discouraged its completion. It is an important incident, for it not only demonstrates how he masks his own disappointment with a generous appreciation of the problems in his father's life, but it also shows how he displaces blame from his father onto someone else—in this case, the woman who appears to be his father's mistress.

Merton's problematic relationship with his father would seem to have undergone some degree of resolution in the well-developed Christology that emerges toward the end of the book, for it is through identification with the atoning Son that the son is reunited with the ultimate Father. Merton comments on his first communion in such a way as to suggest this: "Christ born in me . . . and sacrificed in me . . . and risen in me: offering me to the Father, in Himself, asking the Father, my Father and His, to receive me into His infinite and special love . . ." (*SSM*, 224–25).

This ritualistic reunion with the divine Father is preceded by a developmental series of relationships with paternal figures—archetypal *senes* who progress from the intellectual or artistic to the religious, and who mediate between the lost father and the transcendent God. And in this, the quest of the twentieth-century pilgrim is remarkably similar to that of the fourth-century Augustine. Both authors see their religious quest as initiated by a particular book: for Augustine it is Cicero's *Hortensius;* for Merton it is Etienne Gilson's *The Spirit of Medieval Philosophy*. He takes from Gilson "one big concept . . . that was to revolutionize my whole life" (*SSM*, 172). This is the notion of God's *aseity*, an idea of God as utterly transcendent. This appeals to Merton, first, because it represents God less as a divine father than as an omnipotent, omniscient Being; and second, because it is an idea of God that is so abstract as to be devoid of any projected vestiges of the human emotionality that Merton so feared. The next of his intellectual mentors is Aldous Huxley, from whom he takes "two big concepts"—the reality of a supernatural order, and the possibility of actual contact with God (*SSM*, 186). Thus from Gilson he derives a concept of God that he can believe in, and from Huxley a recognition of his own need for a relationship with God—a God safely defined in abstract terms.

His quest continues as he ransacks Columbia's library for books on Oriental mysticism, writes a Master's thesis on Blake, studies the metaphysical poets, and starts a Ph.D dissertation on Hopkins. The transition from the literary mysticism of Blake to the religious vision of the Jesuit, Hopkins, signifies what is happening: gradually, Merton is turning from intellectual concerns toward those which are more purely religious. Similarly, Merton's intellectual quest eventuates in a progressive narrowing and concentration of his spiritual needs in the institutionalized religion of Roman Catholicism. His encounter with the Hindu monk Bramachari is an image of what Merton would himself become much later in his life, when his quest would lead him to an interest in Eastern mysticism.³³

The same progression from the literary to the religious occurs in the transition from using teachers to using priests as *senex* figures.³⁴ This pattern culminates at Gethsemani, where he is situated in a permanent relationship with another surrogate father, his abbot. It is a fully sacramentalized relationship, one where affective responsiveness is neither encouraged nor denied but instead, sublimated by a ritualized paternity in the higher fidelity to "God alone"—the inscription on the sign over the monastery door (*SSM*, 377). The progression from teachers to priests to abbot mediates, as it reenacts, Merton's progress from the real father to the ideal father; it also marks a transition from the factually experienced to the sacramental.

Even from the perspective of his mature years, as he looks back on his life, it seems important to Merton that his identity be patterned after the values and ideals of his father, and in opposition to those of his mother. But his uncritical devotion to his father may betray a deep, unresolved, and unaccepted yearning for the maternal. Behind the decision to submerge the self in becoming a monk and priest is the maternally inspired wish to elevate the self in becoming a saint. In the end it is the introjected ideals of the mother that triumph—a paradox that even Merton himself may not have accepted. Merton's memories of his mother are few, since she died when he was only six years old. He mentions that he inherited from her "some of her dissatisfaction with the mess the world is in," that she "must have been a person full of insatiable dreams and of great ambition after perfection," and observes that she "wanted me to be independent and not to run with the herd. I was to be original, individual, I was to have a definite character and ideals of my own" (*SSM*, 4,5,11). That he should become a monk, he observes wryly, is "the ultimate paradoxical fulfillment of my mother's ideas for me . . . the boomerang of all her solicitude for an individual development" (*SSM*, 11).

The latent autocentricity that can be observed in Merton's religious development could easily derive from an unconscious internalization of these maternal values of individuality and originality. So, too, his dislike of systematization. His comments later in life on "the false peace that is imposed by means of an arbitrary system" are darkly suggestive of an unresolved and perhaps not fully acknowledged restlessness with monastic life: "We do not respect the living and fruitful contradictions and paradoxes of which true life is full. We destroy them, or try to destroy them, with our obsessive and absurd systematizations. Whether we do this in the name of matter or in the name of spirit makes little difference in the end."[35] His mother's wish that he "have a definite character and ideals of [his] own" is reflected in his paradoxical image of himself as a monk. For what happens is that "Thomas Merton, monk," acquires a special identity—a special idea of selfhood—by virtue of the very anonymity of the monastic life: "My ambition is to be the most insignificant person in this house" he writes, an ambition that he calls "consciously selfish."[36] He is also aware of the specialness conferred on the individual by the monastic vocation itself. The monk, he writes, is "a very strange kind of person, a marginal person . . . [one who] is essentially outside of all establishments, [who] withdraws deliberately to the margin of society with a view to deepening fundamental human experience."[37] But in the autobiography Merton consistently attributes his religious yearnings and his vocational decision to the influence of his father, not his mother.[38]

Given Merton's ambivalence about his mother, the absence of any compelling erotic attachment as he grows up is not surprising. Indeed, the way in which he describes his early amatory experience is always negative, in one way or another. The first of this kind occurs when he is eleven, "a rather desultory affair" with a "mousy" little girl (*SSM*, 48). The next is an unrequited love affair with a "girl" who is twice his age. Merton ironically observes that he made "a declaration of [his] undying love," only to have her respond in terms that humiliated him (*SSM*, 90). Subsequent depictions of himself as the "young man in love" are characterized by this same self-deprecating irony, and also by a greater authorial distance from the experience as lived. He later describes himself, going through another adolescent attachment, "lying in the grass in the front of the old Cistercian abbey, copiously pitying myself for my boredom and for the loneliness of immature love" (*SSM*, 101). As a student at Columbia he finds himself once more in a one-sided love affair, "reduced to this extremity of misery and humiliation" (*SSM*, 164). It is significant that now Merton seems to accept the emotional pain of a failed love relationship as "just punishment" and, furthermore, perceives that punishment as "the will of God."

But the kind of youthful amours that Merton writes about seem fairly innocent; the truth is rather less so. The self-punitive element in some of Merton's writing in the autobiography becomes more easily comprehensible when we learn of an affair at Cambridge that resulted in the girl's pregnancy, responsibility for which Merton evaded through some sort of shady legal settlement.[39] Monica Furlong sees Merton's interest in the Cistercians, with their strong penitential character, as based on this incident: "Merton came to the monastery, as we know, with a strong sense of the need for personal penance, to expiate the sins of his past life—one sin in particular—and there was much in the structuring and outlook of Gethsemani for that wish to feed on."[40]

It would appear that Merton's relationships with women, his mother included, were almost always unsatisfactory. Whereas for Augustine the delights and dangers of the world were personified in the concubine, the problematic relationship for Merton is his younger brother. In fact, it is this relationship with John Paul, one that blends feelings of hostility, guilt, jealousy, rivalry, and underlying affection, that provides the best model for the ambivalence with which he confronted the world. As Edward Rice observes, "Merton saw in John Paul not only a brother but all mankind."[41] The changes in the way that Merton relates to John Paul mirror the development of his attitude toward the world: both progress from an initial disgust and rejection into an attitude of compassion and acceptance.

Merton introduces John Paul in the language of comparison and rivalry: "He was a child with a much serener nature than mine, with not so many obscure drives and impulses. I remember that everyone was impressed by his constant and unruffled happiness" (*SSM*, 8). The next reference occurs when the seven-year-old Merton and his friends pelt John Paul with stones when he tries to join them in their play. It is a vivid memory for Merton. It is also the first time in the narrative that Merton mentions the feeling of love in relation to another human being—a love he characterizes as "disinterested." This episode both parallels and inverts all of Merton's later love affairs. Here it is Merton who rejects love—who "violates . . . so wildly and unjustly . . . the law of love"—a situation that he describes as "the pattern and prototype of all sin" (*SSM*, 23). In his adolescent romances the situation is reversed (with one very significant exception), for there it is Merton who is the hurt and rejected lover. Perhaps, like the "screen memory" of psychoanalysis, Merton's emphasis on this incident with John Paul conceals the later affair with the girl in Cambridge (which was apparently censored out of the manuscript).

At the very end of the autobiography there is a fraternal episode that directly parallels the earlier one. John Paul is visiting Merton at Gethsemani, and preparing for baptism. He has somehow entered the wrong door and gone to the wrong place. The two brothers are separated by a locked door, and by the elder Merton's vow of silence: "At that moment there flashed into my mind all the scores of times in our forgotten childhood when I had chased John Paul away with stones. . . . And now, all of a sudden, here it was all over again: a situation that was externally of the same pattern: John Paul, standing, confused and unhappy, at a distance which he was not able to bridge" (*SSM*, 398). It is a powerful visual image of unconsummated brotherhood—a relationship impeded by doors and locks, physical distance, and an imposed silence. In some sense, by bringing John Paul into the Christian brotherhood, Merton is making reparation for his rejection of him in their childhood.

The autobiography closes with an elegy to John Paul, who has just died in a wartime plane crash in the North Sea. His death occurs in Easter week. The poem is perhaps the most moving, most emotional part of the book. It is about brothers and sons; Thomas, John Paul, and Christ, in whose death and resurrection both Mertons are united in a consecrated fraternity. It is toward John Paul that Merton comes closest to a love that is at the same time "disinterested"—in that it respects the freedom and autonomy of the other—and "interested"—in that it is fully responsible, fully committed to the human being who is flawed, ordinary, and a brother. The union with God that Merton seeks for himself he also wishes for John Paul. Though this fraternal relationship, like the paternal one, is interrupted by death, the elegy represents Merton's gesture toward its fulfillment—reaching past all the barriers of distance and death that still divide them. Perhaps in his writings, themselves a paradoxical inversion of his vows of silence, Merton is speaking to his dead brother.

7

Thomas Merton
Sacramental Conversion

At first glance the tripartite structure of Merton's autobiography and the nature of his conversion would seem to follow the Augustinian model, where the life of the author is seen as either preparatory to or as a consequence of the climatic moment of conversion. The two conversions are similar in many ways. Imagery of sickness and health, bondage and freedom, darkness and light are present in both. Augustine's Catholic conversion is "against" Manichaeism; Merton's sacramentalism is shaped by antipathy to Protestantism. For both, conversion is mediated by the parent archetype—the mother for Augustine and the father for Merton—and further defined by substitute parental figures. The incident in *The Seven Storey Mountain* when Merton first meets his abbot and finds him "deep in a pile of letters which covered the desk before him" is remarkably similar to Augustine's finding Ambrose reading in silence and engrossed in study (*SSM,* 377; *Conf.* 6.3).

However, though conversion is represented in *The Seven Storey Mountain* as the climax of a life of search, there are *crisis*like episodes in other parts of the narrative as well: physical automatisms, such as hearing voices and sensing the presence of spirits; divine decrees to take a new direction; sudden moments of new conviction. Are these episodes, then, also conversions? Is Merton's conversion, like Augustine's, to be considered as the last in a series of conversions? Or does Merton's conversion, like Bunyan's, consist in a repetitive pattern of conversion, relapse, and recovery? Or does it belong to the broader *lysis* category of a gradual process of unification? The answer to all these questions is negative. Although the conversion in Part 2 occurs over the course of several separate events, Merton clearly saw these events as phases of a single *crisis*. Also, experiences that are like conversions occur both before and after Merton's conversion to Roman Catholicism (whereas in the *Confessions*, the protoconversion episodes all precede and culminate in the conversion to Christianity).

Thus Merton's experience is unlike *crisis* conversion because it lacks the definitive, climactic episode; it is unlike the *lysis* type because it does not involve a progressive, gradual change marked by clearly delineated stages. Merton's conversion is best explained by invoking the principle of *epektesis*, where there are a number of *crisis*like episodes related to each other not in progressive stages but as widening or deepening circles. As Merton himself observed: "My conversion is still going on. Conversion is something that is prolonged over a whole lifetime. Its progress leads it over a succession of peaks and valleys, but normally the ascent is continuous in the sense that each new valley is higher than the last one."[1]

In the autobiography the idea of *epektesis* is manifested in the tendency to translate personal into ritual experience, and especially, the individual conversion into the communal sacrament. As I shall show, the visionary experience in Part 1 (where Merton, in a hotel room in Rome, first becomes aware of God in the sensed presence of his dead father) is not a conversion.[2] Clearly, Merton did not perceive it as such; instead, it must be considered as an early manifestation of a religious potential that could be fully realized only later on. The hotel-room experience functions like a dream—in fact it is quite similar to Monica's dream about her converted son; though portentous, it appears to have little or no transformative effect. Similarly, in Part 3 there is an episode that strongly suggests a conversion experience: Merton's decision to become a Trappist. However, this is not so much a conversion as it is a decision, in spite of the fact that it is a decision made (or reconstructed) with all the dramatic trappings of a *crisis* conversion.

Merton's conversion takes place not so much as a series of graduated stages as on successive levels. The first of these is the private visionary experience where he has a unique and direct confrontation with something he considers to be divine—an unmediated form of religious experience that is both canceled by and fulfilled in the "true" conversion later on. The second is the corporate ecclesiastical ritual that serves to validate, assimilate, and give form to this direct mystical experience. And the third is the process of subsequently defining and redefining the converted self within the Roman Catholic hierarchy. Merton's sacramental conversion can thus be discussed as "private vision" (events in Part 1, before conversion), "corporate expression" (events in Part 2, the conversion itself), and "communal experience" (vocational decisions in Part 3). Again, the pattern is that of a spiral—of spiritual change through repetition, though it is a repetition that is always on a more profound level—an *epektesis* of deepening religious faith.

i. The private vision

Merton tells us his father is Anglican and his mother, Quaker. These faiths represent two extreme poles of Protestantism, Anglicanism being the most fully mediated and Quakerism the least. Merton's religiosity can be seen as a synthesis of these two Protestant faiths, although it is a synthesis where the paternal contribution is a conscious one and the maternal influence unconscious and suppressed. For example, his deep hunger for silence, the outer symbol of an inner solitude, could very well be a legacy of his mother's Quakerism; so also his strong and continuous pacifism.[3] Yet nowhere in *The Seven Storey Mountain* (or anywhere else) does Merton link these concerns with silence and pacifism with the values of his mother. Still another evidence of internalized maternal values might be found in Merton's underlying obedience to the "inner guide," the equivalent to the "inner light" of the Quakers, which he calls *logos* or *telos*—and which often exerts a directive energy that contradicts his religious superiors. The sense of an ultimate within the self inevitably restricts total obedience to a religious superior: "That which is most perfect and most individual in each man's life is precisely the element in it which cannot be reduced to a common formula. It is the element which is nobody else's but ours and God's."[4] This is surprisingly close to the unmediated bond between the individual and his God so central to Protestantism.

But Merton consistently refuses any delineation of his life-pattern that would imply an internalization of maternal values. Throughout, the autobiography is shaped to depict an inborn need for a fully mediated religiosity, in accord with his consistent tendency to identify with his father, not with his mother. Thus his mock-characterization of himself as a child of four with "a deep and serious urge to adore the gas-light in the kitchen, with no little ritualistic veneration" has more serious overtones (*SSM*, 5). Similarly, he presents his great love of old churches and ruined monasteries as the early manifestation of his vocation as a Roman Catholic—the "calling" of a future saint. Indeed, Merton's memory of his many early travels seems to center primarily on an ability to recall, in formidable detail, all of the churches in every place he ever visited. He remembers the old Quaker meeting house where his mother went and the "old Zion Church" where his father played the organ (*SSM*, 10, 12). And he writes of his early childhood in Prades: "There were many ruined monasteries in those mountains. My mind goes back with great reverence to the thought of those clean, ancient stone cloisters, those low and mighty rounded arches hewn and set in place by monks who have perhaps prayed me where I now am" (*SSM*, 6). Merton is "barely a year old" when he leaves Prades for America; here we can detect the retrospective imagination actually at work, imposing on the memory the need to see the child as "father of the man."

The paradoxical culmination of this need to sacramentalize his early life is an event that occurs during a trip to Rome when he is eighteen, his father having died some two or three years earlier. He had responded to his father's death with a sense of great freedom—but it is a spurious freedom, which he now sees as "a frightful captivity." It is because of this negative freedom that Merton plunges into "a deep and tremendous apathy." So he writes: "But my soul was simply dead. It was a blank, a nothingness. It was empty, it was a kind of spiritual vacuum." His captivity is total: "What is more, there was nothing I could do for myself. There was absolutely no means, no natural means within reach, for getting out of that state." It is in this state that he takes off for Rome, the archetypal city of pilgrimage.

The language in which he describes himself on this journey is reminiscent of the "sick soul" of James's preconversion psychology: he refers to himself as a "corpse," falls ill repeatedly, becomes "more weary and depressed," and dreams that he is in jail. And he is "bored." As he draws nearer to Rome, he writes, "I was tired of passing through places. I wanted to get to the term of my journey. . . ." When he finally arrives in Rome, these aimless physical wanderings turn into a directed spiritual pilgrimage as he gradually finds himself "looking into churches rather than into ruined temples"—his interest being "in another and a far different Rome."

Merton's experience of the "two Romes" is a manifestation of the archetype of the two cities, as he surely realizes: the pagan temples and their "vapid, boring, semi-pornographic statuary" representing the secular city, and the old churches with their Byzantine mosaics the sacred city (*SSM*, 97–109).

But it is ironically appropriate that this young man who habitually sought out romantic old churches throughout Europe should have the climactic experience of his pilgrimage in the thoroughly secular setting of a hotel room. It is perhaps the most important episode in the entire book:

> I was in my room. It was night. The light was on. Suddenly it seemed to me that Father, who had now been dead more than a year, was there with me. The sense of his presence was as vivid and as real and as startling as if he had touched my arm or spoken to me. The whole thing passed in a flash, but in that flash, instantly, I was overwhelmed with a sudden and profound insight into the misery and corruption of my own soul. . . . And now I think for the first time in my whole life I really began to pray . . . praying to the God I had never known, to reach down towards me out of His darkness and to help me to get free of the thousand terrible things that held my will in their slavery.
>
> There were a lot of tears connected with this, and they did me good, and all the while, although I had lost that first, vivid, agonizing sense of the presence of my father in the room, I had him in my mind, and I was talking to him as well as to God, as though he were a sort of intermediary. (*SSM*, 111–12)

The tears of this incident recall the tears he had to suppress in his dying father's hospital room, the ability to pray to God for help recalls and redeems the feelings of "great helplessness" at his father's deathbed, and the intermediary presence of his father atones for his sense of aloneness after the death of both parents. The experience releases him from the tyranny of the inhibited emotional life that followed upon the death of his parents, and points the way to his future conversion and monastic vocation.

Significantly, it is an event that occurs outside Merton's usual aesthetic-religious expections. Rather than accepting this fact (and perhaps dealing with it as itself a part of the nature of the religious experience), Merton first tries to apologize for the episode, and then tries to sacramentalize it. He is clearly embarrassed about the role played by his father: "How do I know it was not merely my own imagination, or something that could be traced to a purely natural, psychological cause—I mean the part about my father?"

(*SSM*, 112). His ambivalence is evident in his need to affirm, perhaps more for himself than for his reader, that he *really* felt what he has just described himself as feeling: "But whether it was imagination or nerves or whatever else it may have been, I can say truly that I did feel, most vividly, as if my father were present there . . ." (*SSM*, 112).

The way in which he writes about the event is an indication of his difficulty in formulating it. What he does is to bracket the experience with references to churches. Thus, just before the description of the hotel-room experience, he observes: "my love for the old churches and their mosaics grew from day to day. . . . I loved to be in these holy places. . . . my rational nature was filled with profound desires and needs that could only find satisfaction in churches of God" (*SSM*, 110). And just after the event in the hotel room, Merton makes several attempts to account for and sum up the experience with an appropriate ritual action. The first is his observation that the very next morning he "climbed the deserted Aventine, in the spring sun, with my soul broken up with contrition . . ." (*SSM*, 112). Then, in the same paragraph, he moves abruptly away from this to remark upon his conversionlike experience of "capitulation" and "surrender" upon entering a Dominican church, then that he looked "into a tiny, simple cloister, where the sun shone down on an orange tree" and finally that he "walked out into the open feeling as if I had been reborn" and strolled over to "another deserted church." He concludes by mentioning a visit, some ten days later, to the Trappist monastery of Tre Fontaine—a "dark, austere old church." As he walks outside its walls, he tells us that "the thought grew on me: 'I should like to become a Trappist monk'" (*SSM*, 114). The easy proliferation here of ritual commentary points to the intensity of his need for it; but also, the hastiness with which he moves from one symbolic action to another betrays its failure as an explanatory or representational framework.

Merton's early mystical experience in Rome represents a private, almost hallucinatory experience of the implosion of the divine into the natural world. At first it might seem that this experience marks a *crisis* conversion. But it does not. The simplest explanation why this does not constitute a conversion is that he does not see himself as converted, and in fact his life thereafter is not much changed. The event in Rome is followed by a series of inadequate, useless, and blind attempts on two continents to locate that experience of the heart somewhere in the visible structure of the world. So he briefly visits the Episcopal Church of his father and the Quaker meeting-house that his mother used to attend, reads some pamphlets on the Mormons, and then descends into a subjective state where "the stews of my own mental Pompeii" are projected onto Cambridge, "the sweet stench of corruption . . . the keen, thin scent of decay . . . this rotten fruit" (*SSM*, 121, 118). Trying to find something to believe in, he undergoes several proleptic conversions, as did Augustine: first, a partial conversion to psychoanalysis, and then to Communism. But none of these constitutes a successful solution. The narrative material that follows upon the visit to Rome is uniformly anticlimactic, and would seem to indicate that nothing whatsoever really happened to Merton in the Roman hotel room. The truth is that the experience, however deep an impression it may have made on Merton initially, remains somehow unreal and invalid for him—a kind of dissociative state that requires a different form to be rendered psychically potent.

ii. The corporate expression

Part 1 ends with the theologically necessary death of the "natural man," which Merton experiences as *anomie*. But as he succumbs to the "very anguish and helplessness" of his position, he admits to a defeat that is "to be the occasion" of his rescue (*SSM*, 165). It is thus appropriate that part 2, the account of his conversion, should begin with a theological perspective on helplessness: Merton observes that "we were never destined to lead purely natural lives," and offers a theological answer to the problem of the individual's incompleteness in a state of nature, namely, "sanctifying grace."

What happens during the conversion in part 2 is that Merton's visionary experience in the hotel room in Rome finds its form, and therein its validation and meaning, in the corporate expression of Roman Catholicism. For it is Merton's baptism and first Mass— the institutionalized rites of conversion—that represent the fulfillment as well as the valid expression of his early mystical encounter with God. In other words, Merton's individual, direct encounter with the numinous is spiritually impotent; the real transformation is accomplished indirectly, through ritual participation in the death and resurrection of Christ in the transformed substances of the Mass. That Merton downplays the personal, visionary experience while emphasizing the institutionally shared, corporate Mass is a function of his inability to deal with the emotional facts of life without a ritual commentary to make sense of them. This interpretation also accounts for the emotional paralysis he describes when he faces the deaths of his mother and his father without the help of ceremony and ritual.

Part 2, the conversion, is divided into two sections: the subject of the first is the decision to become a Roman Catholic; the subject of the second is the decision to become a priest. In one way or another, both events look back to that original encounter with the numinous in Rome.

The decision to become a Roman Catholic is bracketed by liturgical expressions of conversion—Merton's experience of his first Mass, and his ritual acceptance into the Church. The language with which he describes his growing religious conviction in this section advances from the simple and the subjective (reminiscent of his encounter with God in Rome) to the liturgical and the mystical. In the beginning of the section, he is prompted to attend Mass by an impulse that he characterizes as a voice: "It was something quite new and strange, this voice that seemed to prompt me, this firm, growing interior conviction of what I needed to do. It had a suavity, a simplicity about it that I could not easily account for." When he leaves the Church, after this first Mass, he writes: "All I know is that I walked in a new world. . . ." It is of interest that Merton should introduce his experience of the Mass with an architectural description of the building itself: "It was a gay, clean church, with big plain windows and white columns and pilasters and a well-lighted, simple sanctuary. Its style was a trifle eclectic, but much less perverted with incongruities than the average Catholic church in America. It had a kind of seventeenth-century, oratorian character about it, though with a sort of American colonial tinge of simplicity" (*SSM*, 206–11). In a way, this also describes the self he would like to be.

When Merton actually decides that he wants to become a Roman Catholic, this is also experienced as a subjective phenomenon on the borderline between impulse and voice: "All of a sudden, something began to stir within me, something began to push me, to prompt me. It was a movement that spoke like a voice." And again he expresses his feelings of release when he has acceded to the voice in subjective language: "everything inside me began to sing—to sing with peace, to sing with strength and to sing with conviction" (*SSM*, 215–16).

But during the ritual of admission to the Catholic Church, the language of subjective experience gives way to the language of the liturgy: as Merton describes the ancient Latin rite of the Mass, the inner voices are replaced by that of the priest. The change of language here signals a definite inner change as emotionality is transformed into ritual expression: "I was absorbed in the liturgy . . . I did not have any time to feel how relieved I was when I came stumbling out, as I had to go down to the front of the church. . . ." In addition, no longer does Merton discuss the architecture of the church; instead, he becomes it: "In the Temple of God that I had just become, the One Eternal and Pure Sacrifice was offered up to the God dwelling in me: the sacrifice of God to God . . ." (*SSM*, 220–25).

Characters as well as language are sacramentalized. Merton acts upon his decision to become a Roman Catholic not by contacting a friend, but by seeking out a priest. And in the Mass that ritualizes his acceptance into the Church, individuals are inevitably cast into roles of a conventionally religious and sacramental nature. Even Merton's close friend, Ed Rice, is drawn into the religious drama as a sacramental character. Merton's description of his ritual acceptance emphasizes the aspect of mediation at a variety of levels: Rice acts as godfather, the priest celebrating the sacrament is performing a mediatory role, and Christ himself is the ultimate mediator, incarnate in the person of the priest. The godfather, the priest, and Christ—all three represent a sublimation and transformation of the archetype of paternal mediation that was first manifested in the presence of Merton's own father during the initial, conversionlike experience in the Roman hotel room. For Merton the Mass makes this experience "real" by centering it in an identification with the dead and risen Christ that is both mystical and liturgical.

But however final and lofty this aspect of Merton's conversion seems to him at the time, the conversion to Roman Catholicism is not adequate. He refers to it as the "complete conversion of my intellect" and then goes on to remark, "But the conversion of the intellect is not enough" (*SSM*, 231). The polarities he is here implying are the conventional ones of conversion of the intellect and conversion of the will. The pattern is one that will come to be characteristic of Merton's paradigm of conversion—that any given goal in the spiritual journey, once arrived at, becomes another stage, another starting-place toward a further goal. So Merton realizes that his conversion has been partial not only in regard to orthodox Catholic categories of mind (i.e., intellect and will), but also in regard to persons in the Catholic Holy Family.

Merton begins section ii by observing that "one of the big defects of my spiritual life in that first year was a lack of devotion to the Mother of God" (*SSM*, 229). He goes on to observe that Mary "is the Mother of the supernatural life in us" and that "the one thing I needed most of all was a sense of the supernatural life." Perhaps this emphasis on the supernatural mother is some sort of psychic compromise—a recognition of his lack of feeling (or latent hostility) toward his natural mother and a concomitant sublimation of the natural-maternal into the supernatural-maternal. For the observation that he needs "a high ideal, a difficult aim" (which he identifies as his aspirations toward the priesthood) betrays a resurgence of the perfectionist standards of his own mother. This ambition to become a priest thus unites the secular ideals of the natural mother with the spiritual ideals of the supernatural mother, Mary. Furthermore, this absence of the "Holy Mother" in his religious life he perceives as related to the absence of a conversion of will. For symptomatic of both defects is a failure of trust—the inability to acknowledge his helplessness and dependency; the reluctance to give up his own personal will and yield to the greater will of God. These virtues, for Merton, are symbolized in the person of Mary: "I did not have that sense of dependence or of her power. I did not know what need I had of trust in her" (*SSM*, 230).

The themes of maternal idealism and creaturely trust come together in Merton's decision about the priesthood. Appropriately, he does not perceive this as a personal, willed choice; instead, he writes of it as a "conviction that had suddenly been planted in me full grown . . . a strong and sweet and deep and insistent attraction," or as "the grace that had been suddenly planted in my soul" (*SSM*, 253, 255). Just as celebration of the Mass formalizes Merton's entry into the Church in section 1, so again, in section 2, Merton uses the ritual of the Mass to mark—and to sacramentalize—his decision to become a priest. The principle is one of repetition, but it is a repetition on a higher level. The aspects of mediation so obvious in the earlier decision to become a Roman Catholic are here, in the decision to become a priest, sacramentally abstracted in the dominant presence of the "white Host," upon which Merton fixes his eyes and his attention. His experience here in an underground church, full of lights, which he enters at night, is reminiscent again of his visionary experience in Rome, which also occurred at night and in a lighted hotel room. It was in this place that Merton experienced the presence of his dead father, acting as intermediary between himself and God. Similarly, in the underground church the intermediary presence of the natural father is sublimated into the intermediary presence of the "white Host," which is both an abstract symbol of the body of Christ and an actual substance to be ritually consumed. Thus the rite of the Mass, for Merton, both symbolizes and helps effect a redemption of the original, flawed parental relationships.

The Mass can be thought of as a liturgical equivalent of sacramental conversion. The significance of the Host is that it represents the surrender of personal selfhood in mystical identification with the sacrificial body of Christ. The apparent extinction of the personal will which is a characteristic of conversion—the "death" of the old self—marks an extreme passivity where the self is overwhelmed by an "other" that is both internal and external to the psyche: this "other" can be seen as the unrecognized and unacknowledged configuration of the unconscious part of the psyche, and also as the transcendent divine presence. The image of Christ works for Merton because it is a composite archetypal figure representing at the same time an intrapsychic reality and an external, divine "otherness." Perhaps Jung's observation is especially true for Merton—that "what we seek in visible human form is not man, but the superman, the hero or god, that 'quasi-human' being who symbolizes the ideas, forms, and forces which grip and mould the soul."[5]

iii. The communal experience

In Part 3, the death and rebirth that are experientially real in conversion and sacramentally focused on the Mass become a way of living—the process of decision and transformation by which Merton becomes a monk, and the lifelong dying to the self and renewal in Christ that are the purpose and meaning of monastic life. Merton's conversion to Roman Catholicism seems to have constituted itself as an archetypal model for dealing with subsequent decisions. We see this in the way that he writes of his decision to become a Trappist monk.[6] Once more there are two phases in this conversionlike experience. The first is Merton's decision to become a Franciscan and his subsequent rejection from the Order. The second is the choice between the vocations of Catholic social worker in Harlem and Trappist monk in Kentucky. It is clear that Merton observes these episodes to be analogous. Moreover, he shapes his material in such a way that the parallel that he sees between the initial decision to become a Franciscan and the later decision to become a Trappist is a dialectic between willed, personal decision and unwilled, religious conversion. The pattern is that of an ascending spiral—an *epektesis*—of choice.

Merton describes these two episodes in such a way as to point to his intervening spiritual maturation. For example, the different notions of selfhood that characterize the two experiences are symptomatic of a change in attitude. He spends a good deal of energy in trying to choose a new name for himself as a Franciscan. What he comes up with is "Frater John Spaniard"—a consciously romantic return to the childhood ethos of an artistic and romanticized religiosity. Retrospectively, Merton sees this choice as "a sign of a profound and radical defect in my vocation" (*SSM*, 291). But when he enters Gethsemani, the mark of his spiritual maturation is his obliviousness as to what will be his new name: "I had spent hours trying to choose a name for myself when I thought I was going to become a Franciscan," Merton observes; "now I simply took what I got. In fact, I had been too busy to bother with such trivial thoughts" (*SSM*, 384). Similarly, the difference in his ideas about freedom in the two episodes indicates a process of ongoing spiritual maturation. He characterizes himself as choosing the Franciscan Order because it offered "a sort of freedom from spiritual restraint, from systems and routine" and because he thinks it "the easiest of religious rules" (*SSM*, 261, 262). This negative ideal of freedom later gives way to one more positive: he remarks about his entering Gethsemani to become a Trappist, "So Brother Matthew locked the gate behind me and I was enclosed in the four walls of my new freedom" (*SSM*, 372).

The first phase sets up a dialectic of authorities: rejected by the Franciscans, Merton has been told by his religious superiors that he has no vocation as a priest, and yet his "inner voice" insists that he does have such a vocation. It is worth noting here that in this *psychomachia* of conflicting imperatives it is his own inner consciousness, not the Roman Catholic hierarchy, that turns out to have been the "voice of God." In this, Merton's eventual reliance on his inner voice is similar to Augustine's experience during his conversion, when he obeys the voice that chants *"tolle, lege."* Both Merton and Augustine, in their conversions, learn that there is a higher guide than the teacher or the ecclesiastic to whom they first turn.

The second phase turns on the choice between a life of pastoral social work in Harlem and a life as a Trappist monk in the mountains of Kentucky. Merton chooses the former, although it is a choice that is reversed soon after. What attracts him to the Catholic settlement-house in Harlem, he writes, is the dedication to a "total, uncompromising poverty" (*SSM*, 358). But Merton's response to the Trappist monastery at Gethsemani is also an attraction to a life of poverty—only it is poverty in a spiritual sense; for the Trappist monks, he writes, "were poor, they had nothing, and therefore they were free and possessed everything . . ." (*SSM*, 316). One difference, then, between the two vocations—of social worker and of monk—is the difference between two kinds of poverty: Merton's final choice of a monastic vocation represents a redefinition not only of charity but also of need. So Merton can write that the monk is secluded in his monastery "where the news and desires and appetites and conflicts of the world no longer reached [him]" but also that the secluded monk, by his prayers, "amazingly held back the arm of God from striking and breaking at last the foul world full of greed and avarice and murder and lust and all sin" (*SSM*, 316, 318). In this second phase of vocational conversion, the pattern of Merton's religious life manifests itself as a spiraling movement from a secular to a spiritual idea of compassion. Just as his initial conversion to Communism is transcended by a conversion to Roman Catholicism in part 2, so his decision to deal with the problems of human poverty by dedicating himself to a life of pastoral social work is transcended by the desire to give himself up to the spiritual poverty of the monastic life and the charity of prayer.

But the most important difference between the two vocations is in the process of the choice itself. Merton's decision to go to Harlem is indeed a decision—a considered act of the personal will. But the conviction to become a Trappist is quite different. Accordingly, Merton describes it in the language of religious conversion rather than the psychological language appropriate to decision-making: "Finally, on the Thursday of that week, in the evening," he writes, "I suddenly found myself filled with a vivid conviction: 'The time has come for me to go and be a Trappist.' Where had the thought come from? All I knew was that it was suddenly there" (*SSM*, 363). The conviction is set off by quotation marks—it speaks to him as though it were an autonomous, projected entity. Merton comments on his response to the experience in language that is so conventional to *crisis* conversion as to border on the mimetic: "it was as if scales fell off my own eyes. . . . already I was full of peace and assurance—the consciousness that everything was right, and that a straight road had opened out, clear and smooth, ahead of me. . . . I went upstairs like somebody who had been called back from the dead. . . . Never had I experienced the calm, untroubled peace and certainty that now filled my heart" (*SSM*, 365–66). The organizing structural experience or metaphor (they are here the same thing) is when Merton hears the great bell of Gethsemani, miraculously ringing from a distance of a thousand miles: "The bell seemed to be telling me where I belonged—as if it were calling me home" (*SSM*, 365). It is a marvelous image of the call to pursue one's spiritual quest.[7]

The remainder of *The Seven Storey Mountain* describes Merton's entry into and life in the monastery, where the individual conversion is further sacramentalized in communal life. When Merton enters the novitiate, he emphasizes the ritual stripping of clothing, possessions, and name as symbolic of the death of the self to the world. The monastic life entails the death of the personal self, but it also makes possible a kind of resurrection of the self in a Christ-centered consciousness. It is significant for Merton that he should enter Gethsemani during Advent—the time when the spiritual community awaits the birth of Christ. Thus the garden of the monastery, which is "dead and stripped and bare" when Merton arrives, is the winter of the soul. His trust that his own inner desert—the soul emptied of selfhood—will flower under God's sanctifying grace is very much a part of his sacramentalism. For the unifying symbol of both the exterior cycle of winter and summer and the interior cycle of emptiness and fullness is Christ, whose death and resurrection are sacrificial acts bringing together the seasonal cycles of nature and the spiritual cycles of human nature. When Merton enters into the sacred space of the monastery, he also enters into a new concept of time, whereby both the natural and the psychological cycles of birth and death, joy and sorrow, are incorporated into the "Mystical Body of Christ" and celebrated according to the liturgical calendar. He learns that the "soul of the monk is a Bethlehem where Christ comes to be born" (*SSM*, 379) but also that it is a Calvary where Christ comes to be crucified. This is a mystery that Merton will learn only gradually.

The Seven Storey Mountain concludes not with a happy sense of the joys of the monastic life, but with something rather different. Merton ends his autobiography with a conscious projection of the voice of God speaking to him: it would seem to be the supreme gesture of religious affirmation, and yet it is riddled with ambivalence. By his tense rhetoric Merton conveys the coincidence of need and fear, affirmation and rejection; for the love of God so projected is one that burns, consumes, and destroys:

> Therefore all the things around you will be armed against you, to deny you, to hurt you, to give you pain, and therefore to reduce you to solitude.
> Because of their enmity, you will soon be left alone. They will cast you out and forsake you and reject you and you will be alone. . . .
> Everything that can be desired will sear you, and brand you with a cautery, and you will fly from it in pain, to be alone. Every created joy will only come to you as pain, and you will die to all joy and be left alone. . . .
> You will be praised, and it will be like burning at the stake. You will be loved, and it will murder your heart and drive you into the desert. . . .
> And when you have been praised a little and loved a little I will take away all your gifts and all your love and all your praise and you will be utterly forgotten and abandoned and you will be nothing, a dead thing, a rejection. (*SSM*, 422)

It is not clear whether these remarks are indicative of spiritual heroism or spiritual pathology. For in God's love everything that is most terrifying to Merton in the human intimacies from which he has so resolutely turned is here embraced.

The ambivalence in Merton's relationship to God reflects a deeper ambivalence in his relationship to himself—a situation where the desire for freedom, autonomy, and individuality alternates with the opposite desire for a matrix of security, dependence, and corporate sacramentalism. The juxtaposition of these two kinds of need can be seen as a positive element in Merton's life, where the pattern is not one of conflicting desires that cancel each other out but of complementary desires that complete each other in the figure of a spiral. This pattern is a dialectical one; and as Bamberger observes, it is rooted in "the confidence that the overall pattern of his life would witness to an ultimate authenticity and truth."[8] There is indeed an aspect of the dialectical in the shape of Merton's life, for it is characterized by an attraction to pairs of opposites: social work and the priesthood, the active and the contemplative lives, the self and the nonself; later on, it is Roman Catholicism and Buddhism that are the alternatives. And the pattern of his development turns on his life as being not simply a rotation or oscillation between these opposites but a spiraling movement from the one to the other that constantly forces him toward a higher level of integration. Brother Louis is and is not the same man as Thomas Merton; the psychological pattern remains, but it is raised to another level of humanity and consciousness as if on Dante's spiraling and seven-storied mountain.

Yet this ascent does not end, as does Dante's *Divine Comedy*, in the blinding raptures of mystical communion with God; as we have seen, it ends with that troubling passage where God's love is characterized as consuming and destroying. This emphasis on "last things" toward the end of the autobiography suggests a change that is not simply dialectical but anagogical. For dialectic leads to synthesis, but here synthesis occurs in the mind of God—beyond the perimeters of human understanding and the life of the body. The last words of the autobiography—"*sit finis libri, non finis quaerendi*"—remind us that in the modern spiritual quest, the hero never reaches a final destination, that the "truth" of the religious vision attained never totally satisfies. And this is the meaning of *epektesis:* a continuous process of conversion where resolution is always provisional, and where these plateaus do not mark final synthesis or unity but are found to be stages toward further development, both in the self and in life. The "authenticity and truth" that Bamberger points to in the overall pattern of Merton's life are indeed ultimate; synthesis occurs in the mind of God and the person of Christ.

Conclusion

My reader may question why I have chosen these three particular spiritual autobiographies for examination. One reason is the fullness and richness of each narrative. Another is their diversity: that all three are characterized by the same basic constellation of archetypal patterns is rendered more striking by the fact that they differ markedly in regard to historical and cultural era, religious orientation, and the personality of each author. And it is important that the archetype not be considered as constant and unchanging. Archetypes are not uninflected; rather, they are refracted through a constellation of attitudes, values, and traditions of place or time as well as the sensibility of an individual writer. This triad of very different narratives confirms the recurrence of the archetypes considered while revealing their personal and ideological nuances, variations, and reformulations.

Another reason for my choice is the stature of each author. Though their autobiographies may be of differing literary value, all three are now generally recognized as figures who represent the religious sensibility of their time. And because archetypes *are* subject to historical, cultural, and individual variations, this is important. It goes without saying that Augustine is a major literary and religious figure, embodying the intellectual preoccupations of his period in his indebtedness to classical thought and his seminal influence on nascent Catholic Christianity. Though *Grace Abounding* is in every way a lesser work than the *Confessions*, it is superbly representative of seventeenth-century religious autobiography. And *The Pilgrim's Progress,* which has been shown to be an allegorical reworking of the autobiography, firmly establishes Bunyan as a major literary and religious figure. Since Merton belongs to the modern world, his writings have not yet endured the test of subsequent generations. But his immense popularity surely indicates that his experience is in some important way typical—if not in the answers he gives to the problems of the religious life today, at least in the questions he raises.

The spiritual autobiographies of Augustine, Bunyan, and Merton are useful examples of the archetypal patterns analyzed in this book because they are such extraordinarily rich and comprehensive works. But to stress this complex archetypal texture seems to imply that the three works here suggested as instantiations of a particular archetypal pattern themselves constitute that pattern. The reader will inevitably wonder if these are the only examples or if the archetypes I have traced occur in other spiritual autobiographies as well. I believe they do. As examples one could cite the Renaissance autobiographies of the Spanish St. Teresa (1562) and the English Richard Norwood (1639), or the modern spiritual autobiographies of Dorothy Day (1952) and Malcolm X (1964).[1] A comprehensive examination of autobiographies of conversion such as these would both confirm the recurrence of religious archetypes and show how different parts of the total configuration are emphasized by different individuals and in different historical eras. But an adequate demonstration of this lies outside the purview of this book. A major drawback of archetypal criticism is that, if it is used mechanically or carelessly, the artistic uniqueness of the work one seeks to understand is destroyed. Archetypes are by their very nature universalizing, but what must be preserved in the critical appraisal of an autobiographical life is, in James's words, "that unsharable feeling which each one of us has of the pinch of his individual destiny as he privately feels it rolling out on fortune's wheel."[2] In my commentaries I have tried to embody this "pinch"—the uniqueness of each individual life—but the only way I have been able to do so is to discuss each work at length. It is my hope that readers may be encouraged to test the assumptions of this study by using other works—and not just religious autobiographies but any narrative that describes critical turning points in an individual's life. And possibly, too, the archetypal patterns discussed here in relation to autobiography may be relevant in understanding the kind of experience itself that informs such narratives.

Not many of us will undergo the kind of conversion described by any of these three writers; indeed, most of us will probably never experience a religious conversion. However, we are all likely to pass through some sort of personal crisis that will bring about a radical change. One reason is serious or chronic illness—an experience that has produced its own body of autobiographical narratives. The authors of these books often lament that in the modern world there seems to be no broadly applicable model, no network of myths and practices within which such experiences of radical discontinuity can be endured and integrated into the ongoing personality. But the problem may be not the absence of models or precedents but the fact that we are unaware of them. Perhaps human problems remain similar, or even the same, while the language in which we describe them and the methods for dealing with them change.

What I am suggesting is that the paradigms of a religious conversion might prove helpful in understanding other kinds of drastic change or radical discontinuity. Even though we may not be Catholic like Merton or Puritan like Bunyan, even though we may not be religious at all, there is something deeply affecting about these anguished stories of searching, failing, and finally discovering something that makes it all worth while. What is human in them speaks to what is human in us. The idea of life as an arduous journey, the sense of the divided self, the ways in which other people take on deep, symbolic roles for us at certain times—these are archetypes of action and figure that enact as they represent our yearnings, our guilt, our feelings of relatedness, our sense of purpose. It is these feelings that are the raw materials of a conversion experience, but they are also the substance of any kind of personal change.

We have seen how spiritual autobiographies have often functioned for their readers as mirrors or maps of the inner life. It is possible that they could perform a similar function for the modern reader: the relevance of these books today may depend not so much on their religious content as on the highly patterned way in which they describe personal change. Indeed, experience always seems more comprehensible, and even more meaningful, when it is perceived as a patterned and organized process. Of course, I recognize that there are many differences between religious conversion and other experiences of change, but what I am concerned with here is the ways in which they are alike. Conversion, whether *crisis* or *lysis*, can be thought of as a process that brings about a radically different sense of the self as it restores a "right" relationship between the self and its God. Similarly, in "conversionlike" experiences, what is changed is both the relationship to one's self and one's relationship to the other—whether that "other" is conceived of as God or as the external world. Perhaps it is significant that all three of the authors discussed here go on to write larger, more "global" works after their autobiographies—Augustine, the *City of God;* Bunyan, *The Pilgrim's Progress;* and Merton, the later political and meditative writings that are just now achieving recognition. It may well be that in the process of reordering the world within, one is led to discover, or create, an orderly world without.

Notes

Chapter 1. Introduction

1. For a similar attitude toward autobiographies that describe conversion, see H. Porter Abbott, "Organic Form in the Autobiography of a Convert: The Example of Malcolm X," *College Language Association Journal* 23, no. 2 (December 1979): 125–46. Abbott observes that there is a subgenre of autobiography "of which Augustine's is again the prototype and perhaps greatest example [which] derives its organic cohesiveness directly from the author's experience of conversion. It thus has a uniquely organic character all its own which can be contrasted to other life narratives" (p. 126). Abbott is convinced that this "organic form" that is special to conversion autobiographies arises not from the autobiographical process but from "the character of the conversion" and "the spontaneous operation of the mind itself" (pp. 138, 128).

2. Carl Jung distinguishes between the archetype proper, which is by definition unconscious and unknowable, and the archetypal idea, the images that occur in consciousness and in works of art (see "Archetypes of the Collective Unconscious," in *The Archetypes and the Collective Unconscious*, in *Collected Works*, trans. R. F. C. Hull, Bollingen Series 20, 2d ed., vol. 9, pt. 1 [Princeton, N.J.: Princeton University Press, 1969], pp. 3–5). The archetype itself, he observes, is the psychobiological manifestation of instinct, and is therein similar to "the biological conception of the 'pattern of behavior'" ("On the Nature of the Psyche," in *The Structure and Dynamics of the Psyche*, in *Collected Works*, trans. R. F. C. Hull, Bollingen Series 20, 2d ed., vol. 8 [Princeton, N.J.: Princeton University Press, 1969], pp. 200–201). The archetypal idea, on the other hand, represents a conscious manifestation of archetype—one that is modified by the vagaries of the individual psyche and the particular configurations of a given culture.

The distinction between archetype and archetypal idea would seem to be important, yet it is one that Jung himself frequently ignores. Indeed, if Jung were to conform strictly to his own terminology, he would use the term *archetypal image* or *archetypal idea* throughout, since *archetype proper* is unconscious and unknowable. But Jung's interest is less in definition than in description. Given this inclination, his terminology tends to proliferate, so that in the end, *archetype*, *archetypal idea, archaic mode* or *image, symbol, pattern,* and *organizing dominant* are used more or less indiscriminately to refer to the same thing.

3. Jung, "Archetypes of the Collective Unconscious," p. 4.

4. Jung, "Psychological Aspects of the Mother Archetype," p. 75.

5. Jung, "Psychological Commentary on *The Tibetan Book of the Dead,*" in *Psychology and Religion: West and East,* in *Collected Works,* trans. R. F. C. Hull, Bollingen Series 20, 2d ed., vol. 11 (Princeton, N.J.: Princeton University Press, 1969), pp. 517–18.

6. Jung, "Instinct and the Unconscious," in *The Structure and Dynamics of the Psyche,* p. 137; idem, "Psychological Commentary on *The Tibetan Book of the Dead,*" p. 517; idem, *Psychology and Religion* (New Haven, Conn.: Yale University Press, 1938), p. 63; Jung's preface to *Psyche and Symbol,* ed. Violet S. de Laszlo (New York: Doubleday, 1958), p. xvi.

7. Joseph Havens, observing that the assumptions of modern psychology are materialistic, whereas the nature of God extends beyond the parameters of the material and visible world, concludes that "a satisfactory closure integrating the psychological and the theological perspectives cannot be achieved" ("Notes on Augustine's *Confessions,*" *Journal for the Scientific Study of Religion* 5, no. 1 [Fall 1965]: 141–43). I think that Havens is right. But I do not mean here to reduce religious truth to psychological categories, only to point to an analogy between them. Moreover, to refer to such an analogy seems justifiable in view of the fact that Jung was attempting to find a set of concepts and a vocabulary that would integrate psychology and religion.

8. Thomas Merton, *The Seven Storey Mountain* (New York: Harcourt Brace & Co., 1948), p. 255. All further references will be to this edition and cited within the text. When abbreviated, the book will be referred to as *SSM.*

9. Augustine, *The Confessions,* trans. William Watts, rev. W. H. D. Rouse, The Loeb Classical Library, 2 vols. (London: William Heinemann, 1977), 10.5 and 13.13–16. When abbreviated, *The Confessions* will be referred to as *Conf.* For the most part I have used Watts's translation; where it seemed appropriate, I have substituted my own.

10. Quoted on the back cover of the Signet edition of *The Seven Storey Mountain* (New York: Harcourt, Brace & Co., 1948).

11. Sigmund Freud, "The Question of a Weltanschauung," in *New Introductory Lectures on Psychoanalysis,* trans. James Strachey (New York: Norton, 1965), p. 167.

12. Carl Jung, "The Origins of the Hero," in *Symbols of Transformation,* in *Collected Works,* trans. R. F. C. Hull, Bollingen Series 20, 2d ed., vol. 5 (Princeton, N.J.: Princeton University Press, 1956), esp. p. 204.

13. Erik Erikson, *Young Man Luther,* Austen Riggs Monograph no. 4 (New York: W. W. Norton & Co., 1962), p. 255.

14. Paul W. Pruyser, *A Dynamic Psychology of Religion* (New York: Harper & Row, 1976), p. 7.

15. Heije Faber, *Psychology of Religion,* trans. Margaret Kohl (London: SCM Press, 1976), pp. 320–21.

16. D. W. Winnicott, "Transitional Objects and Transitional Phenomena," in *Collected Papers* (London: Tavistock Publications, 1958), p. 230.

17. Plato, *The Republic,* trans. Francis MacDonald Cornford (New York: Oxford University Press, 1945), p. 232.

18. William James, *The Varieties of Religious Experience* (New York: Long-

mans, Green & Co., 1902), p. 189. My reader may question why I rely here (and elsewhere) so heavily on James's study of conversion. I do so because I believe *The Varieties* still to be the best study of conversion available. Arthur Darby Nock's *Conversion* (London: Oxford University Press, 1933) is a standard authority, but this book really deals with conversion in its classical and early Christian forms. Sante de Sanctis's *Religious Conversion*, trans. Helen Augur (New York: Harcourt, Brace & Co., 1927) is often cited, as is James H. Leuba's *A Psychological Study of Religion* (New York: Macmillan, 1912), Francis Strickland's *The Psychology of Religious Experience* (New York: The Abington Press, 1924), J. B. Pratt's *The Religious Consciousness* (New York: Macmillan, 1920), R. H. Thouless's *An Introduction to the Psychology of Religion* (New York: Macmillan, 1924), and George A. Coe's *The Psychology of Religion* (Chicago: University of Chicago Press, 1916). But these books are for the most part variants on the studies of James and E. D. Starbuck's *The Psychology of Religion* (London: W. Scott, 1903). In addition, all were written before 1930.

More recent studies of conversion are limited by the narrowness of their particular academic biases. Thus the psychiatrist A. R. Christensen views conversion from the standpoint of the psychology of adolescence, using as the basis for his data the conversion experience of ministers with psychiatric disorders ("Religious Conversion," *Archives of General Psychiatry* 9 [September 1963]: 207–16); William Sargant discusses conversion in terms of the physiology of abnormal mental states (*Battle for the Mind* [New York: Harper and Row, 1957]); G. Sedman and G. Hopkinson discuss psychiatric cases where religious conversion provides the content of the psychopathology ("The Psychopathology of Mystical and Religious Conversion Experiences in Psychiatric Patients," 1 and 2 *Confinia psychiatrica* 9, no. 1 [1966]: 1–19 and 9, no. 2 [1966]: 65–76); and the psychoanalyst Leon Salzman discusses conversion in terms of its traditional two categories. The psychiatric population upon which Salzman bases his study leads him to identify the sudden type (the *crisis* paradigm) as regressive and pathological—a "destructive, disintegrating process"—and the gradual model (the *lysis* pattern) as progressive, maturational, and a "constructive and integrating process" ("The Psychology of Religious and Ideological Conversion," *Psychiatry* 16 [1953]: 177–87). The problem with conversion studies based on psychiatric patients is precisely that they are based on individuals encountered in a therapeutic context, and their findings cannot readily be applied to the experiences of others.

For different reasons, the scholarship in the sociology of conversion is also problematic. Some recent studies in this field are of great interest in their description and explanation of contemporary conversion phenomena: e.g., James A. Beckford, "Accounting for Conversion," *British Journal of Sociology* 29 (1978): 249–62, and Robert Balch, "Looking behind the Scenes in a Religious Cult: Implications for the Study of Conversion," *Sociological Analysis* 41 (1980): 137–43. John Lofland and Norman Skonovd attempt to classify six major kinds of "conversion careers" or "conversion types"—the intellectual, mystical, experimental, affectional, revivalist, and coercive—and then discuss the "social psychological and social organizational implications" of those motifs ("Conversion Motifs," *Journal for the Scientific Study of Religion* 20, no. 4 [December 1981]: 373–85). Rodney Stark feels that he is writing in the tradition of William James in his attempt to categorize religious experience using data gathered from a sample of Protestant and Roman Catholic church members ("A Taxonomy of Religious Experience," *Journal for the Scientific Study of Religion* 5, no. 1 [October 1965]:

97–116). But these studies, however interesting, do not shed much light on the architectonics of the conversion process, and the conclusions that their authors reach are not very useful in explaining or describing conversion in literature. Another approach is that of C. Daniel Batson and W. Larry Ventis, who use insights from the literature on the psychology of creativity in an attempt to better understand conversion phenomena. But this study, though thorough and insightful, fails to come to terms with the experienced reality of the divine in conversion (*The Religious Experience: A Social-Psychological Perspective* [New York: Oxford University Press, 1982]).

19. For example, Sante de Sanctis calls the two types of conversion the "fulminant or lightning type, and the progressive type." He also observes that "Starbuck's classification of conversion into the impulsive and the volitional types is a mere paraphrasing of the classic division" (*Religious Conversion*, p. 52).

20. James, *The Varieties*, p. 183.

21. Ibid., pp. 206–10. In the second of these two quotations, James is quoting Starbuck.

22. James does not actually write that Augustine's conversion is an example of *crisis* conversion. The discussion of Augustine occurs in the chapter called "The Divided Self, and the Process of its Unification," which immediately precedes his discussion of the two forms of conversion. Though he was apparently unwilling to commit himself, it is my impression that James's description of *crisis* conversion fits Augustine's experience in almost every way. The exception that seems to have troubled James is not the period before Augustine's conversion, which was characterized by the gradual acquisition of Christian beliefs, but the Neoplatonism in the period directly after his conversion. It is interesting that in his text James writes about Augustine's experience in the garden as conforming to the paradigm of the *crisis* model, seeing it as an experience that "laid the inner storm to rest forever." But he corrects himself in a footnote, where he observes that "the crisis in the garden marked a definitive conversion from his former life, but it was to the neo-platonic spiritualism and only a halfway stage towards Christianity. The latter he appears not fully and radically to have embraced until four years more had passed" (pp. 171–72; James is here using an essay published in 1900 by Louis Gourdon).

23. Ibid., p. 210.

24. James Olney, "Autobiography and the Cultural Moment," in *Autobiography: Essays Theoretical and Critical*, ed. James Olney (Princeton, N.J.: Princeton University Press, 1980), p. 22.

25. Roy Pascal, *Design and Truth in Autobiography* (Cambridge, Mass.: Harvard University Press, 1960), pp. 19,11.

26. Dean Ebner, *Autobiography in Seventeenth-Century England* (The Hague: Mouton, 1971), p. 19; John Morris, *Versions of the Self* (New York: Basic Books, 1966), p. 11; James Olney, *Metaphors of Self* (Princeton, N.J.: Princeton University Press, 1972), p. 3. Olney's recent collection of essays on autobiographical criticism and theory manages to impose its own kind of order and pattern upon the "life history" of writings about autobiography.

27. Benjamin Franklin, *Autobiography*, ed. Russel B. Nye (Boston: Houghton Mifflin, 1958), p. 1.

28. Richard Norwood, *Journal* (New York: Published for the Bermuda historical monuments trust by Scholars' facsimiles & reprints, 1945), p. 3.

29. John S. Dunne, *A Search for God in Time and Memory* (New York: Macmillan, 1969), p. 2.
30. Augustine, *On Christian Doctrine*, trans. D. W. Robertson, The Library of Liberal Arts (Indianapolis, Ind.: Bobbs-Merrill, 1958), p. 10.
31. Stanley E. Fish, *Self-Consuming Artifacts* (Berkeley and Los Angeles: University of California Press, 1972), p. 23.
32. Augustine, *The City of God*, trans. and ed. Marcus Dods, 2 vols. (New York: Harper & Row, 1948), 1.10.14, p. 402.
33. Joseph Anthony Mazzeo, *Renaissance and Seventeenth-Century Studies* (New York: Columbia, 1964), p. 28.

Chapter 2. St. Augustine: The Heroic Paradigm

1. Dunne, *Search for God*, p. 46.
2. Robert J. O'Connell, *St. Augustine's Confessions: The Odyssey of Soul* (Cambridge, Mass.: Harvard University Press, 1969), p. 186.
3. St. Teresa, "Life," in *Complete Works*, trans. E. Allison Peers, 3 vols. (London: Sheed & Ward, 1957), 1: 56.
4. Quoted in Roy W. Battenhouse, "The Life of St. Augustine," in *A Companion to the Study of Augustine*, ed. Roy W. Battenhouse (New York: Oxford, 1955), p. 17.
5. Augustine's *peregrinatio* is a synthesizing word since it is fundamentally an ambiguous term, as O'Connell points out, that can mean either "wandering" or "pilgrimage," depending upon whether one is moving away from or toward God (*St. Augustine's Confessions*, p. 186).
6. Peter Brown, *Augustine of Hippo* (Berkeley & Los Angeles: University of California Press, 1967), p. 80.
7. Romano Guardini, *The Conversion of Augustine*, trans. Elinor Briefs (Westminster, Md.: Newman Press, 1960), p. xv.
8. See Robert J. O'Connell, *St. Augustine's Confessions* and *St. Augustine's Early Theory of Man, A.D. 386–391* (Cambridge, Mass.: Harvard University Press, 1968); also "*Ennead* VI. 4 and 5 in the Works of St. Augustine," *Revue des Études Augustiniennes* 9 (1963): 1–39 and "The *Enneads* and St. Augustine's Image of Happiness," *Vigilae Christianae* 17 (1964): 129–64; and "The Riddle of Augustine's *Confessions*: A Plotinian Key," *International Philosophical Quarterly* 4 (1964): 327–72; Eugene TeSelle, *Augustine the Theologian* (New York: Herder and Herder, 1970). As to the influence of Porphyry, see John J. O'Meara, *The Young Augustine* (London: Longmans, 1954) and articles.
9. O'Connell seems to be aware of this, crediting O'Meara in his observation that the "odyssey image" is "an ancient-world commonplace for the 'wandering soul'" (*St. Augustine's Confessions*, p. 12; also *St. Augustine's Early Theory*, p. 73). But O'Connell then goes on to write that this is a concept "familiar to Augustine from *Ennead* I.6"—thus reducing everything to a Plotinian source *(St. Augustine's Confessions*, p. 6). It seems surprising that O'Connell does not take the next step, which is to see the "odyssey image" in that poem so dear to Augustine, Vergil's *Aeneid.*
10. Brown, *Augustine of Hippo*, pp. 97–98; 168–69.

11. TeSelle, *Augustine the Theologian*, p. 70.
12. *Ennead* 4.3, paraphrased in ibid., p. 70. I have used TeSelle here because his translation of this particular passage seems superior to MacKenna's.
13. Leo Ferrari makes the interesting observation that such words as *lust*, *adultery*, and *harlotry* throughout Augustine's writings often "lose their primary sexual connotations and are used merely to signify the attitude of the soul to God." For Ferrari, the autobiographical analogy with the parable would thus refer far more to Augustine's lengthy infatuation with Manichaeism than to any sexual licentiousness ("The Theme of the Prodigal Son in Augustine's *Confessions*," *Recherches Augustiniennes* 12 [1977]: 112–13).
14. Domenico Comparetti observes that "the hidden meanings which both [pagan and Christian] discovered in Vergil were of a purely ethical and philosophical character, dealing generally with the vicissitudes of human life in its aspirations towards perfection." For example, not long after Augustine, Fulgentius allegorized the *Aeneid* in detail as tracing the life of the soul from the storms of birth (i.e., the shipwreck in book 1, with Juno as the goddess of birth) through childhood (books 2 and 3) and adolescence (book 4, Dido) to maturity and wisdom in the descent to the Underworld (book 6) (*Vergil in the Middle Ages*, trans. E. F. M. Benecke [London: Allen & Unwin, 1966], p. 107). But it is difficult to document precisely the kind of allegorical commentary on the *Aeneid* that was being written prior to and at the same time as the *Confessions*. For, as Comparetti observes, the commentaries that are still extant have been altered by the multitudes of generations that used them: "All have been condensed or rearranged or interpolated from various sources; none has remained in its original form" (pp. 55–56).

Harald Hagendahl observes that Vergil was for the Latin-speaking peoples the equivalent of what Homer was for the Greek world—the *"poeta doctissimus,"* the embodier of learning in all fields, the undisputed authority. Thus from Vergil, as Hagendahl shows, Augustine would have learned "not only correct grammar, literary vocabulary and oratorical art, but also mythology, history, philosophy, even science." Moreover, he would also have received training "in interpreting the poet . . . and exercised [himself] on themes taken from him" (*Augustine and the Latin Classics*, Studia Graeca et Latina Gothoburgensia 20, 2 vols. [Göteborg: University of Göteborg, 1967], 2: 384).

15. Hagendahl shows that Augustine's use and appreciation of pagan authors fluctuates in a wavelike pattern. The wave of classical allusions and quotations is high in the Cassiciacum dialogues and highest in *The City of God*. It falls in the literary works written between 388 and 413, and reaches its lowest ebb in the *Confessions:* "Hardly any work by a Christian writer since Tertullian breathes such a deep-seated hostility to the old cultural tradition as this manifesto of fanatical religiosity" (p. 715). The hostile tone of the *Confessions* reflects the extreme negative side of Augustine's ambivalence toward the classical tradition; the positive side is expressed in other ways.

16. Hagendahl, *Augustine and The Latin Classics*, p. 430.

17. But it must be acknowledged that there exists a complex background of ambivalence, confusion, and contradiction in the minds of Augustine and his contemporaries about the relation between classical and Christian thought. Whatever resonances one might sense between the *Confessions* and the *Aeneid*, one must deal with the fact that the mature Augustine quite consciously and conscientiously tries to abandon his background in classical literature—on the philosoph-

ical ground that it is basically irrelevant to Christian faith, and on the moral ground that it represents a chapter out of the sins of his youth. It is also true that the ambivalence that Christian apologists felt toward pagan philosophy was even more marked toward pagan literature. In the *Confessions,* Augustine expresses this ambivalence in his reference to the *Aeneid* as "a most delightful spectacle of vanity" (1.13).

Augustine's ambivalence as to how to deal with classical poetry permeates his writings. On the one hand, he more than once explicitly repudiates pagan literature as a proper subject of study (or mention) for the Christian; for example, in *Contra Adimantum* (394, quoted in Hagendahl, *Augustine and The Latin Classics,* 2, p. 424) he sets forth the principle that classical authors merit attention only in matters of language and phraseology—"*de verbo, non de re.*" And Augustine's treatment of Vergil in the *City of God* is emphatically ambivalent. He introduces him as "*poeta magnus omniumque praeclarissimus atque optimus*" and yet throughout Vergil is treated as the champion of pagan Rome—the same Rome that Augustine identifies as *civitas terrena* (Hagendahl, ibid., 2: 455–57; Hagendahl is quoting *Contra Academicos* 4.9). On the other hand, in his argument for "Egyptian gold" in *De Doctrina,* Augustine is adopting a completely contradictory principle to the "*de verbo, non de re*" laid down in *Contra Adimantum.* This argument exhorts the Christian apologist to sever himself in spirit from "their miserable society" but to take their treasure (i.e., whatever pagan ideas or institutions are thought to be suitable for Christian assimilation) with him "for the just use of teaching the gospel" (*De Doctrina,* p. 75).

18. Hagendahl, *Augustine and the Latin Classics,* 2: 715.

19. Perhaps it is significant, as E. R. Dodds points out, that for the ancient Romans Carthage was called *Carthago Veneris*—"the city of Our Lady of Love" ("Augustine's *Confessions*: A Study of Spiritual Maladjustment," *The Hibbert Journal* 26 [October 1927–July 1928]: 464).

20. Cicero, *De Inventione,* trans. H. M. Hubbell, The Loeb Classical Library (London: William Heinemann, 1949), 2.53. 161, p. 329.

21. Athanasius, in his *Life of Antony* (which Augustine refers to in the *Confessions*), "intended to oppose the Christian saint who works his way to God with the help of God to the pagan philosopher who is practically a God himself. By imparting a mortal blow to the ideal of the pagan philosopher, he managed to produce an ideal type which became extremely popular among ordinary Christians" (Arnaldo Momigliano, "Paganism and Christian Historiography in the Fourth Century A.D.," in *The Conflict Between Paganism and Christianity in the Fourth Century,* ed. A. Momigliano [Oxford: The Clarendon Press, 1963], p. 98).

22. The *Aeneid* might be called an "epic of return" since Aeneas's Rome is treated as a new Troy—both from the point of view of the hero, who is seeking to reestablish the city he has lost, and also from the point of view of the author, who constantly recalls incidents and motifs from the fighting around Troy in the *Iliad* as he writes about the battles around Latium in the last six books. Behind the first six books is, of course, the *Odyssey,* the archetypal epic of return.

23. Leo Ferrari, "The Arboreal Polarisation in Augustine's *Confessions,*" *Revue des Études Augustiniennes* 25 (1979): 43.

24. Brown, *Augustine of Hippo,* pp. 151–52. Quotations are taken from *de lib. arb.* 2.16.41.

25. Norwood, *Journal,* pp. 67, 60.

26. St. Teresa, "Life," p. 56.

27. James, *The Varieties*, p. 217.
28. B. R. Rees, "The Conversion of St. Augustine," *Trivium* 14 (1979): 13.
29. It is this kind of thinking that governs H. Porter Abbott in his comparison of the conversions of Augustine and Malcolm X: "Perhaps the most striking difference . . . is that whereas Augustine's is the final step in a causal series, Malcolm's is a sudden blinding illumination. . . . Augustine has already undergone a mental ascent which has brought him to the final logic of his conversion. Malcolm, in contrast, undergoes an absolute transformation from ignorance to enlightenment within the space of a few months." ("Example of Malcolm X," pp. 137–38). It is interesting here that Abbott sees Malcolm's, not Augustine's experience in terms of the paradigmatic *crisis* conversion.
30. James, *The Varieties*, pp. 242, 230.
31. Nock, *Conversion*, p. 266.
32. Mircea Eliade, *Rites and Symbols of Initiation*, trans. Willard R. Trask (New York: Harper & Row, 1958), p. 128.
33. See Georg Misch, who observes that the early conversion narratives were based on the Socratic "conversion" to philosophy, as described by Plato in his *Apology*. Thus Dio Chrysostom in the first century and Lucian in the second century recount their typical conversions from rhetoric to philosophy in the Platonic mode. There follows a whole series of autobiographies whose authors describe their conversion to Christianity in the same way as the pagan rhetorician would tell of his conversion to philosophy. In all spiritual autobiographies of this kind, the progress from Neoplatonism to Christianity was a central motif, and was presented as a stage in the quest for truth. (*A History of Autobiography in Antiquity*, trans. E. W. Dickes, 2 vols. [London: Routledge and Kegan Paul, 1950], 1:488–89).

Furthermore, it was Simplicianus, to whom Augustine went for spiritual guidance, who helped Augustine harmonize Christianity with Platonism: "In the Platonists, [Simplicianus said] God and his word are everywhere implied" (*Conf.* 8.2).

34. Brown, *Augustine of Hippo*, p. 69.
35. Ibid., p. 169. As L. J. Daly observes, "emotional impact becomes the criterion of crisis" ("Psychohistory and St. Augustine's Conversion Process," *Augustiniana* 28 [1978]: 231).
36. Ferrari comments at length on the significance of the two trees in "The Arboreal Polarisation in Augustine's *Confessions*" and also in "The Pear-Theft in Augustine's *Confessions*," *Revue des Études Augustiniennes* 16 (1970): 233–42. The fig tree may also represent the fig tree that Christ curses because it bears no fruit; here, it does. Moreover that the tree under which Augustine is converted is a fig tree most certainly reflects the Manichaean myth of the fig tree, which Augustine discusses in 3.10.
37. Augustine's famous story of his conversion in the garden appears to be not at all unique. St. Cyprian's description of his conversion, for example, is remarkably similar to that of Augustine, though he would seem to be describing a ritual rebirth by baptism: "And immediately, in a wonderful way I saw certitude take the place of doubt. The doors that had been shut opened, and light shone in the darkness" (*Ad Donatum*, iii–iv, in Jules Lebreton and Jacques Zeiller, *The History of the Primitive Church*, trans. Ernest C. Messenger, 2 vols. [New York: Macmillan, 1949], 2:844).

38. James, *The Varieties*, pp. 214–15. The terms *self-surrender* and *new determination* are Starbuck's.

39. Although scholars have regularly tended to view conversion as belonging to one or the other of the two conventional categories—the gradual and the abrupt—the difference may well be one that is paradigmatic rather than literally real. As Sante de Sanctis points out: "A conversion may certainly appear sudden and fulminant, but upon serious reflection it will be evident that the suddenness—if any—is only the perception of the significance, the realization of one's destiny . . ." (p. 82). Alfred Underwood also recognizes the limitation of the *crisis/lysis* classification: "At one time two main types [of conversion] were thought of—the gradual and the sudden. Then it was discovered that sudden conversions were sudden in appearance only; the abrupt breakthrough to the new life being the sudden irruption of forces that had long since been maturing in the subconscious" (*Conversion: Christian and Non-Christian* [London: Allen & Unwin, 1925], p. 143).

40. Dunne, *Search for God*, p. 47.

41. Brown, *Augustine of Hippo*, p. 115.

42. Charles Kligerman, M.D., "A Psychoanalytic Study of the *Confessions* of St. Augustine," *Journal of the American Psychoanalytical Association* 5, no. 3 (July 1957): 484. See also James Dittes, "Continuities between the Life and Thought of Augustine," *Journal for the Scientific Study of Religion* 5, no. 1 (Fall 1965): 130–40.

43. Pascal, *Design and Truth*, p. 72.

44. William C. Spengemann, *The Forms of Autobiography* (New Haven, Conn.: Yale University Press, 1980), p. 15.

45. "Matter" reaches its apotheosis in the "Heaven of Heavens"—the *"caelum caeli"*—an "intellectual creature" that "partakes in thy eternity" (*Conf.* 12.9) and precedes the creation of time, being "the rational, intellectual mind of that chaste city of thine, our mother which is above, and is free, and eternal in the heavens . . ." (12.15).

Chapter 3. St. Augustine: Archetypes of Family

1. O'Connell discusses this theme at length in his chapter, *"Fovisti Caput Nescientis,"* in *St. Augustine's Early Theory of Man*.

2. George P. Lawless points out that the theme of "rest" is structurally represented in the *Confessions* in three crucially placed passages: *"donec requiescat in te"* (1.1), *"et tu solus requies"* (6.16), and *"requiescamus in te"* (12.36). "These three passages," he writes, "point to the artistic and theological unity of the *Confessions*. Present time is contrasted with future time in terms of work and rest" ("Interior Peace in the *Confessions* of St. Augustine," *Revue des Études Augustiniennes* 26 [1980]: 59).

3. Jung, "Psychological Aspects of the Mother Archetype," in *Archetypes and the Collective Unconscious*, p. 92.

4. Ibid.

5. Jung, "The Syzygy: Anima and Animus," in *Aion, Collected Works*, trans. R. F. C. Hull, Bollingen Series 20, vol. 9, pt. 2 (Princeton, N.J.: Princeton University Press, 1959), pp. 11, 13.

6. See also Proverbs 5:3–8 on "the strange woman." *Sapientia* and *meretrix* are vividly described in Proverbs 7:7–27 and Proverbs 8 in their parallel roles as crying out to Man for his allegiance. Also see Ferrari, who observes that *meretrix* for Augustine was allegorized as *superstitiones,* and thus an appropriate opposition to *sapientia* ("The Theme of the Prodigal Son," p. 113).

7. Note the imagery in Proverbs 8:30: "Then I [Wisdom] was by him, as one brought up with him" and "I was daily his delight, rejoicing always before him. . . ." Compare this with the imagery in *Confessions* 12.16: "Jerusalem my country, Jerusalem my mother; and thyself that ruleth over it, the Enlightener, the Father, the Guardian, the Husband, the chaste and strong Delight, the solid joy of it. . . ." Note also Wisdom of Solomon (Apoc.) 8:2–3: "I loved her [Wisdom], and sought her out from my youth, I desired to make her my spouse, and I was a lover of her beauty. In that she is conversant with God, she magnifieth her nobility: yea, the Lord of all things himself loved her."

8. *Ep.* 243; in Brown, *Augustine of Hippo,* p. 63.

9. Kligerman sees Augustine as preoccupied with the story of Dido and Aeneas, which he had had to memorize as a child, because it "contains the nuclear conflict of Augustine's infantile neurosis and played a most decisive role in his subsequent career" (p. 472). Here, he remarks, is the infantile sexuality that had been omitted from the narrative of his early years. Augustine identifies himself with Aeneas and his mother with Dido, and "the bitter tears he shed in childhood for poor slain Dido were the tears of rage, frustration and guilt he felt toward his mother" ("A Psychoanalytic Study," p. 479).

10. It is no accident that Venus first appears to her son as a beautiful maiden, garbed like a huntress, as Dido will be in the cave episode. Aeneas mistakes his mother for Diana—ironically, considering her present purpose—and it is to Diana that Vergil compares Dido at her first appearance later in the same book. But Dido is not just an alluring temptress for Aeneas; she is also a motherly figure for him. The widowed queen who offers Aeneas welcome and safety, who feasts and pities him, seems as maternally protective as Venus herself.

11. Vergil, *The Aeneid,* trans. Allen Mandelbaum (New York: Bantam, 1971), bk. 4 109–12, p. 84.

12. Brown, *Augustine of Hippo,* p. 29.

13. It may be impossible to overstate this point, but it is certainly possible to distort it. Not surprisingly, Augustine's representation of his mother in the *Confessions* has served as the basis for a number of psychoanalytic interpretations of a Freudian persuasion. As L. J. Daly observes in an article on Augustine's conversion, which is itself a superb critique of psychoanalytic and historical methods alike, "The deleterious impact of Monica on Augustine's personality from nursery through episcopacy is the idée fixe of psychoanalytic interpretations of his conversion process" (p. 245). Though psychoanalytic studies of the *Confessions* may contribute valuable insights, they are often severely limited by the tendency to see Augustine's life and thought as governed by an unresolved Oedipal situation, and by the unquestioned (and unfounded) assumption that religious phenomena can simply be reduced to the category of the sexual. For Kligerman, Augustine's conversion is the result of "an identification with the mother and a passive feminine attitude to the father displaced to God" ("A Psychoanalytic Study," p. 483) and for Dittes, Augustine's conversion represents a simultaneous surrender to his mother and abandonment of masculine sexuality ("Continuities," p. 139). What these interpretations fail to recognize is that Augustine's abandon-

ment of sexuality is both functional and teleological in the religious framework within which it is grounded. By failing to acknowledge the reality, at least to Augustine, of this religious framework, such interpretations inevitably distort both the autobiography and the experience upon which it is based. And even the vocabulary is wrong: Augustine neither "repressed" nor "suppressed" his sexuality; he renounced it, and moreover did so in order to get something that he believed would offer him deeper pleasure and more complete satisfaction.

It would seem that the archetypal approach is here superior to the Freudian; first, because it assumes an underlying dualism of natural (sexual) and spiritual realities rather than a monism that reduces the spiritual to the sexual; and second, because its quasi-allegorical method is closer to Augustine's own system of thought.

14. Thus Augustine writes of the quest for wisdom, awakened in him by Cicero's *Hortensius*, as a desire that left him free "to love, and seek, and obtain, and hold, and embrace wisdom itself . . ." (3.4). These words will be echoed in Augustine's several visionary apprehensions of God, who is identified with wisdom later on in the book (9.10).

15. O'Connell, *Early Theory*, chap. 8, "Vision"; Teselle, *Augustine the Theologian*, p. 67.

16. Jung, "The Phenomenology of the Spirit in Fairytales," in *Archetypes and the Collective Unconscious*, pp. 217–18. Jung writes that "the psychic manifestations of the spirit indicate at once that they are of an archetypal nature—in other words, the phenomenon we call spirit depends on the existence of an autonomous primordial image which is universally present in the preconscious makeup of the human psyche. . . . It struck me that a certain kind of father-complex has a 'spiritual' character. . . . Mostly, therefore, it is the figure of a 'wise old man' who symbolizes the spiritual factor" (pp. 214–15).

17. The fact that Augustine remembers himself to have been so deeply affected by this story that it serves as a link in his own conversion (a narrative link, at least, for it is at the beginning of the same chapter in which he describes his conversion) may well indicate a wish rather than a reality—an autobiographical emendation of actual events to make them conform to what he wished had happened. On the basis of works written just after his conversion, it has been pointed out by many that there is a discrepancy between the way Augustine "really" professed his Christianity and the description he gives in the *Confessions*. And indeed, there is some ambiguity as to the way in which Augustine made known his newly acquired Christianity. In several of the works written after his conversion he indicates that he resigned his post as teacher of rhetoric because of a *dolor pectoris*, and with the intention of pursuing the study of philosophy; in the *Confessions*, very little is made of the *dolor pectoris*, and nothing of the intent to study philosophy. About this B. R. Rees observes: "He consciously glossed over this, the true reason for his resignation, in order to throw into greater prominence the transformation brought about by his religious conversion" ("The Conversion of St. Augustine," p. 6). Rees is probably right, though there is no indication that this was a "conscious" distortion of the truth, as Rees implies. Again, it is not the literal truth of Augustine's description of these events that is here important; what does matter is the way in which he revises and edits this part of his life to present a truth that is paradigmatic, rather than literally real.

18. Jung, "The Phenomenology of the Spirit in Fairy-Tales," in *The Archetypes and the Collective Unconscious*, p. 215.

19. Carl Jung and Carl Kerényi, "The Psychology of the Child Archetype," in *Essays in a Science of Mythology*, trans. R. F. C. Hull, Bollingen Series 22, 2d ed. (Princeton, N.J.: Princeton University Press, 1969), p. 83.
20. Ibid., p. 82.

Chapter 4. John Bunyan: The Conflictive Paradigm

1. G. A. Starr, *Defoe and Spiritual Autobiography* (Princeton, N.J.: Princeton University Press, 1965), p. 13.
2. William York Tindall, *John Bunyan, Mechanick Preacher* (New York: Columbia University Press, 1934), p. 39; quoting Bunyan's *Building, Nature, Excellency of the House of God*, 2:582.
3. Starr, *Defoe and Spiritual Autobiography*, p. 14; quoting from *The Memoirs of the Rev. Thomas Halyburton*.
4. Henri Talon, *John Bunyan, the Man and his Works*, trans. Barbara Wall (London: Rockliff Publ. Co., Ltd., 1951), p. 26.
5. John Bunyan, *Grace According to the Chief of Sinners*, ed. Roger Sharrock (Oxford: The Clarendon Press, 1962), p. 41. All subsequent references to *Grace Abounding to the Chief of Sinners* will be to this edition and cited within the text. The full title will be shortened to *Grace Abounding* and abbreviated as *GA*.
6. "I will confess that which I know about myself and also that which I know not . . ." (*Conf.* 10.5).
7. The depth psychologist might see the unacceptable self and its personification in the "Tempter" as the archetype of the shadow.
8. Jung uses these terms most often in describing the function and characteristics of anima and animus: "The animus corresponds to the paternal Logos just as the anima corresponds to the maternal Eros" ("The Syzygy: Anima and Animus," in *Aion*, p. 14). Paul Pruyser's notion of "attitudinal transference"—the idea "that belief and unbelief are embedded in, and ideational portrayals of, our actual human object relations"—is most relevant here. The terms *eros* and *logos*, which I have been using to refer to modes of relating to God, can be seen as analogous to concepts in psychoanalytic object-relations theory, *eros* being the anaclitic position, emphasizing blissful union with the mother, and *logos* being what Freud calls the narcissistic position, where union with the love object is achieved by identification. Pruyser, following Michael Balint, sees this second position as one either of idealization of the love object and self-abasement of the subject, or of humiliation of the love object and idealization of the subject (*A Dynamic Psychology of Religion*, pp. 223–24). Both Freud's original idea of this second form of object-choice and Balint's adaptation of it are descriptive of the psychodynamic of *logos* as it is manifested in Bunyan's autobiography.
9. William Haller, *The Rise of Puritanism* (New York: Harper, 1975), p. 88.
10. Géza Róheim, *The Origin and Function of Culture*, Nervous and Mental Disease Monographs 69 (1943; reprint, New York: Johnson Reprint Org., 1968), pp. 39, 38.
11. Jung, "Psychological Aspects of the Mother Archetype," in *Archetypes and the Collective Unconscious*, p. 96.
12. See Joseph Campbell: "As the original intruder into the paradise of the infant with its mother, the father is the archetypal enemy; hence, throughout life all enemies are symbolical (to the unconscious) of the father" (*The Hero with a Thousand Faces* [New York: Meridian, 1956], p. 155).

13. John Dunne writes that "the mediation, whether spiritual or temporal, was mediation between man and God and thus between man and all reality, and all men in the Middle Ages could experience it, including the mediators themselves. Its breakdown, the breakdown of spiritual mediation in the Reformation and the breakdown of temporal mediation in the Revolution, meant a fundamental change in the structure of human life" (*Search for God*, pp. 75–76).

14. Norman O. Brown, *Life Against Death* (Middletown, Conn.: Wesleyan University Press, 1959), pp. 210–11.

15. I am here developing ideas formulated by N. O. Brown in his discussion of Luther: "The positive features in Luther are his diabolism and his eschatology. Actually the diabolism and the eschatology are two sides of the same coin. It would be psychically impossible for Luther to recognize the Devil's dominion over this world . . . without the faith that the Devil's dominion is doomed, and that the history of man on earth will end in the kingdom of God, when grace will be made visible"(Ibid., p. 217). I have substituted "predestinarian anxiety" for Brown's "eschatology" and have discussed it as a modality of disease and therapy. As "this world" is related to "that world" and the ambiguities of time to the clarities of eternity, so is predestinarian anxiety related to eschatological certainty. Indeed, it was Luther who translated the language of eschatology into that of psychology: "Hell, Purgatory and Heaven appear to differ as despair, near-despair, and security" (Thesis 16 of 95 Theses, *Heidelburg Disputations*, quoted in and translated by Dunne, *Search for God*, p. 79).

16. Róheim, *Origin and Function of Culture*, p. 83.

17. Haller, *Rise of Puritanism*, pp. 153–54.

18. Pascal, *Design and Truth in Autobiography*, p. 10.

19. M. Esther Harding, *Journey into Self* (London: Vision, 1958), p. 34. See also L. P. Lerner, who observes that "a confession of one's own weakness . . . is not incompatible with spiritual pride. Puritanism can glory in its own debasement, thanking God that its weaknesses and sinfulness are a sign of its superiority to others" ("Bunyan and the Puritan Culture," *Cambridge Journal* 7 [1954]: 239).

When Bunyan describes himself as "chief of sinners," he is sharing that title with such diverse Puritan saints as Oliver Cromwell, who wrote, "O, I lived in and loved darkness, and hated light; I was a chief, the chief of sinners," with Anna Trapnel, who likewise called herself the "chief of sinners" and with Sarah Wright, who is described in an edition of her life by Henry Jessey as a "chief of sinners." The Cromwell quotation is from Roger Sharrock, *John Bunyan* (London: Hutchinson's University Library, 1954), p. 59; the Trapnel and Wright/Jessey quotations are from Tindall, *John Bunyan, Mechanick Preacher*, pp. 30, 37.

20. Cf. Ebner, who observes that nearly everything Bunyan wrote deals with the psychology of conversion. He remarks that "this is especially true of *The Pilgrim's Progress, Grace Abounding, The Holy War, The Life and Death of Mr. Badman*. Whenever he put his pen to paper, the result was usually another version of the conflict which he had found within his own soul since he was nine years of age" (*Autobiography in Seventeenth-Century England*, p. 22). See also Roger Sharrock: "In [*The Pilgrim's Progress*] all the concrete and anthropomorphic hints of the autobiography are developed. . . . Christian's progress reflects each stage of Bunyan's spiritual history in its due order" ("Personal Vision and Puritan Tradition in Bunyan," *Hibbert Journal* 56 [1957]: 58) and "the narrative of his introspective pilgrimage through doubts and terrors is intimately linked with the allegorical treatment of the Christian life in *The Pilgrim's Progress*." (*Grace Abounding*, introduction, p. xxvi). See also Henri Talon, who writes: "The spiri-

tual development which is found in the autobiography, *Grace Abounding*, appears again in the allegory . . ." ("Space and the Hero in *The Pilgrim's Progress,*" *Etudes Anglaises* 14 [1961]: 124).

21. John Bunyan, *The Pilgrim's Progress*, ed. James Blanton Wharey, rev. Roger Sharrock, 2d ed. (Oxford: The Clarendon Press, 1960), p. 8.

22. Fish, *Self-Consuming Artifacts*, p. 32.

23. One might well at this point sense a contradiction between the idea of the static hero and the motif of forward-moving progress. But my point is precisely that the spiritual life of the seventeenth-century warrior-saint is represented as developing or progressing in terms of a particular metaphorical figure that has distinct formal or narrative limitations. Perhaps this is one important reason why *The Pilgrim's Progress*, the allegory based on the pilgrimage motif, has for generations been a major literary rendition of the Christian life, whereas *The Holy War*, the allegory based on the archetype of *psychomachia*, has never enjoyed this kind of popularity.

24. Jung, "The Battle for Deliverance from the Mother," in *Symbols of Transformation*, p. 286.

25. Almost always, the theology behind such autobiographies as *Grace Abounding* is discussed in relation to Calvin. And this seems appropriate, since the sectarian movement (of which Bunyan's autobiography is a product) was so strongly influenced by Calvinism through the return of the Genevan exiles when Elizabeth succeeded Mary Tudor. Richard Greaves, however, helpfully observes that Bunyan's theology is as much an amalgam of Luther as it is of Calvin: "[Bunyan's] foundation principles were basically Lutheran, but much of his theology was in full accord with the orthodox Calvinism of his period." Moreover, Greaves observes that "on this Lutheran foundation Bunyan built an essentially Calvinist superstructure with the ideas which he assimilated from the writings of Bayly and Dent, the teaching of Gifford and Burton, his ministerial association with men such as Owen, and his contact in general with the recurrent and often controversial discussion of basic Christian principles which absorbed the minds of so many in the seventeenth century" (*John Bunyan*, Courtenay Studies in Reformation Theology 2 [Grand Rapids, Mich.: Eerdmans, 1969], pp. 159, 156).

26. Norman Pettit, *The Heart Prepared: Grace and Conversion in Puritan Spiritual Life* (New Haven, Conn.: Yale University Press, 1966), esp. pp. 51–55, 66–75. But the introduction of the gradual conversion as a valid model in itself raised a new problem. As Pettit observes, "the very fact that spiritual preachers began to think of regeneration as a process, rather than as a moment in time, meant that conversion itself no longer implied immediate assurance of final election. . . . rarely could [an individual] gain election without the agony of doubt" (p. 56).

27. John Calvin, *Institutes of the Christian Religion*, trans. John Allen, rev. and cor. by B. B. Warfield, 7th Amer. ed., 2 vols (Philadelphia: Presbyterian Board of Christian Education, 1813), 3.3.9, p. 658.

28. James, *The Varieties*, pp. 183, 206. Although the two classifications of the sudden and the gradual types of conversion are repeatedly referred to in the literature on the subject, there is far less understanding of the gradual model. The best example of this one-sided treatment of the two categories is James himself, who never discusses *lysis* conversion with the same interest and vigor as he does *crisis* conversion.

29. Margaret Bottrall, *Every Man a Phoenix* (London: John Murray, 1958),

pp. 89, 94; Roger Sharrock, "Spiritual Autobiography in *The Pilgrim's Progress*," *The Review of English Studies* 24, no. 94 (April 1948): 113–14; Ola Elizabeth Winslow, *John Bunyan* (New York: Macmillan, 1961), pp. 48–50; Greaves, *John Bunyan*, p. 17; Ebner, *Autobiography in Seventeenth-Century England*, pp. 58–59.

30. Erik Erikson, *Young Man Luther* (New York: W.W. Norton & Co., 1962), p. 39.

31. The idea of the double conversion is also to be found in other sectarian autobiographies, for example, the Baptist Anna Trapnel's *A Legacy for Saints, Being Several Experiences of the Dealings of God with Anna Trapnel, In and After Her Conversion* (London, 1654) and the Rev. James Fraser's autobiography ("Memoirs of the Rev. James Fraser of Brea, Minister of the Gospel at Culross, Written by Himself," *Select Biographies*, ed. for the Wodrow Society by the Rev. W. K. Tweedie [Edinburgh, 1847]), and in Bunyan's major works. For a fuller discussion of this, see my article "The Double-Conversion in Bunyan's *Grace Abounding*," *Philological Quarterly* 61, no. 3 (Summer 1982): 259–76.

Bunyan's allegory *The Holy War* is exemplary in its allegorical rendition of the double conversion. The story is as follows: The town of Mansoul, built by Shaddai (God) "for his own delight" has a garrisoned castle in the very center, five gates, and a wall that is unique in that it can be penetrated only with the consent of the town's inhabitants. Diabolus (Satan), disguised as a dragon, lays siege to the town, and finally persuades the townspeople to open their gates and let him in. After many years of hardship under his tyranny the citizens repent. Shaddai sends an army, led by Emmanuel (Christ), who finally defeats Diabolus and enters the city in triumph. There is a trial, after which the repentent townspeople are pardoned. But the narrative does not end here; there is a second fall, begun by "Mr. Carnal Security." Emmanuel departs and Diabolus enters the city again. Once more the people repent; once more Emmanuel defeats Diabolus and enters the city. The pattern is thus of conversion, relapse, and reconversion—the same double-conversion paradigm as in *Grace Abounding* (*The Holy War*, ed. Roger Sharrock and James F. Forrest [Oxford: The Clarendon Press, 1980]).

32. Calvin, *Institutes*, 3.3.20, p. 672.

33. Ibid., 3.3.5, p. 654 and 3.3.9, p. 657.

34. William Ames, *The Marrow of Theology*, trans. John D. Eusden (Philadelphia: Pilgrim, 1968), pp. 161–74. I am indebted to Alden T. Vaughan, in whose anthology I first read this material (*The Puritan Tradition in America, 1620–1730* [Columbia, S.C.: The University of South Carolina Press, 1972], pp. 14–20). In his introduction, Vaughn observes that Ames was an influential Puritan writer who "codified more clearly than any of his contemporaries the growing body of Puritan doctrine" (p. 14). Similarly, Eusden writes that "for a century and a half, William Ames' *Marrow of Theology* held sway as a clear persuasive expression of Puritan belief and practice" (p. 1). Ames's work first appeared in Latin in 1623, and underwent many subsequent translations in English and Dutch.

35. Greaves, *John Bunyan*, p. 76; quoting Bunyan's *Solomon's Temple Spiritualiz'd*.

36. Dunne, in *A Search for God*, quotes Max Weber as writing that "both Luther and Calvin believed fundamentally in a double God." Dunne then goes on to observe: "Both believed in a God who had two faces, a wrathful face and a gracious face. The wrathful countenance of God and the gracious countenance alternate throughout the Bible, especially in the Psalms, but one has the feeling

that these are only different expressions, so to speak, which the same face can assume. With Luther and Calvin, however, the opposition of God's wrath and God's grace is carried so far that it is rather like two faces" (p. 95). In *Grace Abounding* the dual face of the deity is rendered somewhere between expression (which conveys an attitude) and reification (which represents a separate autonomous being).

37. James, *The Varieties*, pp. 209, 214–15.

Chapter 5. John Bunyan: God and Family

1. Of course, to write about our images and ideas of God as projections is not in any way to imply that such projections constitute the "reality" of God. As Paul Pruyser remarks in a parallel instance, "this is a functional statement which should not be mistaken for an ontological assertion" (*A Dynamic Psychology of Religion*, p. 224). At the end of this very fine book, Pruyser draws an analogy between the *tremendum* of the dynamic unconscious, from which we shield ourselves by a curtain of repression, and the *tremendum* of ineffable, divine reality. And he does so in a way that preserves the reality of the religious phenomena that are the objects of his scrutiny: ". . . God's own revealing and concealing activities make the human projections of gods possible. For symbols (here gods) participate in the reality to which they point" (pp. 337–38).

2. Calvin, *Institutes*, 3.3.15, p. 665.

3. Compare Jonathan Edwards, for whom the work of redemption is superior to the work of creation: "I am bold to say that the work of God in the conversion of one soul, considered together with the source, foundation, and purchase of it, and also the benefit, end, and eternal issue of it, is a more glorious work of God than the creation of the whole material universe" (in James, *The Varieties*, p. 238).

4. Calvin, *Institutes*, 3.6.2, p. 747.

5. Ibid., 3.7.1, pp. 765–66.

6. Ibid., 3.2.5, p. 659.

7. Bottrall, *Every Man a Phoenix*, p. 89. The quotation that Bottrall attributes to Augustine is rendered in *Grace Abounding* as follows: "so that I see the best way to go thorow sufferings, is to trust in God thorow Christ, as touching the world to come; and as touching this world, to 'count the grave my house, to make my bed in darkness, and to say to Corruption, Thou art my Father, and to the Worm, Thou art my Mother and Sister' . . ." (*GA*, 98).

8. Harding, *Journey into Self*, pp. 34–35.

9. Jung, "The Phenomenology of the Spirit in Fairytales," in *Archetypes and the Collective Unconscious*, pp. 215–18.

10. Campbell, *Hero with a Thousand Faces*, p. 72.

11. Bunyan, *The Pilgrim's Progress*, p. 29.

12. Ibid., p. 29.

Chapter 6. Thomas Merton: A Modern Paradigm

1. John F. Teahan, "Renunciation of Self and World: A Critical Dialectic in Thomas Merton," *Thought* 53, no. 209 (June 1978): 140.

2. Teahan gives a superb summary of all these positions. James Baker, in

Thomas Merton: Social Critic (Lexington: The University Press of Kentucky, 1971), Dennis McInerney, in *Thomas Merton: The Man and His Work* (Washington, D.C.: Cistercian Publications, Consortium Press, 1974), Charles Dumont, in "The Contemplative," *Thomas Merton, Monk; A Monastic Tribute*, ed. Brother Patrick Hart (New York: Sheed & Ward, 1974), and Aldhelm Cameron-Brown, in "Zen Master," *Thomas Merton, Monk*, see a marked discontinuity between Merton's early and late writings. On the other hand, Frederic Kelly, in *Man Before God: Thomas Merton on Social Responsibility* (Garden City, N.Y.: Doubleday, 1974), John Higgins, in *Thomas Merton on Prayer* (Garden City, N.Y.: Doubleday, 1973), and Elena Malits, C.S.C., *The Solitary Explorer* (San Francisco: Harper & Row, 1980), recognize the change as one that is gradual and developmental (pp. 140–42).

3. In Malits, *Solitary Explorer*, p. 141. Monica Furlong observes: "In later years, he became uncomfortable and embarrassed about the book, not wanting to disclaim all memory of it . . . yet uneasy about some of its emphases, and more than a little resentful of the way it had fixed him in a certain mold in the public mind, out of which readers were then unwilling to let him grow" (*Merton: A Biography* [San Francisco: Harper & Row, 1980], p. 158).

4. E.g., Aelred Graham, O.S.B., "Thomas Merton: A Modern Man in Reverse," *Atlantic Monthly* 191 (1953): 70–74.

5. In Peter Brown, *Augustine of Hippo*, p. 175; quoting Augustine, *Sermon* 67, 2.

6. The diversity of Merton's life and thought has been a matter of concern to almost all of his commentators, and a number of hypotheses have been suggested to explain it. Elena Malits, in *Solitary Explorer*, interpreting his life in accord with the journey metaphor, sees it as determined by a "commitment to continuing conversion." The autobiography, she observes, "represented only the beginning of his conversion story. He underwent genuine religious growth all the years of his monastic life. . . . Merton articulated his experience of conversion as an open-ended process, an ongoing development, a dynamic thrust forward and upward" (p. x). Dennis McInerny, in *The Man and His Work*, sees the diversity of Merton's writings as tempered by "his love for balance, his reluctance to go off in any one direction to the extent that he completely lost sight of the possibility that there might be other directions as well." The "incessant expansion of his thought" is modified not only by this instinctive sense of equilibrium, but also by the presence of an inner unity: "There was a certain permanence, a core of stability around which his diverse ideas revolved and from which they gained their focus and coherence" (pp. 120, 79). Monica Furlong, in *Merton: A Biography*, to the contrary, emphasizes Merton's "deep loneliness. . . . the deep emptiness and need of one who has not been securely loved as a child" and sets this in the context of his poignant and lifelong yearning for a home—"a contained and rooted community." The psychological pattern that she observes in his life turns on two very different but equally powerful needs that were fulfilled at Gethsemani—the need for a home and the need for punishment. Furlong also suggests an interpretation of Merton's later life that pivots on the dualities of monastery and world: "Having moved inward to establish his stability and life of prayer at the monastery and to reach the goal of ordination, he was now slowly turning back towards the world he had excluded" (pp. 333, 244, 20, 201). John Bamberger sees Merton's life and thought as governed by a dialectical movement between opposites—a way of thinking that both grew out of and helped resolve the psychological ambivalence of his early years ("The Cistercian," *Continuum* 7, no. 2 [Summer 1969]: 234).

7. But in so consistently defining himself as distinct and apart from the secular world, Merton fails to see the extent to which his religious experience, as well as his religious needs, are shaped by that world. Thus it would appear that his joining the monastic community is an affirmation of an ideal of community as over against an ideal of individualism (and so it seems to Merton). But the latent self-referential quality of Merton's religious ethos tends to place a higher value on individualistic than on communal values, and thus seeds his dissatisfaction with all communities, even the sacramental one.

8. Furlong, *Merton: A Biography*, p. 205. Edward Rice dates this petition as occurring in 1953 (*The Man in the Sycamore Tree* [Garden City, N.Y.: Doubleday, 1970], p. 79). Furlong sees Merton, near the end of his life, as a monk in name only, particularly because he no longer believed in the authority of his abbot (pp. 288–89).

9. Thus in part 1 Merton locates himself as born into a world that was "the picture of Hell"; in part 2, just after baptism, he observes: "I was about to set foot on the shore at the foot of the high, seven-circled mountain of a Purgatory steeper and more arduous than I was able to imagine . . ."; and in part 3 he tells us that he is reading Dante's "Paradiso," and refers to the monastery as a kind of paradise. (*SSM*, 3, 221, 277, 325).

10. Bishop Fulton J. Sheen, on the jacket of the Signet edition of *The Seven Storey Mountain* (New York: Harcourt, Brace & Co., 1948). Malits, in *Solitary Explorer*, p. 32, and Brooke Hopkins, in "Thomas Merton: Language and Silence" (*New Orleans Review* 5 [1979]: 99), compare *The Seven Storey Mountain* to the *Confessions*.

11. Bamberger, "The Cistercian," p. 238.

12. Malits, *Solitary Explorer*, p. 21.

13. John Freccero, discussing the spiral motif in reference to Dante, mentions Plato in the *Timaeus*, Aristotle in *De caelo* and *De anima*, Boethius, Aquinas, and Alanus ab Insulis ("Dante's Pilgrim in a Gyre," *PMLA* 76, pt. 1 [June 1961]: 168–81).

14. Malits, *Solitary Explorer*, p. 155.

15. In Elizabeth Drew, *T. S. Eliot: The Design of his Poetry* (New York: Charles Scribner & Sons, 1949), p. 1. It is a fascinating, though unanswerable question as to whether Merton was imitating Eliot—either consciously or unconsciously—in his use of a critical strategy that is both literary and religious. Though he does not acknowledge Eliot as a source, he mentions reading him in the autobiography (*SSM*, 93); also, there is the fact that at the time Merton's literary tastes were formed and trained at Columbia, Eliot was universally acknowledged as the great modern poet and critic. Perhaps, regardless of his opinion of Eliot, Merton preferred to use the Catholic Dante without reference to the Anglican Eliot.

16. This is, of course, consistent with the Catholic liturgical calendar, where the past is always present, not as the universal in the particular, but as story or event reenacted, recreated.

17. E.g., Merton remarks, "I have had to accept the fact that my life is almost totally paradoxical" (*A Thomas Merton Reader*, ed. Thomas P. McDonnell, rev. ed. [New York: Image Books, Doubleday, 1974], author's preface, p. 16) and "Like Jonas himself I find myself traveling toward my destiny in the belly of a paradox" (Merton, *The Sign of Jonas* [New York: Image, 1956], epigraph).

18. Matthew Kelty, "The Man" in *Thomas Merton, Monk*, p. 48.

19. Graham, *A Modern Man in Reverse,"* p. 71. The quotation is from *The Seven Storey Mountain;* Merton, while on a visit to Gethsemani, is describing his impression of a man entering the monastery in order to become a monk.

20. Ibid., p. 72.

21. This seems to be an inversion of Bunyan's model in *Grace Abounding*, where he characterizes himself as "the chief of sinners" and emphasizes his early depravity.

22. Merton writes: ". . . Father read them aloud, and I learned of Theseus and the Minotaur, of the Medusa, of Perseus and Andromeda. Jason sailed to a far land, after the Golden Fleece. Theseus returned victorious, but forgot to change the black sails, and the King of Athens threw himself down from the rock, believing that his son was dead" (*SSM*, 11). It is interesting that of all the mythic heroes in the Greek legends, Merton should select Jason and Theseus. What he does mention about them mirrors important elements in his own ideas of spiritual heroism: the motif of quest, and the interwoven theme of the father's life and goals as an artist. If the story of Jason connotes for Merton the glorious element in the archetype of the heroic quest, the story of Theseus connotes the sense of tragedy. Though Merton is the religious hero in search of God, he is also the hero whose quest is always somehow incomplete because of the father's absence.

23. Furlong, *Merton: A Biography*, pp. 14–15.

24. Throughout 2.2 in *The Seven Storey Mountain* the biblical phrase "For the Land which thou goest to possess is not like the land of Egypt from whence thou camest out . . ." echoes like a refrain. The identification with the Moses myth is certainly the organizing metaphor of Merton's conversion here. The section is titled "The Waters of Contradiction"; Merton writes of his conversion to Roman Catholicism as a passing "through the Red Sea of Baptism"; and the geographical symbols of desert and promised land are the basis of an extended meditation on their paradoxical similarity.

25. Merton, *The Sign of Jonas*, p. 233. In *The Seven Storey Mountain* Merton writes of his desire to be a saint with complete seriousness; here he does so with a sense of irony.

26. Merton, *Reader*, author's preface, p. 17.

27. I do not mean to imply that social concerns should be transcended, but simply that Merton must transcend this attitude at this particular time in his life and thought.

28. I do not use the term *narcissistic* here, and later, because its psychoanalytic meaning is so layered and thus confusing: it can refer to homosexuality, to a developmental or structural category of psychic life, and is further discussed as "primary" or "secondary." Narcissism, in colloquial usage, is often thought to mean simply "love of the self." But LaPlanche and Pontalis define narcissism as "love directed towards the image of oneself" (*The Language of Psycho-analysis*, trans. Donald Nicholson-Smith [New York: Norton, 1973], p. 255). Egocentrism (to define the relationship to oneself) or autocentrism (to define the relationship to God) seem more appropriate terms to describe the way in which the idea of the self is, for Merton, so central a theme.

29. Herbert Fingarette, *The Self in Transformation* (New York: Harper, 1963), p. 104. Fingarette uses this phrase to refer to doctrines of "self-realization" or "self-actualization": "These notions have a phenomenological basis in that, in moments of existential crisis, we do seem to 'find ourselves,' discover who and what we are" (ibid.).

30. In the *Confessions* the pattern is the idealization of a strong mother and a corresponding devaluation of a weak father. It may be psychologically significant that in both cases it is the parent who dies first—Augustine's father and Merton's mother—who is characterized in negative terms.

31. Raymond Bailey, in *Thomas Merton on Mysticism* (N.Y.: Doubleday & Co., 1975) writes about Merton: "His notebooks reveal a strong sense of failure that he never developed a really intimate relationship with an individual. He could love the world and God and persons as persons, but he had difficulty giving himself completely to any single person. Only the mystical marriage with love itself could grasp him and demand his all" (p. 28).

32. The mature Merton's search for the "perfect place" follows the same pattern, except that he has substituted an ideal group of people for the ideal locale: he comments on his relationship to both the Trappist monastery and the settlement-house in Harlem as "my close and immediate and visible association with any group of those who had banded themselves together to form a small, secret colony of the Kingdom of Heaven in this earth of exile" (*SSM*, 349).

33. Rice comments on there being an uncanny physical resemblance between Merton and Bramachari: "For a moment his face and build [Bramachari's] made him seem almost like Merton reincarnated" (*Man in the Sycamore Tree*, p. 12).

34. The dark potential of the ecclesiastical *senex* is embodied in Merton's encounter with a Capuchin priest, during confession, just after he has been rejected by the Franciscans: the priest, he writes, "began to tell me in very strong terms that I certainly did not belong in the monastery, still less the priesthood" and "that I was simply wasting his time and insulting the Sacrament of Penance by indulging my self-pity in his confessional" (*SSM*, 198). It is an incident of failed mediation within the very ecclesiastical structure that is meant to provide and sacramentalize mediation.

35. Merton, *Reader*, pp. 17–18.

36. In Thérèse Lentfoehr, "The Spiritual Writer," in *Thomas Merton, Monk*, p. 108.

37. Bamberger, "The Cistercian," p. 238.

38. Merton's critics, too, have concurred in seeing Owen Merton as a deeply religious figure; e.g., Furlong observes that Merton's father was "the only one of them in the family with any deep religious faith" (*Merton: A Biography*, p. 44). Perhaps this is true, or perhaps the father is being perceived through the eyes of the son?

39. Furlong, *Merton: A Biography*, pp. 59–60. One wonders if this very important information about Merton's past was a part of the original manuscript of *The Seven Storey Mountain*, subsequently cut by his Trappist censors. It does seem likely. According to Rice, a large portion of the manuscript—"perhaps as much as one third"—was seriously altered or cut (*Man in the Sycamore Tree*, p. 65). Rice and Furlong observe that the major objection of the censors was Merton's frankness in discussing his past life (Rice, ibid., pp. 64-65; Furlong, *Merton: A Biography*, p. 153). The result of this was "a curious imbalance in the book, hinting at terrible sins that never seemed to add up to more than seeing a few girls and getting drunk now and then" (Furlong, *Merton: A Biography*, 154). It seems odd that Malits should commend Merton's censors as performing a helpful editorial service for a too-prolific writer: "Trappist censors appear to have exercised nothing but commonsense judgment." The parts they omitted, she

writes, were sections that were "tedious, adding nothing to the story but length" (*Solitary Explorer,* p. 145).

40. Furlong, *Merton: A Biography,* p. 129.

41. Rice, *Man in the Sycamore Tree,* pp. 63–64.

Chapter 7
Thomas Merton: Sacramental Conversion

1. Quoted in Malits, *Solitary Explorer,* p. x.

2. Furlong observes that this experience is very similar to the Puritan conviction of sin, "an acute awareness of himself in the light of divine grace" (*Merton: A Biography,* p. 55). Were Merton not the Catholic that he is; were he, say, John Bunyan, this particular experience would certainly have received greater emphasis.

3. Bailey observes of Merton's mother: "She was an ardent pacifist who prevailed over her husband's patriotic desire to become a soldier in World War I" (*Thomas Merton on Mysticism,* p. 27).

4. Merton, *The Sign of Jonas,* p. 181.

5. Jung, "The Origin of the Hero," *Symbols of Transformation,* p. 178.

6. Malits sees the vocational choice here as a second conversion: "Everything suggests he regarded the period between his baptism and becoming a Trappist as his second conversion—one that concretized, validated, and made existentially effective the promise of the first. The very structure of the autobiography points to this as the decisive sequence of experiences" (*Solitary Explorer,* p. 30).

In the events of his life after completion of the autobiography, Merton's critics (Merton included) habitually find some particular crisis that they see as marking another conversion. Thus Brooke Hopkins alludes to the spiritual crisis that Merton experienced in 1949–50 as an actual conversion, quoting Merton in his journal entry: "Yesterday, the Feast of St. Thomas was, I think, an important day. . . . I had a kind of sense that the day was building up to some kind of deep decision. . . . There is a conversion of the deep will to God that cannot be effected in words . . ." ("Thomas Merton: Language and Silence," p. 102; quoting *The Sign of Jonas*).

Clearly, Merton experienced conversion as a pattern of repeated cycles of death and rebirth. Rice quotes Merton, in 1951, as remarking: "I have become a very different man from what I used to be. The man who began [*The Sign of Jonas*] is dead, just as the man who finished *The Seven Storey Mountain* when this journal began is also dead, and what is more, the man who was the central figure in *The Seven Storey Mountain* is dead over and over. . . . *The Seven Storey Mountain* is the work of a man I never even heard of" (Rice, *Man in the Sycamore Tree,* p. 76). The tone here nicely balances impatience and a wry humor; certainly it underlines Merton's refusal to be identified with or limited to any particular stage in life or any particular literary persona.

7. Malits comments on the similarity between this episode and Augustine's conversion: both occur in a garden; the beckoning voice of *Continentia* is like the hallucinated bells of Gethsemani; etc. (*Solitary Explorer,* p. 32).

8. Bamberger, "The Cistercian," p. 234.

Conclusion

1. Also, there is the eminently archetypal poetry of T. S. Eliot, who tries to make spiritual autobiography transcend itself by making art its form and archetype its content.
2. James, *The Varieties*, p. 499.

Bibliography

Abbott, H. Porter. "Organic Form in the Autobiography of a Convert: The Example of Malcolm X." *College Language Association Journal* 23, no. 2 (December 1979): 125–46.

Ames, William. *The Marrow of Theology.* Translated by John D. Eusden from the 3d Latin edition. Philadelphia: Pilgrim Press, 1968.

Augustine, Saint. *The City of God.* Translated and edited by Marcus Dods. 2 vols. New York: Hafner Publishing Co., 1948.

——. *On Christian Doctrine.* Translated by D. W. Robertson, Jr. The Library of Liberal Arts. Indianapolis, Ind.: Bobbs-Merrill, 1958.

——. *The Confessions.* Translated by R. S. Pine-Coffin. 1961; reprint, London: Penguin, 1964.

——. *The Confessions.* Translated by William Watts. Revised by W. H. D. Rouse. 2 vols. The Loeb Classical Library. Cambridge & London: William Heinemann, 1977.

Bailey, Raymond. *Thomas Merton on Mysticism.* New York: Doubleday & Co., 1975.

Baker, James T. *Thomas Merton: Social Critic.* Lexington: The University Press of Kentucky, 1971.

Balch, Robert. "Looking behind the Scenes in a Religious Cult: Implications for the Study of Conversion." *Sociological Analysis* 41 (1980): 137–43.

Bamberger, John Etudes, O.C.S.O. "The Cistercian." *Continuum* 7, no. 2 (Summer 1969): 227–41.

Batson, C. Daniel, and W. Larry Ventis. *The Religious Experience: A Social-Psychological Perspective.* New York: Oxford University Press, 1982.

Battenhouse, Roy W. "The Life of St. Augustine." In *A Companion to* the *Study of Augustine*. Edited by Roy W. Battenhouse. New York: Oxford, 1955.

Beckford, James A. "Accounting for Conversion." *British Journal of Sociology* 29 (1978): 249–62.

Bottrall, Margaret. *Every Man a Phoenix*. London: John Murray, 1958.

Brown, Norman O. *Life Against Death*. Middletown, Conn.: Wesleyan University Press, 1959.

Brown, Peter R. *Augustine of Hippo*. Berkeley & Los Angeles: University of California Press, 1967.

Bunyan, John. *Grace Abounding to the Chief of Sinners*. Edited by Roger Sharrock. Oxford: The Clarendon Press, 1962.

———. *The Holy War*. Edited by Roger Sharrock and James F. Forrest. Oxford: The Clarendon Press, 1980.

———. *The Pilgrim's Progress*. Edited by James Blanton Wharey. 2d ed., rev. Roger Sharrock. Oxford: The Clarendon Press, 1960.

Calvin, Jean. *Institutes of the Christian Religion*. Translated by John Allen from the Latin and collated with the author's last edition in French. 1st American ed., 1813; 7th American ed., rev. and corr. Benjamin B. Warfield. 2 vols. Philadelphia: Presbyterian Board of Christian Education, 1936.

Cameron-Brown, Aldhelm. "Zen Master." In *Thomas Merton, Monk; A Monastic Tribute*, edited by Patrick Hart. New York: Sheed & Ward, 1974.

Campbell, Joseph. *The Hero with a Thousand Faces*. New York: Bollingen Foundation, 1949; reprint, New York: Meridian Books, 1956.

"The Castle of Perseverance." In *Chief Pre-Shakespearean Dramas*, edited by John Quincy Adams. Cambridge, Mass.: Houghton Mifflin, 1924.

Christensen, A. R., M. D. "Religious Conversion." *Archives of General Psychiatry* 9 (September 1963): 207–16.

Cicero, Marcus Tullius. *De Inventione*. Translated by H. M. Hubbell. The Loeb Classical Library. London: William Heinemann, 1949.

Coe, George A. *The Psychology of Religion*. Chicago: University of Chicago Press, 1916.

Comparetti, Domenico. *Vergil in the Middle Ages*. Translated by E. F. M. Benecke. London: Allen & Unwin, 1966.

Daly, L. J. "Psychohistory and St. Augustine's Conversion Process." *Augustiniana* 28 (1978): 231–54.

Dante Alighieri. *The Inferno*. Translated by John Ciardi. New York: Mentor, The New American Library, 1954.

———. *The Paradiso.* Translated by John Ciardi. New York: Mentor, The New American Library, 1961.

———. *The Purgatorio.* Translated by John Ciardi. New York: Mentor, The New American Library, 1957.

Day, Dorothy. *The Long Loneliness.* New York: Harper & Row, 1952.

de Sanctis, Sante. *Religious Conversion.* Translated by Helen Augur. New York: Harcourt, Brace & Co., 1927.

Dittes, James. "Continuities between the Life and Thought of Augustine." *Journal for the Scientific Study of Religion* 5, no. 1 (Fall 1965): 130–40.

Dodds, E. R. "Augustine's *Confessions:* A Study of Spiritual Maladjustment." *The Hibbert Journal* 26 (October 1927–July 1928): 459–73.

Drew, Elizabeth. *T. S. Eliot: The Design of his Poetry.* New York: Scribner, 1949.

Dumont, Charles. "The Contemplative." In *Thomas Merton, Monk; A Monastic Tribute,* edited by Patrick Hart. New York: Sheed & Ward, 1974.

Dunne, John S., C.S.C. *A Search for God in Time and Memory.* New York: MacMillan, 1967, 1969.

Ebner, Dean. *Autobiography in Seventeenth-Century England.* The Hague: Mouton & Co., 1971.

Eliade, Mircea. *Rites and Symbols of Initiation.* Translated by Willard R. Trask. New York: Harper & Row, 1958; Harper Torchbooks, 1965.

Erikson, Erik. *Young Man Luther.* Austen Riggs Monograph, no. 4. New York: W. W. Norton & Co., 1958, 1962.

Faber, Heije. *Psychology of Religion.* Translated by Margaret Kohl. London: SCM Press, 1976.

Ferrari, Leo. "The Arboreal Polarisation in Augustine's *Confessions.*" *Revue des Études Augustiniennes* 25 (1979): 35–46.

———. "The Pear-Theft in Augustine's *Confessions.*" *Revue des Études Augustiniennes* 16 (1970): 233–42.

———. "The Theme of the Prodigal Son in Augustine's *Confessions.*" *Recherches Augustiniennes* 12 (1977): 105–18.

Fingarette, Herbert. *The Self in Transformation.* New York: Harper & Row, 1963.

Fish, Stanley E. *Self-Consuming Artifacts.* Berkeley & Los Angeles: The University of California Press, 1972.

Franklin, Benjamin. *Autobiography.* Edited by Russell B. Nye. Boston: Houghton Mifflin, 1958.

Fraser, Rev. James. "Memoirs of the Rev. James Fraser of Brea, Minister of the Gospel at Culross, Written by Himself." In *Select Biographies.* Edited for the Wodrow Society by the Rev. W. K. Tweedie. Edinburgh, 1847.

Freccero, John. "Dante's Pilgrim in a Gyre." *PMLA* 76, pt. 1 (June 1961): 168–81.

Freud, Sigmund. *The Future of an Illusion.* Translated by W. D. Robson-Scott. Garden City, N.Y.: Doubleday, Anchor Books, 1953.

———. "The Question of a Weltanschauung." In *New Introductory Lectures on Psychoanalysis.* Translated by James Strachey. New York: W. W. Norton & Co., 1965.

Furlong, Monica. *Merton: A Biography.* San Francisco: Harper & Row, 1980.

Graham, Aelred, O.S.B. "Thomas Merton: A Modern Man in Reverse." *Atlantic Monthly* 191 (1953): 70–74.

Greaves, Richard. *John Bunyan.* Courtenay Studies in Reformation Theology, 2. Grand Rapids: Eerdmans, 1969.

Guardini, Romano. *The Conversion of St. Augustine.* Translated from German by Elinor Briefs. Westminster, Md.: Newman Press, 1960.

Hagendahl, Harald. *Augustine and the Latin Classics.* 2 vols. Studia Graeca et Latina Gothoburgensia 20. Göteborg: University of Göteburg, 1967.

Haller, William. *The Rise of Puritanism.* New York: Harper & Row, 1975.

Harding, M. Esther. *Journey into Self.* London: Vision Press, 1958.

Hart, Patrick, ed. *Thomas Merton, Monk; A Monastic Tribute.* New York: Sheed & Ward, 1974.

Havens, Joseph. "Notes on Augustine's *Confessions.*" *Journal for the Scientific Study of Religion* 5, no. 1 (Fall 1965): 141–43.

Hawkins, Anne. "The Double-Conversion in Bunyan's *Grace Abounding.*" *Philological Quarterly* 61, no. 3 (Summer 1982): 259–76.

Higgins, John. *Thomas Merton on Prayer.* Garden City, N.Y.: Doubleday, 1973.

Hopkins, Brooke. "Thomas Merton: Language and Silence." *New Orleans Review* 5 (1979): 99–106.

James, William. *The Varieties of Religious Experience.* New York: Longmans, Green & Co., 1902.

Jung, Carl. *Aion.* Vol. 9, pt. 2. *Collected Works.* Translated by R. F. C. Hull, Bollingen Series 20. Princeton, N.J.: Princeton University Press, 1959.

———. *The Archetypes and the Collective Unconscious.* Vol. 9, pt. 1. *Collected Works.* Translated by R. F. C. Hull. Bollingen Series 20. 2d ed. Princeton, N.J.: Princeton University Press, 1968; new material copyright, 1969.

———. *Psyche and Symbol.* Edited by Violet S. de Laszlo. New York: Doubleday, 1958.

———. *Psychology and Religion.* 1938; reprint, New Haven, Conn.: Yale University Press, 1960.

———. *Psychology and Religion: West and East.* Vol. 11. *Collected Works.* Translated by R. F. C. Hull. Bollingen Series 20. 2d ed. Princeton, N.J.: Princeton University Press, 1969.

———. *The Structure and Dynamics of the Psyche.* Vol. 8. *Collected Works.* Translated by R. F. C. Hull. Bollingen Series 20. 2d ed. Princeton University Press, 1969.

———. *Symbols of Transformation.* Vol. 5. *Collected Works.* Translated by R. F. C. Hull. Bollingen Series 20. 2d ed. Princeton, N.J.: Princeton University Press, 1967.

———, and C. Kerényi. *Essays in a Science of Mythology.* Translated by R. F. C. Hull. Bollingen Series 22. 2d ed. Princeton, N.J.: Princeton University Press, 1969.

Kelly, Frederic. *Man Before God: Thomas Merton on Social Responsibility.* Garden City, N.Y.: Doubleday & Co., 1974.

Kelty, Matthew. "The Man." In *Thomas Merton, Monk; A Monastic Tribute*, edited by Patrick Hart. New York: Sheed & Ward, 1974.

Kligerman, Charles, M.D. "A Psychoanalytic Study of the *Confessions* of St. Augustine." *Journal of the American Psychoanalytical Association* 5, no. 3 (July 1957): 469–84.

La Planche, J., and J.-B. Pontalis. *The Language of Psycho-analysis.* Translated by Donald Nicholson-Smith. New York: W. W. Norton & Co., 1973.

Lawless, George P. "Interior Peace in the *Confessions* of St. Augustine." *Revue des Études Augustiniennes* 26 (1980): 45–61.

Lebreton, Jules, and Jacques Zeiller. *The History of the Primitive Church.* Vol. 2. Translated by Ernest C. Messenger. New York: MacMillan, 1949.

Lentfoehr, Thérèse, "The Spiritual Writer," In *Thomas Merton, Monk; A Monastic Tribute*, edited by Patrick Hart. New York: Sheed & Ward, 1974.

Lerner, L. P. "Bunyan and the Puritan Culture." *Cambridge Journal* 7 (1954): 221–42.

Leuba, James H. *A Psychological Study of Religion.* New York: MacMillan, 1912.

Lofland, John, and Norman Skonovd. "Conversion Motifs." *Journal for the Scientific Study of Religion* 20, no. 4 (December 1981): 373–85.

Malcolm X. *The Autobiography.* Edited by Alex Haley. New York: The Grove Press, 1965.

McInerney, Dennis Q. *Thomas Merton: The Man and His Work.* Washington: D.C.: Cistercian Publications, Consortium Press, 1974.

Malits, Elena, C.S.C. *The Solitary Explorer.* San Francisco: Harper & Row, 1980.

Mazzeo, Joseph Anthony. *Renaissance and Seventeenth-Century Studies.* New York: Columbia University Press, 1964.

Merton, Thomas. *The Seven Storey Mountain.* New York: Harcourt Brace & Co., 1948.

———. *The Sign of Jonas.* New York: Harcourt Brace & Co., 1953.

———. *A Thomas Merton Reader.* Edited by Thomas P. McDonnell. rev. ed. New York: Image Books, Doubleday, 1974.

Misch, Georg. *A History of Autobiography in Antiquity.* Translated by E. W. Dickes. 2 vols. London: Routledge & Kegan Paul, 1950.

Momigliano, Arnaldo. "Paganism and Christian Historiography in the Fourth Century A.D." In *The Conflict Between Paganism and Christianity in the Fourth Century.* Edited by Arnaldo Momigliano. Oxford: The Clarendon Press, 1963.

Morris, John N. *Versions of the Self.* New York: Basic Books, 1966.

Nock, Arthur Darby. *Conversion.* London: Oxford University Press, 1933.

Norwood, Richard. *Journal.* New York: Published for the Bermuda Historical Monuments Trust by Scholars' facsimiles & reprints, 1945.

O'Connell, Robert J. "*Ennead* VI, 4–5 in the Works of St. Augustine." *Revue des Études Augustiniennes* 9 (1963): 1–39.

———. "The *Enneads* and St. Augustine's Image of Happiness." *Vigilae Christianae* 17 (1963): 129–64.

———. "The Riddle of Augustine's *Confessions*: A Plotinian Key." *International Philosophical Quarterly* 4 (1964): 327–72.

———. *St. Augustine's Confessions: The Odyssey of Soul.* Cambridge, Mass.: Harvard University Press, 1969.

———. *St. Augustine's Early Theory of Man, A.D. 386–391.* Cambridge, Mass.: Harvard University Press, 1968.

Olney, James. "Autobiography and the Cultural Moment." In *Autobiography: Essays Theoretical and Critical,* edited by James Olney. Princeton, N.J.: Princeton University Press, 1980.

———. *Metaphors of Self.* Princeton, N.J.: Princeton University Press, 1972.

O'Meara, John J. *The Young Augustine.* London: Longmans, 1954.

Pascal, Roy. *Design and Truth in Autobiography.* Cambridge, Mass.: Harvard University Press, 1960.

Pettit, Norman. *The Heart Prepared: Grace and Conversion in Puritan Spiritual Life.* New Haven, Conn.: Yale University Press, 1966.

Plato. *The Republic.* Translated by Francis MacDonald Cornford. New York: Oxford University Press, 1945.

Plotinus. *The Enneads.* Translated by Stephen MacKenna. Revised by B. S. Page. 3rd ed. London: Faber & Faber, 1962.

Pratt, J. B. *The Religious Consciousness.* New York: MacMillan, 1920.

Pruyser, Paul. *Between Belief and Unbelief.* 1968; reprint, New York: Harper & Row, 1974.

———. *A Dynamic Psychology of Religion.* New York: Harper & Row, 1968, 1976.

———. "Psychological Examination: Augustine." *Journal for the Scientific Study of Religion* 5, no. 2 (Spring 1966): 284–89.

Rees, B. R. "The Conversion of St. Augustine." *Trivium* 14 (1979): 1–17.

Rice, Edward. *The Man in the Sycamore Tree.* Garden City, N.Y.: Doubleday & Co., 1970.

Róheim, Géza. *The Origin and Function of Culture.* Nervous and Mental Disease Monographs, 69. 1943; reprint, New York: Johnson Reprint Org., 1948.

Salzman, Leon. "The Psychology of Religious and Ideological Conversion." *Psychiatry* 16 (1953): 177–87.

Sargant, William. *Battle for the Mind.* New York: Harper & Row, 1957; Perennial Library edition, 1971.

Sedman, G. and G. Hopkinson. "The Psychopathology of Mystical and Religious Conversion Experiences in Psychiatric Patients." I and II *Confinia psychiatrica* 9, no. 1 (1966): 1–19 and 9, no. 2 (1966): 65–76.

Sharrock, Roger. *John Bunyan.* London: Hutchinson's University Library, 1954.

———. "Personal Vision and Puritan Tradition in Bunyan." *Hibbert Journal* 56 (1957): 47–60.

———. "Spiritual Autobiography in the *Pilgrim's Progress.*" *The Review of English Studies* 24, no. 94 (April 1948): 102–20.

Spengemann, William C. *The Forms of Autobiography.* New Haven, Conn., Yale University Press, 1980.

Stark, Rodney. "A Taxonomy of Religious Experience." *Journal for the Scientific Study of Religion* 5, no. 1 (Fall 1965): 97–116.

Starbuck, E. D. *The Psychology of Religion.* London: W. Scott, 1903.

Starr, G. A. *Defoe and Spiritual Autobiography.* Princeton, N.J.: Princeton University Press, 1965.

Strickland, Francis. *The Psychology of Religious Experience*. New York: The Abingdon Press, 1924.

Talon, Henri A. *John Bunyan*. Translated by Barbara Wall. London: Rockliff Publishing Corp. Ltd., 1951.

———. "Space and the Hero in *The Pilgrim's Progress*." *Études Anglaises* 14 (1961): 124–30.

Teahan, John F. "Renunciation of Self and World: A Critical Dialectic in Thomas Merton." *Thought* 53, no. 209 (June 1978): 133–50.

Teresa, Saint. "Life." In *Complete Works*, translated by E. Allison Peers from the critical edition of P. Silverio de Santa Teresa, C.D. vol. 1. London: Sheed and Ward, 1957.

TeSelle, Eugene. *Augustine the Theologian*. New York: Herder & Herder, 1970.

Thouless, Robert H. *An Introduction to the Psychology of Religion*. 2d ed. New York: Macmillan & Co., 1924.

Tindall, William York. *John Bunyan, Mechanick Preacher*. New York: Columbia University Press, 1934.

Trapnel, Anna. *A Legacy for Saints, Being Several Experiences of the Dealings of God with Anna Trapnel, In and After Her Conversion*. London, 1654.

Underwood, Alfred C. *Conversion: Christian and Non-Christian*. London: Allen & Unwin, 1925.

Vaughan, Alden T. *The Puritan Tradition in America, 1620–1730*. Columbia, S.C.: University of South Carolina Press, 1972.

Vergil, *The Aeneid*. Translated by Allen Mandelbaum. New York: Bantam Books, 1971.

Winnicott, D. W. "Transitional Objects and Transitional Phenomena." In *Collected Papers*. London: Tavistock Publications, 1958.

Winslow, Ola Elizabeth. *John Bunyan*. New York: Macmillan & Co., 1961.

Index

Academics, 31, 32
Adeodatus, 66
Aeneas, *Aeneid*. *See* Vergil
Alypius, 27, 42, 50
Ambrose, Saint, 31, 46–47, 66; reading in silence, 26, 139; as *senex*, 31, 69, 70–71, 110–11
Ames, William, 96
Anchises. *See* Vergil
Antony, Saint, 50, 53
Archetypal method, 14–16, 156, 168–69 n. 13
Archetypes, 13, 14, 159–60 n.2. *See also* Augustine—individual works: family, *psychomachia*, quest: Bunyan—individual works: family, *psychomachia*, quest; Merton—individual works: family, *psychomachia*, quest
Augustine, Saint, 13, 15
—*City of God*, 157–58
—*Confessions*, 16, 26, 74, 108, 110, 120, 124, 131, 132, 155; allegorical method, 24–27; *confessio*, 114; conversion in, 21–22, 30–32, 36, 39, 41–43, 44–55, 63–64, 162nn. 22 and 37; family, archetypes of, 31, 56–72; garden, symbol of, 39–41; ideas of God, 100–102, 104, 130; Prodigal son, story of; 33–34, 38–39, 78; *psychomachia*, 49–50, 85–86; quest, 16, 29–44, 81, 85, 87, 88–89, 117, 122; sense of closure, 118; visionary episodes in, 41–43
—*De Doctrina*, 25

—and the doctrine of *privatio boni*, 80–82
—*Soliloquies*, 52
Autobiographical theory, 22–24

Bamberger, John, 118, 153, 154
Bottrall, Margaret, 93–94, 105
Brown, Norman O., 79
Brown, Peter, 31, 43–44, 48, 63
Bunyan, John, 13, 15
—*Grace Abounding*, 26, 115, 155, 156, 158; conversion in, 21–22, 84–85, 88, 90, 92–99, 106–8; family, archetypes of, 104–9, 110–12; his father and mother, 105–6, ideas of God, 130; *psychomachia*, 16–17, 82–92, 119, 128; quest, 16–17, 85; structure in, 25
—*Holy War, The*, 86, 173 n. 31; *psychomachia*, 86
—*Pilgrim's Progress, The*, 74, 104, 108, 110, 111–12, 155, 158; Celestial City, 108; Doubting Castle, 102–3; quest, 16, 86–87, 89; Valley of Humiliation, 101

Calvin, Jean, 93, 95–96, 100–102, 103; idea of God, 104; theology of, 13, 79, 115
Calvinist, 84, 97, 101, 105, 110, 112; anxiety, 80, 98; the elect, 91; ideas of regeneration, 22, 93
Campbell, Joseph, 110
Carthusian Order, 116
Castle of Perseverance, The, 86

Cicero, 50; *De Inventione,* 37; *Hortensius,* 31, 63, 134; and wisdom, 46, 50
Confessions. See Augustine, Saint
Conversion, 13–14, 19–22, 157–58, 160–62 n.18, 166 n.33, 167 n.39; *See also* Augustine; Bunyan; *Crisis* and *lysis* conversion; Merton
Crisis and *lysis* conversion, 20–22, 39, 44–48, 51–54, 92–99

Dante: *The Divine Comedy,* 117, 118–19, 120–22, 127, 131, 154
Day, Dorothy, 156
Dido. *See* Vergil
Donatism, 46, 52–53
Dunne, John S., 24, 29, 32, 35

Ebner, Dean, 23, 94
Eliade, Mircea, 46
Eliot, T. S., 40, 120–21
Epektesis, 115, 118–19, 123, 140–41, 150, 154
Erikson, Erik, 18, 94, 119
Eros: mode of, 75–79, 102, 104, 170 n.8

Faber, Heije, 18–19
Faustus. *See* Manichaeism
Ferrari, Leo, 40
Fish, Stanley, 25–26, 87
Franciscan Order, 149–50, 116, 124
Franklin, Benjamin, 23–24
Freud, 17, 18
Furlong, Monica, 127, 137

Gifford, John, 84, 90, 109–12
Gilson, Etienne, 134
Grace Abounding to the Chief of Sinners. See Bunyan, John
Graham, Aelred, 122–23, 125–26
Greaves, Richard, 94
Gregory of Nyssa, 118
Guardini, Romano, 32

Hagendahl, Harald, 35–36, 164 nn. 14, and 15
Haller, William, 75–76, 80–81
Halyburton, Thomas, 73
Harding, Esther, 83, 107
Hegel, Georg Wilhelm Friedrich, 24–25

Hortensius, *See* Cicero
Huxley, Aldous, 13

James, William, 20–21, 97–98, 142, 156; *crisis* conversion, 45–46, 52; *lysis* conversion, 93–94
Joyce, James, 120, 121
Jung, Carl Gustav, 14–16, 17, 76, 129; *logos* and *eros,* 90, 129; mother archetype, 57–58; *senex* and child, 69, 72, 169 n.16. *See also* Archetypes

Kligerman, Charles, 52

logos: mode of, 75–79, 102, 104, 108, 109, 170 n.8
Luther, Martin, 13, 22, 74, 79, 80, 94

Malcolm X, 156, 166 n.29
Malits, Elena, 118, 119
Manichaeism, 31, 48, 49, 50, 57, 60, 80, 115, 139; Augustine's conversion to, 31, 32, 46, 52, 89; dualism of, 49, 62; and Faustus, 31, 70
Mazzeo, Joseph Anthony, 27
Merton, Thomas, 13, 15, 113–14, 155–56, 158
—*Seven Storey Mountain, The,* 16, 26, 27, 113; his brother John Paul, 129, 137–38; conversion in, 22, 99, 126, 139–54; family, archetypes of, 130–38; his father, 123, 129, 130, 132–34, 136, 139, 141, 142; the hotel-room experience, 140, 143–44, 148–49; *logos* and *eros,* 78; his mother, 129, 130, 132, 135–37, 140, 141, 143, 148–49; *psychomachia,* 125–30; quest, 17, 115–25; structure in, 25
—*Sign of Jonas, The,* 128
Monica, 31, 32, 63–67, 68, 69, 72, 89, 111, 139, 168–69 n.13; her dream, 64, 140; and maternal archetype, 58–60; in Milan, 47–48; and Vergil, 35, 37, 60–62; and visionary experience, 40, 42–43
Morris, John, 23

Neoplatonism, 32–33, 48–49, 50, 52, 65, 109, 115; books of, 27, 41, 42;

conversion to, 46, 51, 52, 89; dualism of, 62; vision in, 38, 41–43
Nock, Arthur Darby, 46

O'Connell, Robert, 29, 32, 35
Olney, James, 23

Pascal, Roy, 23, 53, 82
Patricius, 31, 66, 67–69, 72, 105
Paul, Saint, 41; conversion of, 17, 20, 21, 45–46, 51–54; *Epistles*, 26, 48–50, 51, 71
Pelagianism, 46, 78
Petrarch, 29–30, 32, 35, 74
Pettit, Norman, 92
Pilgrim's Progress, The. See Bunyan, John
Plato, 14–15, 33, 36, 69; *Republic*, 19–20
Platonism. See Neoplatonism
Plotinus, 32–34, 38, 67. *Se also* Neoplatonism
Ponticianus, 33–34, 53, 71
Prodigal Son, parable of, 33–34, 38, 78
Pruyser, Paul, 18, 170 n.8, 174 n.1

Rees, B. R., 45
Rice, Edward, 137, 147
Rogers, Richard, 93
Róheim, Géza, 76, 80

Senex, 69, 169 n.16. *See also* Augustine—*Confessions:* family, archetypes of; Bunyan—*Grace Abounding:* family, archetypes of; Merton—*The Seven Storey Mountain:* family, archetypes of
Seven Storey Mountain, The. See Merton, Thomas
Sharrock, Roger, 94
Sheen, Bishop Fulton, 17
Sibbes, Richard, 93
Simplicianus, 69, 70–71, 110–11
Spengemann, William, 54
Starbuck, E. D., 20
Starr, G. A., 73

Talon, Henri, 74
Teahan, John, 113
Teresa, Saint, 29, 32, 35, 44, 74, 156
TeSelle, Eugene, 33
Trappist Order, 27, 116, 124, 128, 136, 137, 149–51

Vergil, 33–38, 42, 60–62, 68, 117, 121–22, 164 n.14, 164–65 n.17, 165 n.22, 168 n.10
Victorinus, 33–34, 71
Vindicianus, 70

Winnicott, D. W., 19
Winslow, Ola, 94